City and Sanctuary

Religion and Architecture in the Roman Near East

Peter Richardson

scm press

British Library Cataloguing in Publication data

A catalogue record for this book is available
from the British Library

0 334 028841

First published in 2002 by SCM Press
9–17 St Albans Place, London N1 0NX

www.scm-canterburypress.co.uk

SCM Press is a division of
SCM-Canterbury Press Ltd

Typeset by Regent Typesetting
Printed and bound in Great Britain by
Biddles Ltd, Guildford and King's Lynn

THE JOHN ALBERT HALL LECTURES

Churchman, chemist, pioneer, soldier, businessman and philanthropist, John Albert Hall (1869–1933) emigrated from Britain to Canada in the last decade of the nineteenth century and made his home in Victoria, British Columbia. He left a legacy to the Diocese of British Columbia to found a lectureship to stimulate harmony between the Christian religion and contemporary thought. Colonel Hall's generosity sustained the work of three successive Canon Lecturers: Michael Coleman, Hilary Butler and Thomas Bailey. It also helped found the Greater Victoria Lay School of Theology. Since 1995 it has been supporting the lectureship's partnership between the Diocese of British Columbia and the University of Victoria's Centre for Studies in Religion and Society.

The Centre was established in 1991 to foster the scholarly study of religion in relation to the sciences, ethics, social and economic development, and other aspects of culture. As Co-sponsor of the John Albert Hall Lecture Series it assists in the fulfilment of the terms of the trust.

John Albert Hall lecturers are outstanding Christian theologians who address themselves to the church, the university and the community during a two-week Fellowship in Victoria, Canada. Publication of these lectures allows a wider audience to benefit from both the lecture series and the work of the Centre.

To

Jean Lois (Handy) Cameron
22 March 1912 –

In memory of

Donald James Cameron
17 May 1910 – 22 December 1993

Margaret Louise (Everett) Richardson
7 June 1902 – 8 May 1983

George Grainger Richardson
13 August 1904 – 28 January 1974

Contents

Illustrations

Plans

Plates

Palmyra

Petra

Preface and acknowledgments

I should like to express my warm thanks to all who made possible the lectures on which this book is based: to the committee that organizes the John Albert Hall Lectures for their very kind invitation; to the Diocese of British Columbia of the Anglican Church in Canada, which generously provided the resources for the lectureship and publication costs; and to Connie Carter and Moira Hill, who graciously assisted with the daily administrative tasks that needed attention. Those thanks extend especially to Harold Coward, Director of the Institute for Religion and Society of the University of Victoria, who made all the arrangements and acted as go-between. He was about to retire from his position as the book went to press. He has been an unfailingly courteous and gracious colleague over many years, as he has promoted the collective good of those disciplines in Canada that have contributed to an understanding of religion and society. All his friends will wish him a happy and productive retirement. Alex Wright, recently appointed editor of SCM Press, has also been most cooperative, as has his skilled staff. It was a pleasure to learn of his arrival at the press not long before the publication arrangements were being finalized.

For assistance with some of the research, whether before or after the lectures, I am obligated to students both in courses and in the Work-Study Programme at the University of Toronto: Lawrence Broadhurst, Leda Costaki, Tymen deVries, Debby Donnelly, Andrew Duffy, Jonathan Ferguson, Alana Foley, Debra Foran, Philip Harland, Mona Lafosse, Fleur Leslie, Eileen Morrison, Michele Murray, Elaine Myers, Melissa Prado, Rachel Urowitz and others. Colleagues have prodded me over many years: Bill Klassen (Waterloo, Ont.), with whom I have led tour groups to the Near

East; Jerome Murphy-O'Connor (Ecole Biblique, Jerusalem), who has been most welcoming whenever I have been privileged to stay there; Sy Gitin (Albright Institute, Jerusalem), who has been equally welcoming to my students and me; Ehud Netzer (Hebrew University, Jerusalem), who has taught me about Herod and more recently about Araq al-Emir both in conversation and through his writings; Ken Russell, who, in the year before he died so suddenly and tragically, was forthcoming about his insights into Petra when we were at ACOR in Amman. I am regularly in the debt of senior Canadian colleagues who may recognize much here, especially those connected with the ongoing Seminar on Religious Rivalries: Richard Ascough, Roger Beck, Michel Desjardins, Terence Donaldson, Lloyd Gaston, John Kloppenborg Verbin, Jack Lightstone, Steve Mason, Bradley McLean, Harold Remus, Stephen Wilson, Leif Vaage, among others.

Many share my interests in archaeology, religion and history and continue to instruct me: Donald Ariel (Israel Antiquities Authority), Mordechai Aviam (Kfar Vradim, Galilee), Douglas Edwards (University of Puget Sound), Seán Freyne (Trinity College, Dublin), William Scott Green (University of Rochester), Richard Horsley (University of Massachusetts, Boston), Lee Levine (Hebrew University, Jerusalem), Jodi Magness (Tufts University), Eric Meyers (Duke University), Doug Oakman (Pacific Lutheran University), Jack Olive (Seattle), Wendy Pullan (Cambridge), Jonathan Reed (LaVerne University), Anders Runesson (Lund University). I owe them and many others much for insights into particular issues or ways of thinking about the material cultures which lie at the heart of this book.

My largest immediate debt, architecturally speaking, is to Aaro Söderlund of Helsinki University of Technology. When we met in 1998 we began immediately talking about our mutual interest in Herod the Great's architecture. It seems we have hardly stopped for breath. I am constantly impressed with his detailed knowledge of the whole Near East and his admirable ability to convert this knowledge into three-dimensional and four-dimensional QTVR computer studies of buildings that allow viewers to walk or fly through them. He has read and commented on an earlier version, often at greater length than the draft, and a considerable number of his suggestions are incorporated without explicit acknowledgment.

The book is dedicated to my wife's and my parents, who have been constructive and encouraging at countless points along the way. Paying tribute in this small way to their collective support is hardly an adequate expression of the debt of gratitude that Nancy and I feel. It was a great pleasure for our children and grandchildren that Jean Cameron recently celebrated her ninetieth birthday, full of years, patient wisdom and joyful busyness. Donald Cameron, who always delighted in the opportunities we had to visit the Middle East – though he never quite understood our fascination – taught me love of the land and respect for rural values, along with a healthy scepticism about received opinions. Louise Richardson was born exactly a century ago; she always took great pleasure in 'her boys' and their education, and would have been happy to see this indirect fruit of the result of years of learning from others. George Richardson never complained of not attending university, though he must often have wondered how his life would have been different had he had the opportunity; he enjoyed both religion and architecture as avocations, but regrettably did not live long enough to see how I have struggled in the last two decades to connect intelligently two of our shared interests in my own work.

Peter Richardson
Toronto

Abbreviations

ABD	*Anchor Bible Dictionary*, ed. David Noel Freedman, 6 vols, New York, London, Toronto, Sydney and Auckland: Doubleday, 1992
ACOR	American Center for Oriental Research, Amman, Jordan
ADAJ	*Annual of the Department of Antiquities of Jordan*
ASOR	American Schools of Oriental Research, Jerusalem
BAR	British Archaeology Reports
BCE	Before the Common Era
BASOR	*Bulletin of the American Schools of Oriental Research*
CAHEP	Caesarea Ancient Harbor Excavation Project
CE	Common Era
CIJ	*Corpus inscriptionum iudaicarum*
ESCJ	Studies in Christianity and Judaism/Etudes sur le christianisme et le judaïsme
IEJ	*Israel Exploration Journal*
JRA	*Journal of Roman Archaeology*
NEAEHL	*New Encyclopedia of Archaeological Excavations in the Holy Land*, ed. Ephraim Stern, 4 vols, Jerusalem: Carta/Israel Exploration Society, 1993
OEANE	*The Oxford Encyclopedia of Archaeology in the Near East*, ed. Eric M. Meyers, 5 vols, New York and Oxford: Oxford University Press, 1997
PECS	*Princeton Encyclopedia of Classical Sites*
Schürer	Emil Schürer, *The History of the Jewish People in the Age of Jesus Christ (175 BC – AD 135)*, new rev. edn, ed. Geza Vermes and Fergus Millar, 4 vols, Edinburgh: T. & T. Clark, 1973–87
ZDPV	*Zeitschrift des Deutschen Palästina-Vereins*

Chronological outline

General periods in the Levant

Bronze Age	3300–1200 BCE
Iron Age	1200–520 BCE
Persian period	520–332 BCE
Hellenistic period	332–63 BCE
Early Roman period	63 BCE – 135 CE
Middle Roman period	135–250 CE
Late Roman period	250–363 CE
Byzantine period	363–638 CE
Arab period	638–1099 CE

Local periods

Seleucid period	300–63 BCE
Nabatean period	*c.*300 BCE – 106 CE
Hasmonean period	167–40 BCE
Herodian period	40–4 BCE
Descendants of Herod	4 BCE – *c.*100 CE

Specific dates

Annexation of Syria and Judea by Pompey	64/63 BCE
Caesar's assassination	44 BCE
Parthians invade Syria	37 BCE
Battle of Actium (Octavian defeats Antony and Cleopatra)	31 BCE

Beginning of Principate (Octavian given title Augustus)	27 BCE
Aelius Gallus's expedition to Arabia Felix with Syllaeus	26/25 BCE
Judea governed by procurators	6 CE
Jewish Revolt	66–74 CE
Annexation of Nabatea, creation of province of Arabia	106 CE
Trajan's Parthian Wars	114–17 CE
Hadrian in the east	128–32 CE
Founding of Aelia Capitolina (Jerusalem)	130 CE
Second Jewish Revolt (Bar Kochba Revolt)	132–5 CE
Septimius Severus's Parthian Wars	195–9 CE
Caracalla in the east	214–17 CE
Persian invasion	253–60 CE
Palmyrene Revolt (Queen Zenobia)	270–72 CE
Empire reorganized by Diocletian	294 CE
Constantine	306–37 CE

Introduction

The lectures that lie behind this book had a time and place. They were given in Victoria, British Columbia, in late October and early November 2001, not long after the unspeakable attacks on New York and Washington on 11 September. I was preparing an introduction for them on that ignominious day. The next day I had to wrestle with what to say to a group of first-year students in their first class in a course on 'Ancient Mediterranean Cities and Towns and the Place of Religion' at the University of Toronto. The comments would form a first impression of the relevance of the course and maybe of university education generally. Coming so soon after those horrific events it seemed essential to reflect on the previous day's events in the USA from the vantage point of a Canadian neighbour.

The mind of an ancient historian goes to ancient analogies in such circumstances. My comments were partly instinctive and partly thought-out. The main burden of my comments that day in a course on 'sanctuaries and cities' in the ancient Roman world was how Rome looked to its restless citizens. It was the major superpower in terms of the effective deployment of military might, challenged only by Parthia; it dominated world trade, from which many benefited; its political power included regions reluctantly within its orbit. I focused on analogies between the United States and Rome as superpowers or 'imperial' powers, though I tried to avoid overly blunt comparisons between the USA's role in modern world affairs and Rome's dominance, since both the process and results were very different.

One of the points in my class comments was that just as there had been resistance movements against Rome's dominance, so there has been opposition to the American developments. On the day after the attacks it was not at all clear whether the culprits in the New York, Washington and Pennsylvania terrorist attacks were homegrown far-right movements, far-left movements, Afghani, Saudi, Iraqi or Palestinian movements, or extremists from other countries. Attention was already beginning to focus on Afghanistan as a possible point of origin, so a secondary comment had to do with the extreme difficulty military leaders had had in wresting control of the region from its indigenous peoples. One of the few who had managed to lead an army through Afghanistan had been Alexander the Great, a task he had not found at all easy in that harsh environment. Indeed, Alexander married Roxane (from Bactria; an 'Afghani'?) and had many of his men marry eastern locals to aid in the task. A third observation focused on cultural influence. Just as a number of the leaders of revolts against Rome were citizens of Rome, deeply influenced by its culture, so it would not be surprising if the attacks on the USA had originated with some who were closely familiar with American culture, 'friends' of the USA. The main point was that developments welcomed in some circles elicited horror and resistance in other circles.

Individuals sought singular power, as Pompey had set out to do in the 60s and as Octavian was to do more subtly later in the 30s BCE. Old-fashioned republicans in Rome opposed the concentration of power. Political conspirators – well-intentioned, perhaps, but conspirators nonetheless – murdered Julius Caesar in 44 BCE, following his being named 'dictator for life'. The triumvirate of Octavian, Mark Antony and Lepidus that was formed in 43 BCE to deal with the emergency created by Caesar's assassination aimed for tighter control. The period was volatile as political processes adapted to the new world order that came as a result of Roman expansion. With Octavian's assuming control a kind of stability had settled on the new institution of the Principate, and Rome came to terms with the new order.

More interesting and relevant than internal reactions was external opposition to Rome in subject territories. It should be no surprise to social historians – though it seems to have surprised

Romans – that numerous local resistance movements broke out into open revolt especially in the Julio-Claudian period. Local leaders emerged who sought to redress the wrongs done to them over the years by brutal, grasping or merely thoughtless local agents of a controlling power far away in Rome. Whether motivated by attempts to get even, opportunism, religious goals, revulsion at the suffering and subjugation of their peoples, or other causes, armed rebellion against Rome's dominance was a feature of the early Roman period. Some of the most far-reaching were the following. In 9 CE Arminius, a 28-year-old Roman citizen, with the German tribes united under him, ambushed Roman troops in the Teutoburgerwald under Varus, with the horrifying loss of some 15,000 troops in one day. Elsewhere in continental Europe Illyrians and Pannonians (today's Hungary and roughly what was Yugoslavia) also revolted in 9 CE. Thracians (roughly Bulgaria) revolted in 26 CE; Frisians, along the North Sea coastline, revolted in 28 CE and again in 68–9 CE. Batavia (today's Netherlands/Belgium) rose in revolt under C. Julius Civilis, a Roman citizen, in 69–70 CE. In 61–2 CE the warrior Queen Boudicca, another Roman citizen, galvanized the Celtic tribes, leading them in terrorist attacks on Camulodunum (Colchester), Londinium (London) and Verulamium (St Albans). The uprising stemmed from the cruel treatment, tyranny and greed that resulted from Roman rule, according to Tacitus; it led to the loss of 70,000 Roman and perhaps 80,000 British lives (Tacitus, *Annals* 14.31, 33, 37):

> Egged on by such mutual encouragements, the whole island rose under the leadership of Boudicca, a lady of royal descent – for Britons make no distinction of sex in their appointment of commanders. They hunted down the Roman troops in their scattered posts, stormed the forts, and assaulted the colony itself, which they saw as the citadel of their servitude.
>
> (Tacitus, *Agricola* 16)

A few years later in the Near East the famous Jewish Revolt of 66–74 CE was surprisingly successful (Josephus, *Jewish War*). The revolt eventually resulted in the destruction of Jerusalem and its temple on 9 Ab in the year 70 CE, with men, women and children leaping into the flames of the burning city to escape a worse death. Tens of thousands were killed in a few days. Two generations later the revolt was repeated elsewhere in less well-documented diaspora revolts that occurred between 115 and 117 CE in Egypt, Cyrene, Cyprus and Mesopotamia, again with great loss of life. A generation later there was another Jewish revolt in the homeland, the Bar Kokhba Revolt (132–5 CE), with destructive results.

Later still, in 269/70, the warrior Queen Zenobia of Palmyra, yet another Roman citizen, rose against Claudius II, though in this case the conditions that led to the military actions stemmed more from ambition and opportunity (possibly fuelled by roles she was given as regent for her son) than from a deep sense of grievance, as in the other cases. She was remarkably successful in pursuing her goal as far as Egypt and central Asia Minor. In each of the above cases irresistible Roman retaliation resulted in the inevitable end of the revolt. With the military victory of overwhelming Roman forces, the leaders of the revolts died or were executed, the main cities were besieged and destroyed, and a devastating loss of life followed.

It is ironic that some of the revolts and the revolutionaries have had a better press than Rome and its leaders. History has glorified and mythologized several of the revolts, and their reverberations continue strongly to this day. Bismarck mythologized Arminius in a huge monument overlooking the Teutoburgerwald, built intentionally to reflect German imperial aims of the late nineteenth century. Arminius was a nationalist rallying point, a fact Tacitus had appreciated much earlier when he referred to 'the freedom of Germany', which cost the Republic five consular armies and Augustus three legions (Tacitus, *Germania* 37). British glorification of Boudicca's revolutionary movement, which looked for an end to brutality and humiliation, has interpreted her actions as a glorious chapter in defining the nation. And Jews have recalled the Jewish Revolt persistently everywhere, though especially of course in the state of Israel. The ninth of Ab was mythologized as the date for the destruction of both First and Second Temple and has now been turned into a day of national mourning in Israel, with Masada, the last Jewish stronghold, a nationalist rallying cry. Queen Zenobia lives on as a mighty warrior queen, when her captor has been all but forgotten.

Rome, of course, saw the uprisings as barbaric actions of rebels who had to be crushed by mighty retaliatory armies. But in the perspective of two millennia it is the revolutionaries who appear as heroes of the people, fighting for self-determination, upholding the social, religious and political values of indigenous peoples against the power of the oppressor. This is a modern interpretive gloss on the events, utilizing modern ideals and aspirations as the touchstone, yet it is not altogether false.

Revolution was prompted in part by Roman atrocities and in part by the clash of cultures brought about by fast social and cultural and religious change, change that was endemic as imperial Rome absorbed new territories. Resistance to change with uprisings against Rome could be fervent, as the revolts in Judea and Palmyra show. Palmyra was an Arabian civilization of high culture that had been gradually assimilated into Rome's provincial system through a period of more than two centuries. Its leaders were Roman citizens who enjoyed a substantial degree of independence, which they had used vigorously in Rome's support. Judea was a Semitic country with a long devotion to monotheism and particular cultural and religious markers; it had been within the Roman orbit for over a century and had come to tolerate, not always happily, Rome's influence. Judaism's recollection of the revolt shows the strong modern reverberations of these intense clashes with Roman imperialism. Perhaps in modern Arab political and social sensibilities we also hear reverberations of Zenobia's revolt.

Great powers usually think they are making the world safer and better and more prosperous. Indeed, Rome did make the Mediterranean a huge 'free trade' region, around which merchants could travel for the most part safely, where huge fortunes could be made, and where Roman cultural institutions were spread so broadly that one felt at home almost anywhere (not unlike today's fast food outlets, designer clothes, English-language newspapers and the ubiquitous CNN). But to indigenous religions and cultures homogenization is a distinct disadvantage, not something sought. Cultural, religious, economic and political forces that run roughshod over local aspirations, history, religion, social organization and – to be anachronistic for a moment – drive to self-determination will often be resisted.

The lectures had been intended to focus on the religious and architectural ambiguities of the Levant, including its cultural tensions, an intention given extra point by 11 September 2001. The aftermath of that day inevitably influenced how the lectures were delivered and heard, accounting for some of the preliminary comments on Romanization. Those comments have been expanded for publication and broadened to include additional issues such as frontiers, borders and administration. The events have also heightened my interest in the resistance of local religions to Rome's challenge. While I had studied architectural expressions of religion for years, I found myself giving it more significance than I might earlier have done.

The published form of the lectures is substantially different from the oral form. Lecture 1 was divided into two chapters. The four cities considered in the lectures (Palmyra, Petra, Gerasa and Jerusalem) are included here in the same order, except that Caesarea Maritima has been added between Gerasa and Jerusalem. That chapter is a slightly revised version of an essay that appeared as chapter 2, 'Archaeological evidence for religion and urbanism in Caesarea Maritima', pages 11–34 in Terence L. Donaldson (ed.), *Religious Rivalries and the Struggle for Success in Caesarea Maritima*, ESCJ 8, Waterloo, Ont.: Wilfrid Laurier University Press, 2000. I am grateful to both editor and Press for their permission to include it here.

I have provided a glossary of unfamiliar terms. Chronological tables of building projects are included to assist in understanding the cities' developmental processes; Table 7.1 permits some gross comparisons of those developments. References have been kept to a minimum, with the emphasis on secondary studies that may be widely available.

1

Roman expansion and Romanization

Rome's expansion

Rome had acquired most of Italy and Sicily by the third century BCE; it then began to expand eastwards using a slow and episodic combination of intimidation, negotiation and conquest. The sequence of states taken over and new provinces in the east shows the progression:

- Macedonia was conquered in 167 BCE; initially it was split into four territories but in 146 BCE it was created a province.
- Achaia was created following the Achaian Confederacy's resistance to Rome and the destruction of Corinth in 146 BCE.
- Asia was absorbed in 133 BCE, when King Attalus III of Pergamum willed his extensive kingdom to Rome, partly because he had no successors and partly, perhaps, because he saw where Asia's future lay.
- Pamphylia became a part of Asia in 133 BCE; later (*c.*80 BCE) it was attached to Cilicia, then it rejoined Asia, and later it was added to Galatia (25 BCE).
- Cilicia was taken over about 80 BCE, to a large extent because of the threat of pirates.
- Cyrenaica passed to Rome by bequest on the death of Ptolemy Apion in 96 BCE and was formally annexed in 75/74 BCE.
- Crete was taken by military conquest in 68/67 BCE, partly because of its role as a major pirate base.
- Syria (64 BCE) and Judea (63 BCE) were invaded because both were weakened by internecine royal struggles, in the one case between Antiochus XIII Asiaticus and Philip II, in the other

between Hyrcanus II and Aristobulus II; these rivalries created a pretext to annex Syria as a province and to adopt Judea as a client state, initially with Hyrcanus II as ethnarch and then with Herod as the new king (40 BCE).

- Cappadocia, which had long been pro-Roman, was a client kingdom under Archelaus from about 36 BCE, then annexed as a province in 17 CE.
- Galatia was adopted as a client kingdom with Amyntas II as client king in 25 BCE.
- Egypt was annexed as a province in 30 BCE, after the deaths of Cleopatra VII and Mark Antony, following their defeat at the Battle of Actium (31 BCE).
- Chalcis, Iturea and Abila had complex histories and connections; all came under Rome's indirect control in the Julio-Claudian period.
- Arabia was simply annexed as a province in 106 CE, though it may have been dominated by Rome at earlier periods; it may even have been a client kingdom for a brief period under Aretas IV.

In all cases the events were much more complex than a simple list makes them appear, and the motives were wider-ranging than the brief descriptions suggest. The simplicity and length of this list obscures the fact that a variety of strategies were used: annexation as a province following conquest, as in the cases of Crete, Achaia and Macedonia; acquisition by bequest as in the cases of Cyrenaica and Pergamum; identification of a tractable client king as in the cases of Galatia and Cappadocia and Judea; indirect control, as in the case of Pamphylia, Iturea, Chalcis, Abila and Nabatea. Rome used a range of 'provocations' to justify its actions: external disorder due to piracy, political incompetence, internecine strife that destabilized the region and so on. The net effect was a steady expansion of Rome eastwards, matched by similar movements to west, north and south. Strabo summarized the result at the conclusion of his long geographical work:

> Of this whole country that is subject to the Romans, some parts are indeed ruled by kings, but the Romans retain others

> themselves, calling them provinces, and send to them prefects and collectors of tribute. But there are also some free cities, of which some came over to the Romans at the outset as friends, whereas others were set free by the Romans themselves as a mark of honour. There are also some potentates and phylarchs and priests subject to them. Now these live in accordance with their ancestral laws.
>
> (Strabo, *Geography* 17.3.24)

Syria

Rome's expansion, though hardly planned as a set of strategic moves (Isaac, *Limits*, 416), in retrospect must have seemed inevitable. In the various arrangements noted above there was one simple but often unstated goal, to extend Rome's influence in whatever ways were most appropriate. Behind it, however, this might involve the need for food, the search for private wealth, or punishment of Rome's enemies. But the deeper political and military goal through much of the period was checkmating Parthia, which came to be Rome's major rival from its original base south-east of the Caspian Sea. Rome's relations with Parthia were complicated (Debevoise, *Parthia*). As Rome moved eastwards and took over much of the old Seleucid Kingdom from the west, Parthia had moved westwards, taking over most of Iran and Mesopotamia, until its empire was centred at Ctesiphon on the Tigris. It was a major force to be reckoned with during the late-Hellenistic period (Richardson, *Herod*, 119–29). The two powers abutted – and occasionally came into conflict – more or less along a line east of the Mediterranean coastline: Strabo catches the essence well when he says, 'of the interior and the country deep inland, one part is held by the Romans themselves and another by the Parthians and the barbarians beyond them' (Strabo, *Geography* 17.3.24). Parthia overwhelmed Rome disastrously in Crassus' crushing defeat at the Battle of Carrhae in 53 BCE, with the loss of legionary signa. It was almost inevitable that they would continue to come into conflict in the same region, and the securing of new territories in the Levant may have been a part of Rome's anticipatory preparations. The province of Syria bore the brunt of the military build-up, with two or three legions (ten to fifteen thousand soldiers) stationed there. Following 27 BCE, when a distinction between senatorial and imperial provinces was drawn, it was an imperial province (i.e. it had governors whose responsibility and allegiance were to the emperor), with the emperor effectively in charge of all or most Roman troops. Likewise, the choice of Herod as client king of Judea in place of the weakened and Parthian-leaning Hasmoneans fitted that goal, for he was a strong and well-known Romanophile.

Judea and client kingship

Client rulers who owed their allegiance to the emperor (earlier they owed their allegiance to or were authorized by the senate) were an important part of Roman policy, used in cases where there was some doubt about Rome's ability to govern a population peacefully and well. Less fully Romanized regions – or areas less predictably amenable to Romanization – might be allowed to retain a degree of local independence for a period of time (always presupposing conformity to Roman long-term goals and foreign policy), usually not more than a few generations. It was assumed that, having been drawn into the Roman sphere and exposed to the advantages of Roman culture and religion and society, the population of a client state would want to become fully Roman. This might happen relatively quickly or slowly or not at all. Strabo chooses to end his long work with these words:

> [Augustus] divided the whole of his empire into two parts, and assigned one portion to himself and the other to the Roman people; to himself all parts that had need of a military guard (that is, the part that was barbarian and in the neighbourhood of tribes not yet subdued, or lands that were sterile and difficult to bring under cultivation, so that, being unprovided with everything else but well provided with strongholds, they would try to throw off the bridle and refuse obedience), and to the Roman people all the rest . . . [numerous examples follow]. Kings also, and potentates and decarchies are now, and always have been, in Caesar's portion.
>
> (Strabo, *Geography* 17.3.25)

For example, Judea was a client kingdom, initially under Herod the Great (40–4 BCE) and later divided between three of his sons, and then under a grandson. While Herod's strong rule resulted in Judea's full inclusion into the economic and social benefits of the Empire, when the kingdom was split in three at his death conditions suited the promotion of Roman ways less well than nurturing fissiparous Judean movements aiming for autonomy. The safeguarding of local traditions, which client rule – as a transitional phase to a more stable Roman set of conditions – made possible, did not always work to Rome's advantage. Augustus made a serious mistake in Judea. Having participated with Marc Antony in installing Herod as king in 40 BCE, Augustus might have opted for a single successor in place of three successors in 4 BCE when Herod died. Or alternatively, as some Jewish leaders argued, Rome might simply have included Judea with Syria as part of the Roman provincial system. The least satisfactory arrangement from Rome's point of view was a three-part division with competing rulers; this merely encouraged the nationalist sentiment that Rome was trying to finesse by opting for a client kingdom in the first place.

Areas that became provinces were already more Romanized – or at least more open to Romanization – than areas that were dealt with as client kingdoms. Provinces had already reached the point where full inclusion in the Roman world was possible. With client kingdoms, where local social or political conditions made the process of Romanization more difficult, incorporation as a province was not yet possible.

The Decapolis

The Decapolis was a loose association of about ten cities, though the number varied over its lifetime. The boundaries of the cities and the status of territory, if any, between them remain unclear. To a close approximation they occupied a region in southern Syria and northern Jordan, with one city, Scythopolis (Beth Shean), lying west of the Jordan. East and south of the Decapolis cities was Nabatea; north of them was Syria; west of them were Judea, Samaria and Galilee (along with Perea, Galilee's other half, in the first centuries BCE and CE). Their cultural, civic and political backgrounds were varied and complicated. Their founding as outposts of Hellenistic civilization, intended to promote Alexander the Great's programme of Hellenization, and their development during the Ptolemaic and Seleucid periods has come in for close critical scrutiny recently. It now appears that the crucial set of developments came only under Augustus (Graf, 'Hellenisation'). Each was an independent polis with an attached chôra; that is, each city was self-governing, with the requisite civic institutions (often relatively late) and enough countryside under its control to be self-supporting agriculturally.

For a short period of time the Decapolis cities may have included Damascus, but for the majority of the time during which they were an important factor in the region, the largest and most important were Scythopolis (Beth Shean), surrounded by Jewish and Samaritan territory, Gerasa (Jerash) and Philadelphia (Amman), east of the Jordan, bounded mainly by Nabatean territory. As centres of Greek and Roman culture they played a disproportionately large cultural role. The Decapolis came to an end, even as a loose association, with the creation of the Province of Arabia in 106 CE: the cities were included administratively and politically in Arabia (e.g. Gerasa, Philadelphia, Adraa, Capitolias), Judea (probably Scythopolis, Pella, Gadara, Hippos) and Syria (the remainder).

Nabatea and Arabia

While Nabatea has come to be relatively well known in the last generation or so, the author of a recent book on Arabia laments that 'the many centuries of Arabian history that precede the death of Muhammad are little studied and little known in the West', and much of what was written previously is made 'all but obsolete by recent archaeological discoveries' (Holyland, *Arabia*, 1, 2; cf. Bowersock, *Roman Arabia*, ch. 1). Holyland provides a modern survey of the state of the field that draws on the relevant literary and archaeological resources. He portrays a group of closely related sophisticated Arab cultures, occupying parts of an area larger than the size of Europe, sharing languages related to north

Arabian and having in common other cultural features. Most were nomadic pastoralists, whose homeland was north and central Arabia, who enter the historical record clearly through Assyrian and Israelite sources in the ninth and eighth centuries BCE because of trade between Arabia and the Mediterranean world. Many were animal herders and agriculturalists; specific groups became sedentary in north-west Arabia in the final centuries before the Common Era: Nabateans, Idumeans, Itureans, Palmyrenes, as well as Emesenes, Abgarids of Edessa, and others (Richardson, *Herod*, 52–72; Holyland, *Arabia*, 69).

Nabatean culture began to flower in the second century BCE and came to a peak in the late first century BCE and through the first century CE, when it absorbed Hellenistic artistic conventions from Alexandria and wedded them to its own remarkable technological skills. It came under the influence of Rome – perhaps even under direct control – in the late first century BCE. Bowersock has made a case for Nabatea being annexed as a province during a short period (3–1 BCE), after which it was returned to Aretas as a client king (Bowersock, *Roman Arabia*, 54–8). Strabo's comment, however, is not as clear as Bowersock suggests: 'They often overran Syria before they became subject to the Romans; but at present both they and the Syrians are subject to the Romans' (*nun de kakeinoi Rômaios eisin hypêkooi kai Syroi*; *Geography* 16.4.21). When Strabo says in the same paragraph that 'it is exceedingly well governed' and that 'their government' was admired, he does not seem to allude to a Roman provincial arrangement parallel to Syria. The more usual view is that Nabatea retained essential independence throughout the first century CE and was only annexed in 106 CE as a province. Still, even if that were so, there was strong Roman interest and even presence in Nabatea during earlier periods, for Strabo specifically alludes to 'many Romans and many other foreigners sojourning there'. It should be noted that it cooperated with Rome militarily at Ascalon and Alexandria (47 BCE), on the Red Sea (31/30 BCE) and in the expedition to Mariba (25/24 BCE; Josephus, *Ant.* 15.317; Strabo, *Geography* 16.4.22–4).

Roman frontiers

The increase in Roman territory created a major difficulty for Rome's understanding of itself. Was Vitruvius correct about Rome's perception even in the time of Augustus: 'Thus the divine intelligence established the state of the Roman People as an outstanding and balanced region – so that it could take command over the earthly orb' (Vitruvius, *Ten Books* 6.1.11)? Was its need for additional territory insatiable? Was there some defined limit to the growing Roman world? Was it possible at any given moment to mark a boundary?

In the Levant, as elsewhere, the notion of a *limes* (originally 'crosspath' or 'byway' and then 'road') came to have the sense of boundary during the middle Empire, a mark of how far the Roman state extended (Whittaker, *Frontiers,* 200–1). It has often been suggested that in the region where Parthia and Rome met as rivals there was precisely such a static sense of frontier. As Whittaker points out, however, both archaeological and literary evidence show that frontiers were boundaries only in the sense of a region that might be easily navigated in either direction, even in the Levant. Palmyra was a completely ambiguous case: it is not possible to know whether it was inside or outside the empire, 'a perfect example of control without rule or of ideology before reality'. 'In other words, the Arabian frontier was a true limes, a road for movement and not a blocking, defensive system . . . [W]e do not find in this sector anything that could be called a frontier "system"' (Whittaker, *Frontiers,* 49–59; quotations from 54–5, 59; Bowersock, *Roman Arabia,* 103–5). This general view of frontiers primarily as roads is exemplified by the Via Nova Traiana extending from Bostra (Bosra) to Aila (Aqabah) in the south, built connecting the major cities of Syria and Arabia, though missing Gerasa. 'The only natural and logical way, then, of looking at the Trajanic road is to see it as a link between southern Syria and the northern part of the Arabian peninsula. To describe it as a line of defence is speculative and implausible' (Isaac, *Limits,* 121). As Lintott says, 'The empire thus remained for centuries open-ended geographically as well as conceptually, and even when in the second century AD it tended to become a fortress, remained permeable to outside influences. Indeed the frontier could be viewed as a controlled environment in which contact with the outside world could be facilitated' (Lintott, *Imperium Romanum*, 42).

A consequence of the permeability of frontiers is that they did not define cultural or ethnic boundaries. Border peoples took advantage of their liminal positions to play both sides of the game, as Appian says explicitly of Palmyra (in the context of Antony's raid in 41 BCE): 'being on the frontier between the Romans and the Parthians they had avoided taking sides between them' (Appian, *Civil Wars* 5.1.9). Some of the accounts of 'brigands' in the border regions of Syria, Galilee, Iturea and Arabia doubtless stem from the extensive trade coupled with frontier permeability (Richardson and Edwards, 'Social protest').

Roman administration

The organization of the Roman Empire to a large extent supports the above emphasis on flexibility and permeability. 'The earliest contemporary evidence for the existence of a technical term for a geographical area ruled by Rome comes with the creation of the province of Macedonia in 148–7 and its Greek annexes in 146–5.' Though *provincia/eparcheia* had some spatial connotations, the primary meaning was the 'assigning of specific functions to magistrates' (Lintott, *Imperium Romanum*, both quotations from p. 23). Spatial limitations for officials were, of course, particularly important between adjacent provinces, though even in those cases there could be overlapping of jurisdictions, as was true during Herod's and his sons' reigns in Judea when responsibilities extended into Syria and perhaps Nabatea, too. The local initiatives and roles of Roman officials in frontier provinces were ambiguous and uncertain, though it was clear that Roman officials, including client kings and presumably even those who were only loosely under Roman control, could not engage independently in military or political adventures in neighbouring provinces. Rome's disciplinary hand was quickly felt in such cases.

Roman flexibility was reflected in the multiplicity of ways it might govern its territories directly and indirectly. There was no one organizational structure, not even in contiguous areas. In a single region Rome could have a province (Syria), an ambiguous arrangement (Palmyra), a polis with chôra (Gerasa), a client king (Herod of Judea), a territory under that client king (Iturea), and a semi-independent kingdom not yet clearly incorporated (Nabatea/Arabia). This lack of fixed views on governance was part of the genius of the Roman Empire.

Rome was not always a conqueror that imposed unwanted rule on states as it expanded. Many in Rome's territories found its rule both benign and beneficent. It almost goes without saying that those involved in trade and commerce (often a formidable group) appreciated Rome's control. Trade flourished after Octavian's solution to the unrest of the period of the civil wars; the pax romana brought with it a period of prosperity. Many must have welcomed the conditions Rome had created – conditions that were reflected both in the general expansion of the cities examined below and also in the numerous benefactions that were bestowed on the cities by grateful citizens. Clear evidence of this gratitude at an elite level can be seen in the response of Herod to his patrons, Marc Antony, Augustus, Livia and Marcus Agrippa: the naming of numerous projects after them and especially the construction of three large temples to Roma and Augustus speaks to the sense of obligation and to the generosity with which that obligation was reciprocated (Richardson, *Herod*, ch. 8). Others who shared in the benefits felt the same gratitude. Of course, as noted in the Introduction, there was also opposition to Rome, for reactions both at home and abroad were very mixed. Not everyone had a share of the benefits and many resisted the notion of 'Romanization' that seemed to lie behind Rome's policies.

Romanization

As with questions of frontiers and administrative issues, scholarly attitudes on Romanization have been changing in recent decades.[1] A. H. M. Jones's influential book on the cities of the eastern provinces is still essential, but the field has developed since its time (Jones, *Cities*). The situation has been assessed recently by Ramsay MacMullen, who holds a variant of the classical view: 'Roman civilization eventually appeared everywhere as one single thing' although it was 'sometimes imperfectly achieved' (MacMullen, *Romanization*, p. ix). Rome was engaged in an extensive effort to promote its culture, as observed for example in the large number of *municipia* and *coloniae* founded in the time of Caesar and Augustus (Millar, *Roman Near East*, ch. 2). On the 'classic' view, this effort was so successful that Roman culture developed almost homogeneously throughout the empire. It is tempting to fall into this view, especially when describing similarities in plan and design between various baths or theatres or stadia or basilicas (e.g. the baths at Hammat Gader in the Golan Heights and at Bath, England). The view has some force, though there were differences between east and west (Keay and Terrenato, *Italy and the West*).

Warwick Ball has proposed another view, in a big book written in the same year as MacMullen's book but arguing a fundamentally different view from the consensus (*Rome in the East*). Ball argues aggressively that 'Romanization' is largely a western scholarly construct and he claims that to a significant extent Rome's efforts at Romanization were unsuccessful. Much of what is seen as evidence of Romanization was originally a product of eastern civilization, he says, which was exported to the west and only later in a third stage exported east again. Colonnaded streets are his prime example: they originated in Antioch in the late first century BCE, then moved to the west, and later became popular again in the east (Ward-Perkins, *Roman Imperial Architecture*, 286). The example is especially interesting; according to Josephus (*War* 1.425; *Ant.* 16.148), Herod was the builder of Antioch's colonnaded street and thus the innovator of this civic element. Ball's most useful other examples, for our purposes, are the layout of cities and the design of temples. Some of his discussion is exaggerated, to be sure, but enough is on target to suggest the usual view falls short.

A third broader book appeared the same year, dealing fundamentally with the same issue. Its contributors examine 'the idea of the city as an instrument of Romanization', in ways that are diverse in strategy, geography and topical focus (Fentress, *Romanization*, 7). Yet the volume is not a disjointed, haphazard, conglomerate of papers; it makes a valiant effort to evaluate the 'heroic myths' of previous scholarship – focused on celebrated excavations at Cosa –

by attending to those achievements and wrestling with new definitional problems. The participants move in various directions, but the content is governed by a careful editorial reticence that precludes 'an over-exuberant paradigm swing'; the papers make use of comparative strategies to deal with 'myth-making and myth-breaking about cities and their role in the Roman world' (Alcock in Fentress, *Romanization*, 221–6; cf. Barrett, 'Romanization'). Two quotations on the general topic of Romanization from Mary Downs will illustrate the crucial point:

> The notion of a Mediterranean-wide unity in Roman culture, or in Roman material culture, can no longer be sustained. Today, greater attention is focused on the multiple cultural and ethnic experiences across the empire, on the active role that indigenous populations played in the evolution of their own cultural landscapes, on regional variability, and on adaptations – in material culture, technology, language and forms of expression – on a local scale.
>
> . . . [T]here was no active 'Romanizing' on the part of Rome. In recent years, scholars have stressed that the gradual adoption of Latin language and Roman customs, and assimilation to Roman institutions, varied greatly in time and space and was driven by the interests of the local indigenous aristocracy. But, in the absence of documents that would provide more detail about the motivations and behavior of the indigenous elite in their relations with Rome, scholars have sought refuge in the creation of a stereotype, a vague construct with ho historical flesh on his bones – the semi-Romanized native. The construct of the 'semi-Romanized' native makes the analysis of frontier demographics much easier.
>
> (Downs, 'Refiguring colonial categories', 198, 207)

Something is in the wind when a number of books appear in such a short space of time on closely related topics and with overlapping hypotheses. A major premise is being rethought. With respect to Ball and MacMullen, one reason for their substantial differences is that their notions of 'the east' vary. In the classical view the east is from Achaia eastwards, while for Ball the Roman east is essentially the Near East, the Levant, from the eastern end of the Mediterranean to the Euphrates, 'corresponding broadly to the Roman provinces of Syria, Palestine, Arabia and (briefly) Mesopotamia' (Ball, *Rome in the East*, 6). This definitional difference, of course, affects deeply both the evidence and the generalizations drawn from the evidence.

This study adopts the more limited definition, so the discussion is limited to cities of the Near East or the Levant (by which I mean the same region as that on which Ball focuses). The term 'Levant' has an archaic and Eurocentric ring to it, as dictionaries note, but it may still be useful to describe this region (modern Syria, Lebanon, Jordan, Israel, the West Bank, parts of Turkey and Saudi Arabia). When I refer to the Roman east, then, I intend consistently to refer to the larger area – from Greece, or the Aegean coast of Turkey, eastwards – to which classical scholars refer in that phrase; I refer to the narrower region as the Levant or Near East.

In the broader Roman east, the developments in administrative organization, technology and communications helped to create a single Roman world. The effort was extensive and successful. In other matters such as language and philosophy, however, Rome was unable to resist the continued pull of Greece: 'captive Greece took Rome captive', to use familiar words (MacMullen, *Romanization*, 29). The primary data in this present study is architecture. Along the eastern Mediterranean coastline – the Levant or the Near East – Romanization, judging from the architecture and urban design, was less extensive, deep-rooted and successful (see Downs's caveat above). This general stance may seem odd, given MacMullen's appeal to Herod's architecture as an example of an eastern ruler who was much influenced by Rome and whose programme of change seems to have included substantial allegiance to Rome. Herod was an important ruler, whose architecture is still the most important example of a major architectural patron in the region (Richardson, *Herod*). His architecture obviously owes much to Roman technology and architectural vocabulary (below, Chapters 5 and 6); but his oeuvre as a whole does not support MacMullen's thesis as strongly as he might wish. An analysis of Herod's works, which decisively affect one's views on more general questions, shows that the influences on him were very mixed (Richardson, *Herod*, ch. 8; Roller, *Building Program*, passim; Lichtenberger, *Baupolitik*, passim). There is much more to trace than simply similarities with the Roman canon of architecture and engineering. That is another story, but there is reason to look again at some of the material in these eastern regions, including areas under Herod's influence.

Five cities are selected here to test views of Romanization and earlier dependence on Hellenization in this limited region based on one kind of evidence. The situation will almost certainly be different in Ionia (Asia) or Achaia or Alexandria, or in the west (White, 'Urban development', 30–3). The focus of the present study is on material culture, especially urban culture, the setting where Romanization might be most effectively expressed. The prevailing mood together with my own inclinations suggests that rural areas ought to be included as well; to understand popular expressions of indigenous culture requires turning from the great civic agglomerations to the small towns and villages, where more extensive continuity with traditional civilizations would be found. Much of my own work has focused in the last decade on precisely this type of study, particularly in the Galilee, where one of the great revolts against Rome took strong root (Richardson, *Judaism*). This was a region where there was considerable tension between rural areas and poleis such as Tiberias, Sepphoris, Gadara, Hippos and Scythopolis. To assess the success of the Roman 'programme', however, one must look not to the rural areas where it was likely to be weakest but to the places where it was strongest: Palmyra, Petra, Gerasa, Caesarea Maritima and Jerusalem.

Arabs and Jews

In dealing with issues at the point of intersection of several cultural and ethnic areas there is a scholarly temptation to imagine that influences were one-directional: Rome influenced the Levant (Romanization) but not the other way around. Such a view tends to assume that the provincial areas were a *tabula rasa* (Holyland, *Arabia*, 167), able to be written upon easily and clearly by a stronger and more sophisticated culture. But this was not so either with Arabs or Jews. The point is often recognized when dealing with

Jews and Judaism, when there is a dynamic understanding of an ongoing indigenous culture with Hellenistic and Roman influences – whether intense or marginal – over a long period of time.

It is more difficult, however, to value fully Arab cultural inheritance and influence. It has not been so extensively studied and western scholars are not so fully attuned to it. A recent study observes that classical historians such as Strabo 'did not normally refer to them by the generic term Arab, but by specific designations'; he suggests modern historians do something similar (Shahîd, *Rome and the Arabs*, 6). Arab culture was vibrant and longstanding, with religious, linguistic and artistic accomplishments. It was influenced by Hellenistic and Roman culture – sometimes intense, sometimes marginal – over a long period of time. That the relationships and influences were bi-directional is symbolized by the fact that by the late second century CE, before the crisis into which the Empire soon fell, the Near East had deeply influenced the imperial family. (1) Septimius Severus married Julia Domna in 187 CE, daughter of a priest of Emesa. (2) Her two sons, Caracalla (211–17 CE) and Geta (211 CE), were thus partly eastern in their outlook. (3) She herself was made Augusta in 193 CE. (4) After a small gap, two emperors in succession were from the east, Elagabalus (218–22 CE), who was hereditary priest of the Sanctuary of Elagabalus in Emesa, and his cousin Alexander Severus (222–35 CE). (5) Not much later, Philip the Arab (244–9 CE, who may have 'dabbled in Christianity' (Bowersock, *Roman Arabia*, 127) assumed the imperial throne. This imperial history during the unsettled days bridging the Empire's high point and its eventual restoration reflected the importance of the Levant and Arab influence upon the west. The dominance of the west was not broken, but it had to reckon with the Levant in ways that earlier it had not had to do.

Rome never had a Jewish emperor analogous to Philip the Arab. Yet there was a short period in the first century CE when such a prospect was almost imaginable. During the late first century BCE and the mid-first century CE Herod's royal sons were virtual members of the imperial family. His children – half Arab and half Jewish – and grandchildren and great-grandchildren were educated alongside sons of the emperors (Richardson, *Herod*, 231–2). More important were four other imperial associations.

(1) Poppaea, Nero's mistress from about 58 CE and then wife from 62/3 CE, was alleged, perhaps correctly, to have Jewish sympathies (Josephus, *Ant.* 20.195, 252; *Life* 16). She may have influenced the outcome of a Jewish delegation to Nero in 61 CE, one of whose members was Josephus, as well as the selection of Gessius Florus as procurator of Judea in 64 CE, an appointment that turned out badly for Jews. (2) Berenice, great-granddaughter of Herod and sister of Agrippa II, who had been married three times (twice to kings), had a long affair with Titus before being forced to break it off on his accession to the imperial throne in 79 CE, partly because her being called queen offended Roman sensibilities. (3) When Domitian's only child died, he named as heirs two sons of his cousin Flavius Clemens (consul 95 CE) and his wife Flavia Domitilla. Flavius Clemens, however, was soon executed for *atheotês*, which probably meant the practice of Judaism (Cassius Dio 67.14.1; Suetonius, *Domitian* 15.1; Jones, *Domitian*, 47–8). The boys disappeared from the record; had one or other succeeded, a young man might have occupied the throne with strong attachments to Judaism. (4) Finally, one of Nerva's first actions following his accession after Domitian's death was to mint a coin with the suggestive legend, FISCI IUDAICI CALUMNIA SUBLATA ('the offence of the Jewish tax has been suppressed'; Richardson, 'Barnabas, Nerva'), announcing a change in the Flavian programme to appropriate the Jewish half-shekel tax for Roman purposes from 70 CE onwards.

These incidents suggest the strength of the bi-directional influences at work: on the one hand, Arab influences upon the imperial family and the succession from the late second century CE for three-quarters of a century; on the other, a persistent intertwining of Jewish and Roman families from the late first century BCE through first century CE for over a century. Rome was open both to Jews and Arabs, even at the centre of imperial politics and the succession. These influences anticipate in social, political and religious dimensions the discussion that will follow on an architectural and urban level. It is simplistic to think of uni-directional influences in what was a rather complicated world. Oversimplifications are attractive because of the west's strong attachment to its Roman inheritance and the Christianization of that inheritance following Constantine. In fact, the Levant's antiquity and strength, and Rome's tolerance of it, resulted in Rome being open to and influenced by the Levant. That was true of both major cultures and religious groups, Arabs and Jews, touched on in this study. The subsequent Byzantine period shows just as clearly this openness to influences from the Near East.

Architecture and urban design

The Roman Empire, and especially the Near East, defies simple homogenization. It is almost a truism that social, cultural and political conditions differed in various regions. This was as true of architecture and urban design as it was of religion and other features of cultural life on which one might focus. Given the situation noted above with respect to roads and frontiers, ethnic groups and regional differences, administration and technology, it might be thought that the selection of Palmyra and Petra as the two lead examples skews the evidence of cultural infusion. There may be some truth to this, for both cities exemplify as clearly as any the recently developed views of frontier studies and limits of empire. By including other less liminal cities, however, I intend to provide alternative examples, suggesting the inherent complexity of the situation. Gerasa, for example, with its earlier Hellenistic form on the edge of civilization close to the desert, did not show the same pattern as Jerusalem. The latter was much closer to the coast but less influenced by Hellenism and Rome; it had more in common with Petra and Palmyra, both farther inland. Caesarea Maritima was a clear example of a Romanized city, built as a showcase of the symbiosis of Rome and Judea, yet it had unusual features in the early Roman period that bear close examination.

The touchstone of much that follows is religion. Roman society was based on religion and ritual as much as on politics and economics. 'The architecture of the Romans was, from first to last, an art of shaping space around ritual. It stemmed directly from the Roman propensity to transform the raw stuff of experience and behavior into rituals, formal patterns of action and reaction' (Fentress, quoting Brown, in *Romanization*, 23). Romanization of the city focuses on 'the realization of certain abstract ideals in the built environment' (Zanker, 'City as symbol', 25), yet the monumental Roman structures typical of the state-sponsored city plan under the Principate 'could never be truly integrated into the rigorously severe template of the early city plan . . . New buildings were added as individual donations, and neither their architectural form nor their siting within the city was usually derived from a model in the city of Rome' (Zanker, 'City as symbol', 40). No doubt it is true that Egypt 'throws into high relief the actual interaction between so-called "classical" and "oriental" civilizations in the ancient Mediterranean world and the differences of approach to the subject employed by modern classical historians and oriental specialists' (Bowman, 'Urbanisation', 174–5). But it is just as true that a number of the cities of the Levant also throw into relief these differences of approach and that the conjunction of architecture and religious studies with archaeology contribute to understanding those differences. The religious and artistic dimensions of antiquity, above all, emphasize the region's cultural longevity and artistic self-confidence. Far from obliterating the Levant's indigenous cultures, Rome's influence was limited and constrained. Or, as Susan Gelb puts it, the Romanization of architecture following Hadrian's visit was the 'trickle-up' model of architectural development (Gelb, 'Architecture and Romanization').

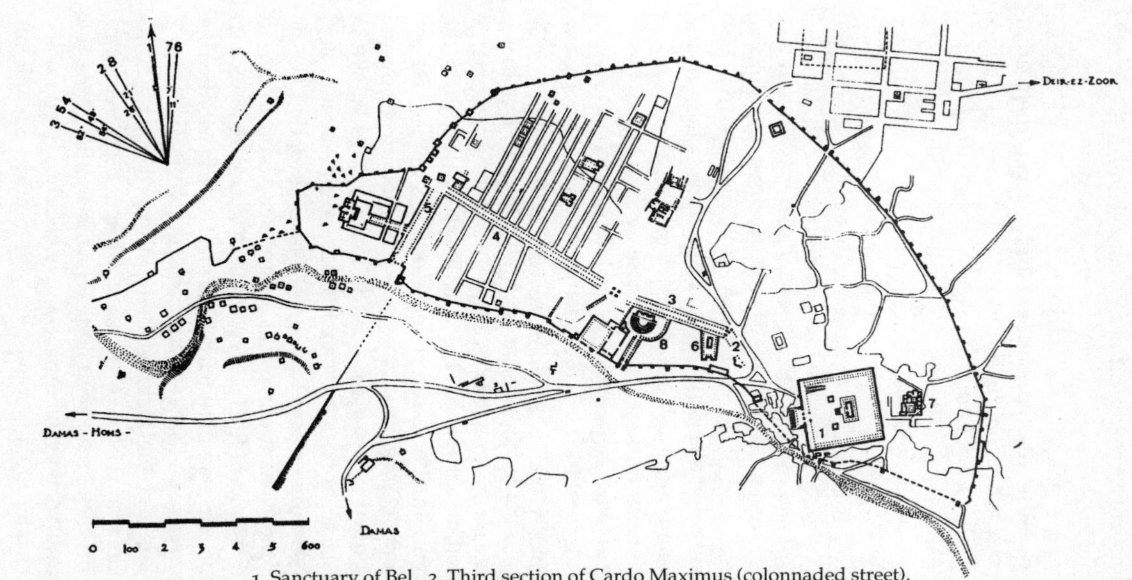

1. Sanctuary of Bel. 2. Third section of Cardo Maximus (colonnaded street).
3. Second section of Cardo Maximus. 4. First section of Cardo Maximus.
5. Western Decumanus (transverse colonnaded street). 6. Sanctuary of Nebo.
7. Houses east of the Bel sanctuary. 8. Houses south and east of the theatre.
Above to the left, comparison of different orientations

Plan of Palmyra, from Frezouls, E. 'Questions d'urbanisme Palmyrenien', in *Palmyre: Bilan et perspectives*, 193.

2

Palmyra: Rome and the Levant

Introduction

Driving through the Syrian Desert beyond the urban sprawl of Damascus there are few settlements of note. The road goes through starkly beautiful landscape for almost 250 kilometres until one comes to a small ridge where the ground drops away. In front and to the right is an enormous oasis of palm groves; ahead are the architectural remains of the ancient city; nearer, the tall towers of its unique necropolis rise; to the left is the hill from which an Arab castle dominates the site. It is a remarkable approach to a remarkable city, one of the great sites of the ancient world, which makes the same unforgettable impression on the modern visitor that it must have made on ancient visitors. Its location beside a very large desert oasis halfway between the Mediterranean Sea and the Euphrates River, in the northern part of the Arabian Desert, explains its importance near the edge of Roman territorial interests. Settlement in Palmyra – or Tadmor as it was known in earlier periods – went back to the early second millennium BCE, though there are earlier traces back to the Neolithic period. It was mentioned in the Mari archives, at Kültepe in Cappadocia, in Assyrian archives and in the Hebrew Bible. A major reason for its location was the presence of two fresh springs, the Efqa spring that runs into a deep cave on the west side being the stronger.

Both Josephus and the Hebrew Bible incorrectly attribute its founding to Solomon (*Ant.* 8.153–4; 2 Chron. 8.4); the word 'Tadmor' in Chronicles may be a confusion with another place, but Josephus's account makes the same claim explicitly. His summary is a not inaccurate explanation of its significance, even if his history is wrong in attributing both the city and its fortifications to Solomon.

> [Solomon] also advanced into the desert of Upper Syria and, having taken possession of it, founded there a very great city at a distance of two days' journey from Upper Syria and one day's journey from the Euphrates, while from the great Babylon the distance was a journey of six days. Now the reason for founding the city so far from the inhabited parts of Syria was that further down there was no water anywhere in the land and that only in this place were springs and wells to be found. And so, when he had built this city and surrounded it with very strong walls, he named it Thadamora [Tadmor], as it is still called by the Syrians, while the Greeks call it Palmyra.
>
> (*Ant.* 8.153–4)

The Seleucid dynasty (third to first century BCE), one of the three main successors to Alexander the Great's conquests, generally ignored Palmyra, though there are some remains of the Seleucid city south of the excavated areas (Grainger, *Seleukid Syria*). Its growth as a major city postdated Pompey's destruction of Seleucid power in 64 BCE, when Rome asserted control over Syria. This must also have been the point at which Palmyra began actively to influence trade between the Mediterranean region and Parthia. The city became a wealthy entrepôt for eastern and western traders; in fact it was a kind of neutral and semi-independent zone between the two ambitious rivals, Rome and Parthia. Pliny the Elder comments:

> Palmyra is a city famous for its situation, for the richness of its soil and for its agreeable springs. Its fields are surrounded on every side by a vast circuit of sand, and it is as it were isolated by nature from the world, having a destiny of its own between the two mighty empires of Rome and Parthia, and at the first moment of a quarrel between them always attracting the attention of both sides.
>
> (Pliny, *Natural History* 5.88)

Palmyra's key location was economically and commercially

beneficial in the spice and aromatics trade, especially myrrh and frankincense production centred in the southern parts of the Arabian Peninsula (Holyland, *Arabia*, 103–7). Some of this sought-after trade went overland up the Arabian caravan routes (including the Wadi Sirhan) or alternatively up the Red Sea to Petra and other trading centres, while some went up the Arabian Gulf and thence up the Euphrates River. So Palmyra became a major stop on caravan routes – eventually including the fabled Silk Road – because the oasis permitted caravans to take a shorter route across the Arabian Desert or, later, to avoid the instability of the upper Euphrates. 'Being merchants, they bring the products of India and Arabia from Persia and dispose of them in the Roman territory' (Appian, *Civil Wars*, 5.1.9); 'Palmyra was a true caravan city, for it owed its prosperity to its ability to channel the commerce passing between the two empires on either side of it' (Holyland, *Arabia*, 107). Strangely, Strabo does not mention Palmyra, but he refers frequently to the Scenitae, who occupied this part of northern Arabia in his account of the geographical, historical and ethnographic facts, as he knew them. He believed that much but not all of the region west of the Euphrates was under Roman control: 'the parts this side the river are held by the Romans and the chieftains of the Arabians as far as Babylonia, some of these chieftains preferring to give ear to the Parthians and others to the Romans, to whom they are neighbours' (*Geography* 16.1.28; cf. 16.4.21; 16.2.1). His view of the Parthians, who were 'in former times eager for friendship with the Romans' (*Geography* 16.1.28), is relatively benign.

Palmyra resisted Mark Antony's attack in 41 BCE, and thereafter it gradually developed close links with Rome, so that by the time of Tiberius – and as a result of Germanicus's time in the east (18–19 CE; attested by Palmyrene inscriptions) – there was some measure of Roman control, though not full incorporation into the Empire, since there were no Roman troops and no Roman collection of taxes (Millar, *Roman Near East*, 34–5). Exactly when it was fully incorporated within the Province of Syria is unclear, but Trajan (when he was legate of Syria under Vespasian) erected a Roman milestone north-east of Palmyra in 75 CE, suggesting an increasing degree of Roman control at least from that time (Millar, *Roman Near East*, 84–5). Hadrian visited the city in 130/31 CE; it was during this period, with strong but still ambiguous Roman influences, that Palmyra flourished.

When the Parthian menace lessened in the late second and early third centuries, Rome seized substantial additional territories, taking the important step of conferring the status of colonia on Palmyra sometime in the early third century under either Severus or Caracalla. As Millar points out, this development complicates the assessment of Palmyra in the mid-third century: it was 'Oriental', 'Greek' and 'Roman' all at once (Millar, *Roman Near East*, 143–4). Persia soon became a threat as it moved westwards, while Rome was in a weakened state because of troubles elsewhere. This left the Palmyrene king Odainath (Odenathus) to fill the breach by leading the defence of the eastern provinces in Rome's support, at the same time reasserting Palmyrene interests. After his murder (267 CE) his wife Queen Zenobia, who had been named Empress of the East, led what is often viewed as a full-scale revolt (270–2 CE) but was in reality an attempt to seize the imperial throne on behalf of her son Vaballathus (Wahaballat). Her action may well be viewed as part of the ascendancy of Philip the Arab (Bowersock, *Roman Arabia*, 128–31). Aurelian (270–5 CE) moved against Zenobia in 272; Palmyra was besieged but not destroyed until a second minor revolt and renewed siege in 274 CE. Zenobia was led in triumph through Rome. Diocletian (284–305 CE) refortified the city, but a period of instability and decline followed. Following the Christianizing of the empire under Constantine and his successors there was a period of resurgence. Justinian (527–65 CE) strengthened the city's defences again, but it fell in 634 to the Islamic Conquest and played only unimportant roles thereafter; eventually shrinking to a village confined to the Temple of Bel, with a mosque in the naos.

'Urbanism' and urban design

One of the most important political instruments in the Roman quiver was the development of new cities or the conferring of Roman benefits upon existing cities (Stambaugh, *Roman City*, ch. 15). Some cities of the Levant had been poleis – the classic form of self-governing urban organization with appropriate countryside or chôra to support them – from the time of Alexander or his successors. Rome made some cities in the Near East coloniae, which were somewhat similar (e.g. Palmyra, Edessa, Ptolemais, Neapolis, Jerusalem), and founded one or two others (e.g. Berytus). Inhabitants of coloniae may have been Roman citizens, while those of other smaller places (municipia) were generally not Roman citizens, unlike the case in Italy. The majority of settlements where people lived, of course, were much smaller towns and villages.

This study looks at the differences within the largest class of urban settlements, poleis or coloniae. It should be noted parenthetically that an equally suggestive and methodologically interesting way to examine cultures of the Levant would have involved urban–rural relationships and the character of small towns and villages (Burns and Eadie, *Urban Centers*; Alcock, *Early Roman Empire*; Richardson, *Judaism*). Although I focus on cities in this study, I recognize the deep importance of villages and small towns in the social makeup of the Roman Empire, especially in the east where populations remained close to their traditional roots.

Cities are human artefacts that draw people into permanent social relationships with each other, usually in ever-larger groups. Urbanism began about 7,500 to 10,000 years ago in the Levant, in fact, though whether in Damascus, Jericho or Byblos, or somewhere else, is unclear and unimportant for us. There was no one pattern for very early cities; in some early eastern examples the city was laid out in a more or less rectangular fashion (Ball, *Rome in the East*, 246–72). The traditional Greek – and later the Hellenistic – city was organized on the so-called Hippodamian plan, named after Hippodamus of Miletus (born about 500 BCE) and exemplified in his work at Miletus, Pireus and Rhodes especially. Ball suggests that 'Miletus received its idea of town planning from (or via) the Iranians' (pp. 253, 255–6). But his main point is the long tradition of Near-Eastern practices analogous to Hellenistic and Roman practices.

The Roman city followed Hellenistic practice, but tended to emphasize the major circulation routes, the Cardo Maximus and the Decumanus, the main street and the principal cross street, partly because of the organization of the typical Roman military camp. This had the advantage of sorting out the city into discrete areas, with Roman institutions appropriately distributed throughout. There is no question that Rome exported some of these urban organizational features to cities of the Empire, many of which were originally military bases.

Palmyra, however, does not follow this model at all obviously, even though on first sight the city strikes the casual visitor as a Roman city set down in the midst of the desert. Many features of the city's urban design can be only weakly, if at all, brought into the Roman range of practices (Perring, 'Spatial organisation'). Its overall plan, even following the period when Rome's influence was strongest, shows that it was different. Palmyra did not have the straightforward classical paved Cardo Maximus with one or two decumani; its cardo did not extend seamlessly through city gates and connect with main roads to neighbouring cities. Instead the cardo was east to west, bent and unpaved – for camel caravans preferred sand – with decumani at eccentric angles to the cardo, reflecting the earlier and traditional design of Palmyra from long before Roman influence (Will, 'Développement'). This arrangement had parallels within the Roman world in places such as Side, Perge and Ephesus, but it was not especially common. The cardo (1.2 km long, 40 m or 30 m wide in its different sections) followed the pattern of some other cities of the east – though mainly of the east – in being colonnaded; this followed the pattern of Herod's and Tiberius's construction of a colonnaded street at Damascus, which should possibly be dated to 20 BCE when Tiberius was in the east recovering the standards that Crassus had lost, the date when Herod was named *epitropos* of Syria (Richardson, *Herod*, 232–4). Ball has made effective use of the indigenous colonnaded street as one of his main arguments for turning the common view of Rome and the Near East on its ear (Ball, *Rome in the East*, 256–72).

The Palmyra cardo with its three different orientations was largely second century CE: the western section, over 30 m wide, was built in the early second century, the middle section was mid-second century, and the eastern section, which was 40 m wide and led to the Temple of Bel, was late second or early third century, suggesting that the city grew from west to east. The cardo now seems to bisect the city and reflect a common Roman practice, but two factors modify this impression: first, the surviving walls of the city are later than the time of the cardo (in their present form they are by Justinian, 527–65 CE, on the earlier walls of Diocletian, 284–305 CE); second, at the time the present cardo was constructed, which was at the height of the city, the urban conglomeration was much larger, with other walls dating to the first century BCE much to the south of the present line of walls; so it seems almost certain that another main street lay south of the present south wall. This earlier main street would then have paralleled the wadi that bisects the city, another slightly unusual feature partially paralleled in the layouts of both Petra and Gerasa, and to a lesser extent Jerusalem. The Temple of Nebo, the agora, the Tariff Court and the Temple of Bel all imply from their layout and orientation to the south that from the Seleucid period and beyond the main street originally lay outside the present south wall. The history of construction and reconstruction suggests an early southerly cardo and a later northerly cardo.

The street layout of Palmyra, then, was conservatively eastern in several respects: first, it respected older street patterns, of which the cross streets still provide evidence; second, it retained the locations and orientations of important religious and civic structures, especially the Temple of Bel with its orientation to the Seleucid civic areas and the Temple of Nebo (around which the cardo had to bend), resulting in a reduced size and trapezoidal shape to its temenos; third, there were two foci at the ends of the cardo, the Temple of Bel and a Funerary Temple (see below), an arrangement that can be paralleled (e.g. Ephesus, Petra), but a not altogether typical piece of Roman urban design, even given Rome's flexibility in approach.

The broad and colonnaded western decumanus was particularly important in the streetscape. It was laid out on an earlier orientation, almost at right angles to the western section of the cardo but at an oblique angle to other nearby features of the plan such as 'Diocletian's Camp' and presumably the earlier building (palace?) below it, as well as the later insulae north of the cardo. The chronology is uncertain, but it is very likely that a rather timid oval plaza was built in 129 CE just inside a gate that led to the road to Damascus (compare the earlier more spectacular oval piazza at

Gerasa, Chapter 4). The wide colonnaded street that connects with the oval piazza probably dates from the same period. Another decumanus farther to the east connected with the cardo by a semicircular plaza around the cavea of the theatre, so that it met the cardo at two points marked by large arches in the cardo's south colonnade. This decumanus may also have reflected the earlier street pattern of the city, for it was neither on the same orientation as other streets in the area nor on the axis of the theatre. In fact it was closer to the orientation of the agora and Tariff Court beside it.

North of the cardo the street layout was more regular, with long narrow insulae between north–south streets and relatively few east–west streets. The streets in this part of the city do not seem differentiated, so that it is difficult to say even if there are decumani. For example, one might think that one of the two streets bounding the Temple of Ba'al Shamim to the north would have been a true decumanus, but neither seems to have filled that role. And one might also wonder how the second-century cardo connected with the road that left the city on the way to the Euphrates?

Two dramatic devices made the new alignment of the cardo, with its dog-legs, a success in expressing civic order. A small ovoid plaza marked one of the points where the cardo changed orientation; in its centre was a tetrakionion, a structure with four freestanding columns at each of its four corners (mid-second century CE). It comprised sixteen pink granite columns from Aswan, with Corinthian capitals and vividly embellished architraves, the whole structure sitting on a raised base. Such a device could be found in other cities, to be sure, though only rarely highlighting and ameliorating a shift in the cardo; it was a typically Syrian piece (Gerasa, Bostra, Philippopolis, Jerusalem). With its exaggerated height, it contrasted strongly with the height of the adjacent colonnades and made a powerful impact in this flat city. A minor street went north from near the tetrakionion to the Temple of Ba'al Shamim; another transverse street – a decumanus? – went south from it on an eccentric orientation. The ovoid plaza and the transverse street may have borne some relationship to the other unrecovered parts of the city plan south of the wadi and Justinian's walls.

Even more important for Palmyra's urban character was the monumental arch (between 193 and 211 CE), a triple arch of unusual design, which successfully achieved a 30-degree shift in the cardo's axis. The change in direction took place between the two angled triple arches within the structure (cf. also the North Gate at Gerasa). Walking east along the cardo the Temple of Bel was hidden until, almost imperceptibly, the direction changed and the focus shifted onto the propylaea of the Temple of Bel. Moving east, the roadway occupied only the higher central arch and the sidewalks beyond the colonnades communicated with the lower side arches. Going west, back from Bel's temple towards the arch, all three arches opened onto this wider section of roadway (about 40 m compared with 30+ m). It was a subtle and sophisticated piece of street architecture that deliberately emphasized Bel's importance.

The columns not only of the cardo and decumani but also of some of the individual buildings had horizontal consoles about halfway up to take statues of local benefactors and patrons. One still has a piece of its sculpture in place; it is clear from the many inscriptions that most carried the burden of promoting their patron throughout antiquity. Two adjacent to the tetrakionion were dedicated to King Odainath and Queen Zenobia; a third from the Temple of Bel was more exaggerated in its praise:

> The council and people honour Soados son of Boliades, son of Soados son of Taymisamos for his piety and love of his city, and the nobility and munificence that he has on many important occasions shown to the merchants and the caravans and the citizens at Volgesias. For these services he received testimonial letters from the divine Hadrian and from the most divine emperor Antoninus his son . . . And now he alone of all citizens of all time is on account of his continuous and cumulative good services honoured by his city at public expense by four statues mounted on pillars in the tetradeion of the city, and by decision of the council and people another three, at Spasinou Charax, Volgesias and the caravanserai of Gennaes.
>
> (*Syria* 12.106–7; quoted from Holyland, *Arabia*, 210)

> To Odainath, King of Kings and Corrector of all the east.
>
> Statue of Septimia Bat-Zabbai [Zenobia], most illustrious and pious queen; the excellent Septimii Zabda, general in chief, and Zabbai, military governor of Palmyra, have raised it to their lady in the year 582 (= 271 CE).

Other important features of the main streets were nymphaea, one just west of the tetrakionion and one just east of it. In the eastern section of the cardo (early third century CE) there was a large semi-circular exedra. The streets were of course lined with shops. Most of these elements of streetscape, while not unparalleled in Roman urban design, were especially characteristic of the east and of the urbanization of the second century CE. For example, the consoles, which were distinctive to Palmyra, were relatively rare and found nowhere else in the same profuse numbers (there are a few at Olba in the Taurus Mountains, a few at Apamea on the Orontes, and possibly in the Temple of Augustus and Livia at Vienne). The evidence of streets and layout suggests that Roman urban design was not imposed on Palmyra as a matter of Roman policy in order to 'Romanize' it but rather that some of its urban design elements were borrowed, joined with other elements and freely adapted to local needs by local architects and craftsmen. They brilliantly manipulated what they had to work with, whether indigenous or Roman, so the result was something between Rome and Arabia. Palmyra had a slightly familiar Roman 'feel', but it was more a case of influences than deliberate imposition of Roman practices.

Indigenous and imported religion

Religion in Palmyra comprised a rich blend of religious attachments borrowed from other places: Bel and Nebo (or Nabu) from Babylon, Ba'al Shamim from Canaan and Phoenicia, Allat from Arabia; they might be associated with others, as Bel was with Yarhibol and Aglibol. Some eventually became assimilated to Roman deities: both Bel and Ba'al could be assimilated to Zeus since both meant 'lord'. In fact, however, the character of the cults in most instances retained strong traditional eastern associations and the iconographic representations were generally also strongly eastern. Alongside these long-standing cults, there were two obviously Roman religious cults: there was a small Caesareum near the tetrakionion that probably served as a centre for the imperial cult, and at the west side of the city was the impressive Camp of Diocletian with its shrine for the standards of the Roman legions serving the region (Michalowski, *Palmyra*). Deriving from about the same time as the latter, two other commonly found cults, Judaism and Christianity, originated from within the Near East. It is worth noting that Palmyrene religion had wider local influence, for at Dura Europos, a Roman garrison town on the Euphrates, there was a Temple to the Palmyrene Gods (along with a church and a synagogue and other cults such as Mithra) in the late Roman period. Palmyra had still other religious structures, of course, but the ones just noted are central and well known.

The Temple of Bel

With its traditional Syrian design, Bel was not only the most important religious monument in Palmyra, as both its size and location showed, but it was also the earliest to be built in hard limestone. The site was traditional; the archaeological evidence goes back to the second millennium BCE, about the time when Bel had been imported from Babylon. He was an Akkadian sky god whose name is found as a theophoric element in such names as Belshazzar and Belteshazzar. He appears in two biblical works from the exile in Babylon: in Isaiah 46.1 in the context of an image carried in a procession and in Jeremiah 50.2; 51.44 (E. R. Dalglish, 'Bel', *ABD* 1.652–3). Bel was assimilated to Marduk as Bel Marduk, the protector of Babylon, but he could also form a triad, as at Palmyra, with Yarhibol (an oasis deity) and Aglibol (a north Syrian deity), a triad that was found even in Rome (Teixidor, *Pantheon*, 1–13). Bel must have been thought of as a god indigenous to Palmyra by the time Bel's magnificent temple was built.

The temple closed the cardo at its east end, with its propylaea or gateway at an acute angle at the end of the vista from the monumental arch. The monumental entrance was 35 m wide, an eight-columned portico with a large central arch, preceded by an impressive set of steps. The details of the propylaea (mid-second century CE) have been obscured by later fortifications (twelfth century CE), but some of the characteristic architectural detailing of both the great central door and the side doors with associated niches remains. The temenos was 205 m by 210 m. There had been a Hellenistic temple on the east side of the site, whose remains show that its naos had steps on all four sides and that only later was the courtyard levelled to its current height. The orientation of the first/second-century building was retained from this earlier structure and long predates the cardo, as is clear both from the way the cardo bends in order to lead, not altogether successfully, to the propylaea and from the way the axis of the Temple of Bel is directed towards the Seleucid-period city. The naos was dedicated 6 April 32 CE; the north, east and south colonnades were built between 80 and 120 CE; the western colonnade and the propylaea were constructed at about the same time in mid-second century CE. It was over a century in the building.

The western colonnade, of which the propylaea formed a part, was a single colonnade of the same width as the others but with higher columns, and without an intermediate line of columns, forming a huge hall. The other three were double colonnades, with an intermediate column supporting the roof. The columns of all four colonnades had the same kind of consoles found along the cardo. There were stairs to the roof in the corners. On the exterior of the peribolos wall enclosing the temenos, pilasters alternated with framed windows surmounted by triangular pediments; the same motifs were repeated on the interior. An arched entrance below the western colonnade led to a sunken ramp to conduct animals to the altar. This very unusual sunken passageway was a brilliant solution to the problem of separating sacrificial animals from the crowds of worshippers in the temenos.

The naos was located on the central axis of the propylaea, but somewhat east of the centre point. While the colonnades had rather strong Roman elements, the naos combined design elements from east and west in an attractive blend. Most noticeably, the axis of the naos or holy place was at right-angles to the axis of the precinct, so that its long side-wall faced the propylaea. The entrance to the naos was in this side-wall, on the axis of the propylaea, though the monumental door was in fact off-centre. This very untypical design was, in its general layout, repeated in the layouts of the Temple in Jerusalem and the Temple of Dushara in Petra (below, Chapters 3 and 6), though unique in Syria. Two features of the roof design of the naos were also eastern and were also shared with both the Temple of Dushara and the Temple in Jerusalem. First, it was capped with crow-stepped merlons, strongly reminiscent of one of the dominant design motifs of Petra (and especially its tombs) and probably similar to the treatment of the eaves in the Jerusalem naos. Second, parts of the roof were flat, with stairs giving access to it (one beside the north adyton or holy place and two flanking the south adyton), again like temples in Petra, Jerusalem and other sites in Syria and Jordan. The roof must have been used for liturgical acts requiring a view of the heavens.

The naos was peripteral, eight columns by fifteen columns, with gilded bronze Corinthian capitals – all of which have disappeared because of the value of the bronze – with acanthus leaves and above that a frieze of winged spirits with garlands and fruits (J.-P. Rey-Coquais, *PECS*, s.v. 'Palmyra'). The walls of the naos were punctured with windows, another untypical design feature found in the east. Spanning between the columns and the naos walls were deep lateral stone roof beams, the tops of which were about 18 m above the ground level. Though visible only with difficulty, the beams were richly decorated with low relief sculptures on the vertical surfaces and the soffits with hieratic and historiated motifs, reflecting Palmyra's religious, social and economic character: a dromedary with a draped image, presumably Bel under a canopy, sacrificial altars, veiled women and hunting scenes.

Inside the door of the naos, one had to turn either left or right to the adyton or sacred place; there were two, one to the north with an Ionic façade and one to the south with a Corinthian façade. The northern adyton was the more interesting, for its monolithic ceiling had a central bust of the great god, surrounded by busts of the seven planetary gods and flanked by the signs of the zodiac in two rows. This was an early instance of an imported decorative motif from Iran that not long afterwards featured prominently in

Mithraism, Judaism and Christianity. On the underside of the opening's lintel was a magnificent eagle with outstretched wings against a background of stars, representing either Ba'al Shamim (literally 'Lord of the Heavens') or, more likely, Bel as lord of the heavens. The southern adyton, also with a richly decorated monolithic ceiling, was approached by a ramp, so this was probably where the portable cult statue was located that would have been used in ritual processions. Thus, while Roman features were found in the propylaea and the colonnades of the peribolos, the holy place was largely eastern in character, with windows, double adyton, lateral axis relative to the main axis, and ramp to the adyton.

As one approached the naos up a slight incline from the propylaea there was a large altar for animal sacrifice on the left or north, to which the below-grade ramp for animals led. A channel to carry away the blood from the sacrifices matched this thoughtful functional piece of design. Opposite the altar on the south or right of the approach was a lustration pool. The disposition of altar and lustration pool, to left and right of the approach to the holy place, was reminiscent of the Temple in Jerusalem, where the altar and basin were left and right of the main axis.

A large dining room or banqueting hall, designed for smaller group celebrations, was situated in front of the altar, between it and the propylaea. The banqueting hall implies the complexity of religious life of Palmyra and how it was organized. Thousands of small clay tokens have been found that gave the bearer admission to banquets in honour of Bel. Though we do not know precisely the character or frequency of the dining activities, the social importance of eating a meal together in the house of the god was underscored by the important place occupied by the hall (see Holyland, *Arabia*, 134–8). Bel's very large courtyard provided for large numbers of the citizens of Palmyra on grand occasions; the dining room within the sanctuary would have been used for smaller, more intimate family or group celebrations.

The Temple of Ba'al Shamim

A temple had been established dedicated to Ba'al Shamim ('lord of the heavens') early in the first century CE, at about the same time as the building of the Temple of Bel. As the name implies, he was associated with weather – a fertility and storm god – who had been worshipped in Canaanite and Phoenician coastal areas of the Near East since the second millennium BCE. He was the most active of the Canaanite gods, attested at an early period in places such as Sidon, Tyre, Ebla and Ugarit (Ras Shamra); he could be associated with other gods such as Bel, Malakbel and Aglibol (John Day, 'Baal', *ABD* 1.545–9).

It has already been pointed out how the street pattern of Palmyra did not emphasize the location or importance of the Temple of Ba'al Shamim; this is surprising, given that the streets were probably laid out later. The sanctuary lay north of the tetrakionion, squeezed between two north–south streets, neither of which gave it much prominence. The main door had little that established it visually as the main entrance; it was tucked away in the south-west corner of the south courtyard. The construction history, though complex, roughly paralleled the period of construction of the Temple of Bel. As in the case of Bel, an earlier late-Hellenistic building preceded the attractive Temple of Ba'al Shamim. The earliest portion was the north court (about 50 m by 60 m), parts of which date from 17 CE. A ritual triclinium at one time occupied the space immediately beside what later came to be the naos, fronting onto this north court from about 67 CE. The west portico of the north court dates from the time of Odenathus in the mid-third century CE. The construction of the naos (130 CE) required the destruction of the dining room. A number of inscriptions attest its date, and one column, which mentions the completion of parts of the structure of the portico, refers to 'the Divine Hadrian', whose visit that same year must have triggered the continuing work on the project. The south court that flanks it on the other side was built 149 CE (Collart and Vicari, *Sanctuaire*, for details). This unusual arrangement of two courtyards with surrounding colonnades was complicated even more by a small central courtyard in front of the naos for the altar (dated 115 CE). A bilingual inscription equates 'Ba'al Shamim, great and merciful' in Palmyrene Aramaic with 'Zeus most high who hears' in Greek.

The relatively deep tetrastyle porch or pronaos and the pilastered sides of the nearly square naos were decorated in an exuberant Corinthian order. The square form is similar to Nabatean temples at many places (below, Chapter 3). The naos was small, at the level of the courtyard rather than raised above it on a podium, and windowed. It had a wonderfully baroque feel, for the central exedra of the naos, with flanking side chambers, was marked by a number of fluid shifts in the plan at the various wall heights (Lyttelton, *Baroque Architecture*, 247–54): almost cruciform at ground level, then hexagonal, then curved and finally semi-circular. The completed project was quite unusually different from standard Roman taste, with its triple courtyard, naos at courtyard level, corner entrance to the sanctuary, no visual emphasis on the approach to the naos, windowed holy place. The naos and small courtyard were converted into a Christian church in the fifth century CE.

The Temple of Nebo

The Temple of Nebo (or Nabu) honoured a Mesopotamian god – the son of Marduk or Bel – who could be assimilated to Apollo. Though rarely attested in the second millennium, he became important in the first millennium BCE. Devotion to Nebo peaked in the neo-Babylonian period, at the time of the exile (see Isa. 46.1); indications of his worship can be found through Syria and into Egypt, and in Palmyra as late as the first century CE, perhaps the latest evidence. The name Nebo or Nabu is found as a theophoric element in names such as Nebuchadnezzar and Nebuzaradan. Its etymological meaning appears to be 'one who is called' (E. R. Dalglish, 'Nebo', *ABD* 4.1054–6). A lively sense of devotion emerges from the hymns and prayers of the Assyrian and neo-Babylonian records.

The Syrian-style sanctuary (late first century CE), which was entered from the south, occupied a favourable central location presumably across the central wadi from an earlier main street. When the cardo was built in the second century CE in its dog-leg form, Nebo's position was seriously compromised, for the sanctuary lost some of its temenos on the north, turning it into a rather lop-sided polygon (roughly 44 m on the south, 60 m on the north, by 85 m). What must have been worse, its propylaea on the south was now away from the main street, almost against the later city walls. This was certainly not how it was meant to sit within the city plan; in fact, the locations of the sanctuaries of both Bel and Nebo speak strongly to a main street parallel to and perhaps just south of the wadi, so that at one time the two sanctuaries had a much closer relationship than later was the case. These alterations may imply an improvement of Bel's position and downgrading of Nebo's importance in the first and second centuries CE.

The unusual six-columned propylaea in the Corinthian order had a richly decorated entrance, behind columns, which were surmounted by a decorated architrave, that were in the same plane as a series of flanking rooms that opened to the south. The polygonal temenos, with no two sides parallel and no corner at right angles, had colonnades on south and west sides from the same period with uncharacteristic pseudo-Doric capitals; there was a later colonnade on the east and a revision to the north side along the newly constructed cardo, though without a colonnade, in order to save space. Shops faced onto the new line of the cardo, one of which was used to create a minor new doorway into the temenos from the cardo. The back walls of the colonnades had brightly coloured frescoes with religious scenes. The naos of the temple itself (20.6 m by 9.15 m) was raised on a high podium (2+ m high) and axially related both to the propylaea and to the small monument and well in front. It employed the more usual Corinthian columns on a 6 by 12 layout. Like the Temple of Bel, part of its roof was flat and crowned with merlons, accessed by a stair from the holy place. Despite its unusual shape and slightly closed-in atmosphere, the splayed areas between the naos and the colonnades gave it the feel of a larger space than it actually was, so that in many respects it was a handsome sanctuary with significant indigenous features.

Caesareum

The sanctuary that comes closest to occupying a central location, indicative of a simple Roman fact of life, was the Caesareum, situated immediately south-east of the tetrakionion and between two colonnaded decumani. Its peristyle courtyard, perhaps initially a rather grand peristyle house, had fine fluted columns behind a typical row of shops. The south stoa had bases, apparently for imperial statues. Its small size may symbolize the nature and degree of Romanization at Palmyra. Roman religion jostled with but did not seem to outrank Arabian and eastern cults in the Palmyrene arrangement.

Other sanctuaries

Funerary Temple

At the west end of the city on the axis of the cardo a magnificently carved Funerary Temple (late second century CE) acted as the focus of the western and earlier portion of the cardo. Though it was not far from the north-west necropolis, and now looks as if it should be part of it, it was built soon after the cardo was built, and so must be interpreted as part of the streetscape. In this position it anchored the west end of the cardo, in somewhat the same way the Temple of Bel anchored its east end, though it was nothing like as dominant. Its porch had six columns at the top of a stair; the most prominent feature of its ornamented façade was the wonderfully natural carved grape-leaf decoration on the antae (projecting side-walls of the naos). Both the interior and the crypt, which was entered by a door at the back on a lower level, had bays that formed loculi for burials. The main floor had niches for statuary.

Diocletian's Camp

Following the destruction of Palmyra after Zenobia's revolt, the Camp of Diocletian was built to contain the facilities needed for the military presence of Legion I Illyricorum (293–303 CE). The complex was built over one of the oldest parts of the city, perhaps on top of an earlier palace, whose orientation must have determined the oblique orientation of the new buildings (Bounni and al-As'ad, *Palmyra*, 84). The precinct was a self-contained area west of the western colonnaded decumanus, more or less at right-angles to the cardo. Its main avenue, which was entered through a triple gateway at the decumanus, may have predated the Camp (second century CE). In its final form, it led to a large rectangular courtyard (principia), with an extremely imposing wide and high stair on its west side leading up to a wide gallery. On the street's axis was a wide room (60 m wide by 12 m deep) with an apse for the Temple of the Signa (standards). The apsidal room was flanked by administrative offices; stairs led to the second floor and roof.

Allat

Crossing this wide avenue (about 20 m) was a slightly narrower north–south avenue (about 13 m), the intersection being covered by a special kind of tetrapylon. Facing onto the north–south street was the Temple of Allat, now in a ruinous state (first and second centuries CE), dedicated to one of the great Arab goddesses. The tetrastyle prostyle naos sat inside a small colonnaded temenos. An inscription equates her to Artemis, and a later statue portrays her as Athena. The most remarkable sculptural find was a Henry Moore-like lion (first century CE), whose inscription asks Allat 'to bless the one who does not spill blood against the temple'.

These temples were each different, demonstrating a wide range of local solutions to the building of sanctuaries. All showed Roman influences, especially in the temenos, in column orders and in minor details, but more rarely in the naos; none was purely Roman. All were mixed structures, with varying degrees of local influences, though these indigenous elements, because they were concentrated in the holy place, tended to influence the overall effect more profoundly. They were situated in the urban plan in unusual ways, with two being at the focal points of the cardo. The traditional cults to Bel, Allat and Ba'al Shamim occupied peripheral sites, not quite but almost on the four sides of the city, perhaps an intentional distribution in the four quarters of the city, which may have been identified by tribes (Costaki, 'Palmyra'). Nebo and the Caesareum were the most centrally located sanctuaries.

Judaism and Christianity

Byzantine-period Christianity is archaeologically attested by two basilicas, both west of Ba'al Shamim, one is fifth century CE and the other sixth century CE. Christianity may of course have come earlier, as in the neighbouring city of Dura Europos, whose third-century church is the earliest archaeologically certain and datable evidence of church buildings, leaving to one side the still uncertain excavated building at Aila (Aqaba). The presence of both Christianity and Judaism at Palmyra is merely one facet of the general picture of religious influences at Palmyra, mainly eastern rather than western.

Judaism spread to Palmyra, though when is unclear. Inscriptions in Scythopolis and Beth Shearim testify to Palmyrene Jews who maintained links with the homeland or were buried there. A long third-century CE Hebrew inscription on the lintel and door-jambs of a house confirms Jewish presence (Berger, 'Inscriptions hébraïques'; Mittwoch, 'Hebraische Inschriften'). Whether this was a communal building or a house (so J.-B. Frey, *CIJ* 2.821–3), or indeed a house that became a communal building, has been debated. I have been unable to locate the building for its location seems unrecorded. A house located north of the cardo, between the seventh and eighth streets west of the Temple of Ba'al Shamim, may have been reused sequentially as a Jewish, Christian and Muslim sanctuary. The most recent phase had a niche that faced south-east to Mecca in an apse; the apse itself is directed to the east; benches and doors and paving and courtyard are all reminiscent of the synagogue at Dura. This was originally a large domestic building that has been adapted in several successive stages, so that it is possible that it served as a synagogue at some point. In any case it is an instance of a religious building that was clearly a result of a wealthy benefaction, probably a case of a gift of a house to a group, who then subsequently renovated and adapted it for their needs. The insula that contained it was about 66 m by 22 m; the flagstoned cultic room was roughly 12.3 m by 20.3 m. The main entrance was from the south, where eight columns, two of which survive partially, created a monumentalized approach, up two steps.

Public, commercial and private

Palmyra had an attractive small council chamber or bouleutêrion (early second century CE), marked by a small peristyle and a room with semicircular tiered seats. Part of the rear wall was cut off to create room for the semicircular theatre plaza. Palmyra's theatre (second century CE) sat in the middle of and gave form to the wide colonnaded semicircular plaza. The rear of its stage was parallel to the cardo, and large arches marked the plaza entrances in the cardo's south colonnade. A subordinate street ran tangent to the curve of the theatre plaza on the west side and gave access to the bouleutêrion, the agora and the Tariff Court, with shops along its west side. The agora (71 m by 84 m) with colonnades on all four sides, again with statuary on the consoles, suggests a date in early to middle second century CE. The adjacent 'tariff court' (roughly 35 m by 70 m with walls 10 m high; also early second century) or caravanserai had no colonnades or roofs. It is named after a 5 m-long stone with inscription dated 137 CE that lays out Palmyrene tariffs in detail. Off the agora at the south-west corner was a nicely proportioned banquet hall (roughly 12 m by 15 m), decorated with a Greek key motif in a continuous border halfway up the wall.

On the north side of the cardo, east of the tetrakionion and almost directly across from the western arch of the theatre plaza, was a nymphaeum with semicircular façade. Four large columns projected out to the line of the columns of the cardo. There was another nymphaeum in the western section of the cardo, leading towards the Funerary Temple. And either an exedra or nymphaeum in the eastern section of the cardo, near the Temple of Bel. Between the theatre and the monumental arch was a bath on the north side of the street, identified in the streetscape by the imported monolithic red granite columns of the propylaea that projected into the street. An inscription dates this portion of the building to the period of Diocletian (293–303 CE), but the major parts of the bath were probably built a century earlier in the time of Septimius Severus (193–211 CE), including the very fine octagonal room with octagonal basin, probably an *apodyterium* or dressing room.

Other parts of the city were filled with houses. The almost regular layout of insulae to the north of the cardo in the north-west part of the city was largely residential. There were large houses south and east of the theatre on the theatre plaza. And some upper-class third-century CE houses were excavated behind the Temple of Bel in the eastern part of the city.

The necropolis

The most striking feature of Palmyra was its necropolis ('city of the dead') or cemetery, which spread along several wadis, prominently west of the city but also to north and east (Schmidt-Colinet, 'Aspects of "Romanization"'). There were three main tomb types, temple or house tombs (the latest form to develop), *hypogeum* tombs ('underground') and tower tombs (the earliest form; of these the earliest dated one was built 9 BCE). The latter were the most unusual though all types shared the same underlying organizational arrangement. Along one wadi alone there were more than 50 tower tombs, up to four storeys high, square towers with burial niches (*loculi*) on each floor. The largest tower tomb contained 300 burial niches, each of which was sealed with a square blocking-stone that had the person's name and portrait. Each tower tomb housed a family or kin-group, and offered the possibility of a complete family tree. The Tomb of Elhabel and his three brothers (Ma'ani, Shokayi and Maliku, the family that constructed the Temple of Nebo), for example, was built in 103 CE. It combined hypogeum and tower, one floor below ground level and four above. Its plain exterior was decorated with a window holding a funerary bed, and below it an inscription. The ceilings were deeply coffered painted stone; nicely fluted posts separated the *loculi* and provided supports for the coffins, which were arranged six high. Some tombs had provision for celebrating funeral meals in the tombs, and just such a burial feast is depicted in statuary.

The hypogeum tombs were more generous but more informal in layout, with more emphasis on decorative features. Yarhai's Hypogeum has been reconstructed in the National Museum in Damascus; the easiest accessible in Palmyra is the Hypogeum of the Three Brothers (about 140 CE), with over 300 loculi and very high-quality frescoes. The Hypogeum of Atenatan has a triclinium and exedra from 229 CE.

The house tombs, of which the Funerary Temple inside the city was noted earlier, tend to be third century CE; most are in the north necropolis. All these tombs offer a wealth of information about the peoples of Palmyra. It was a remarkable fact of life that women were treated like men in the grave sculptures that closed off the loculi, so that we have a stunning collection of female busts, richly attired, staring out from the surface of the blocking-stones, with names and family connections. 'They commission inscriptions, make offerings to the gods in their own right, act as administrative officers, . . . and construct public buildings and tombs' (Holyland, *Arabia*, 132). The grave goods, art and sculpture that have been found and studied from these tombs have shed a bright light on Palmyrene culture, and inscriptions have permitted close study of Palmyrene Aramaic, one of the dialects of the tribes of the Arabian plateau.

Conclusion

Palmyra shows the vitality and complexity of the religious, artistic and architectural traditions of the Levant. It synthesized traditions as diverse as Babylonian, Canaanite, Phoenician, Hellenistic and Roman, not to mention Arab and Parthian sensibilities, the latter especially with respect to modes of dress and formalized portraiture with their strong frontal expression suggesting a kind of timelessly passive view on the world. The architecture, with its deeply decorated mouldings and spatial playfulness gave a baroque character to some of the buildings, especially the Temple of Ba'al Shamim. Even the streetscape had a dynamic baroque quality to it, with hundreds of consoles projecting from the columns, each supporting the statue of a patron. The special details of arches, nymphaea, projecting propylaea, added to this liveliness, as did the unexpected shifts in the axis of the cardo. It is not, then, correct to say that 'the architectural language of Palmyra is a mannered, but in its essentials orthodox, provincial classicism' (Ward-Perkins, *Roman Imperial Architecture*, 354; cf. Ward-Perkins, *Roman Architecture*, 174).

In the long term the art, and also the architecture, later influenced the art of the new imperial centre in Constantinople, with its stiff and mainly frontal depictions and with its increasingly baroque architecture. Palmyra was not a remote oddity in the Syrian Desert; it was a bridge from the Semitic east to the increasingly Christian west. As an important part of Rome's control of the Arabian Near East it showed how the Levant thought of its location between the influences of Rome and those earlier influences that continued to shape it decisively. Not surprisingly, then, it remained relatively strongly eastern in its religious expression, so perhaps it is also unsurprising that Zenobia filled the vacuum when Roman power collapsed. Palmyra's independence shows in its seeking to establish an eastern Empire from which to control part or all of the west. Without too much exaggeration, there was a homology between Palmyra's location and its religious traditions as those were embedded in its architecture and sculpture, just as there was a homology in its trade-related roles between the Mediterranean and the east and a homology in its role in the Byzantine period mediating influences from Levantine (and Christian) traditions to the new Rome in Constantinople.

Roman influences in Palmyra tended to be superficial. It had maintained a long tradition of eastern, Arabian and Hellenistic influences; its religious life was essentially a religious life centred in the Levant, with influences extending from Canaan to Babylon, giving a blend of imported and indigenous religions. In the interplay of Near Eastern and western influences, where it sided totally with neither, there is a strong contrast between its baroque exuberance and its 'ascetic' desert location.

Table 2.1 Palmyra chronology

First centuries BCE and CE	
Ba'al Shamim N court	17 CE
Nebo	inscription 32 CE; late 1st c. CE and later
Bel naos	32 CE
Honorary column	64 CE
Agora	mid-1st c. CE
Banqueting hall (agora)	mid-1st c. CE?
Ba'al Shamim triclinium	begun 67 CE
Bel colonnades (N, E, S)	80–120 CE
Tariff Court	late 1st/early 2nd c. CE
Tower tombs	1st and early 2nd c. CE
Trajan and after	
Ba'al Shamim altar	115 CE
Cardo western section	early 2nd c. CE
Nymphaeum	early 2nd c. CE?
Senate House	early 2nd c. CE
Theatre cavea	early 2nd c. CE;
Oval piazza	129 CE?
Ba'al Shamim naos	130 CE
West decumanus	early 2nd c. CE
Ba'al Shamim	dedicated 132 CE
Cardo middle	mid-2nd c. CE
Tetrakionion	mid-2nd c. CE
Cardo eastern section	late 2nd or early 3rd c. CE
Ba'al Shamim S court	149 CE/33 CE
Bel colonnade (W)	150 CE
'Ain Efqa (water supply)	altar 162 CE
Allat	2nd c. CE building (lion statue from beg. 1st c. CE)
Monumental arch	Septimius Severus (193–211 CE)
Theatre scaenae frons	late 2nd c. CE
Funerary temple	late 2nd/3rd c. CE

Bath	late 2nd/early 3rd c. CE
Hypogea	2nd c. CE
Synagogue	3rd c. CE?

Zenobia and after

North wall	Queen Zenobia?
Baths of Diocletian, colonnade	284–305 CE
Camp of Diocletian	293–303 CE

Constantine and after

Basilicas	5th c. CE; 6th c. CE

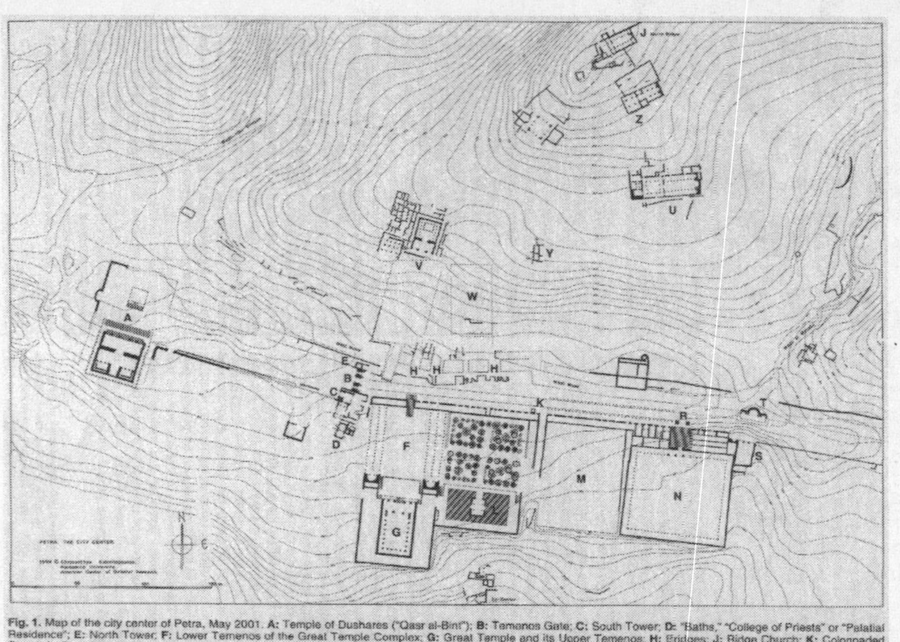

Fig. 1. Map of the city center of Petra, May 2001. A: Temple of Dushares ("Qasr al-Bint"); B: Temenos Gate; C: South Tower; D: "Baths," "College of Priests" or "Palatial Residence"; E: North Tower; F: Lower Temenos of the Great Temple Complex; G: Great Temple and its Upper Temenos; H: Bridges; J: Ridge Church; K: Colonnaded Street; L: Pool Complex ("Lower Market"); M: "Middle Market"; N: "Upper Market" ("Agora"); P: "Byzantine Tower"; R: "Trajanic" Arch; S: South Nymphaeon; T: North Nymphaeon; U: The Petra Church; V: Temple of the Winged Lions or Temple of Al-'Uzza ("Gymnasium") W: "Royal Palace"; Y: Area A; Z: Blue Chapel.

Plan of Petra, © Chrysanthos Kanellopoulos

3

Petra: Rome and Arabia

Introduction

The walk into Petra along the Siq – the 1.2 km natural fracture in the rock that forms the entrance to the city – strikes everyone, from casually uninformed tourist to veteran archaeologist, with its high natural drama and impressive monumental built forms. Right at the outset, the Bab es-Siq ('gateway of the Siq') – with its combination of naturally rugged wadis and sheer-sided crevices together with well-constructed reservoir and dam, niches and monumental arch, tombs and Roman road, baetyls and 'god blocks' – underscores that this was a remarkable civilization, with strong cultural and religiously expressive forms. As the capital of the Nabatean Kingdom, it was a late addition to the Roman Empire, added in a peaceful fashion – though by exactly what mechanism is not known – as the Province of Arabia in 106 CE, though Strabo (born *c*.64 BCE) claims it was a part of Rome already in his day:

> [T]he Nabataeans and the Sabaeans . . . often overran Syria before they became subject to the Romans; but at present both they and the Syrians are subject to the Romans. The metropolis of the Nabataeans is Petra, as it is called; for it lies on a site which is otherwise smooth and level, but it is fortified all around by a rock, the outside parts of the site being precipitous and sheer, and the inside parts having springs in abundance, both for domestic purposes and for watering gardens.
>
> (Strabo, *Geography* 16.4.21)

The degree of Roman influence is uncertain, but it coheres with Strabo's view that Josephus records that Augustus 'was angry that

Aretas had taken the throne [in 9 BCE] before writing to him for permission' (*Ant.* 16.295). Both Palmyra and Nabatea were Arab cultures, Nabatea in the south and Palmyra in the north. By the late first century BCE Nabatea had accommodated its structures and designs to late-Hellenistic practices and models. The importing of Hellenism in Petra's case came mainly from Egypt and especially from Alexandria, with which its connections were close (McKenzie, *Architecture,* passim), whereas Palmyra's western influences came mainly from Antioch or Emesa and Asia Minor. Like Palmyra, Petra's raison d'être lay in its position at a nodal point of the international trade routes of the ancient world. Desirable spices and perfumes could be brought from the areas around Yemen and the Persian Gulf to the Mediterranean world: 'the loads of aromatics are conveyed from Leucê Comê to Petra, and thence to Rhinocolura, which is in Phoenicia near Egypt' (Strabo, *Geography* 16.4.24). Strabo adds that the most important were frankincense and myrrh, along with cinnamon and nard (*Geography* 16.4.25). The trade routes between Petra and the Mediterranean then connected with areas farther east, south India and East Asia; the exchange of goods is archaeologically attested in sites in both Asia and the Mediterranean.

Petra's exploitation of the benefits of trade came a little earlier than Palmyra's, as its Hellenizing influences may also have. Though more remote than Palmyra, Petra's economic role was more important, though Petra did not have as decisive a position in international relations as Palmyra had, given the latter's position between Rome and Parthia. Their roles altered, however, after Rome made Bostra the capital of its newly incorporated Province of Arabia. Petra slowly declined as the main trading centre shifted to Palmyra in the second century CE, although Petra's loss of status was not intended: 'It had become clear from Trajan's grant of the title of metropolis to Petra by 114 that it was not his intention, in placing the capital of the province at Bostra, to diminish the role of Petra' (Bowersock, *Roman Arabia*, 85).

The geographical reasons for Petra's location in a bowl-like depression (elevation about 870 m) on the high Jordanian plateau south-east of the Dead Sea were the combination of a well-protected site, arable land and a plentiful water supply from Ain

Musa (Moses' Spring) 5 km east. There was a practical reason for its location: it was located near the intersection of an ancient north–south road from the Gulf of Aqaba (the biblical King's Highway) with an overland caravan route across the Arabian Plateau. From Petra's entrepôt traders could go south to the Red Sea, west across the Negev to the Mediterranean, north through the Decapolis cities to Damascus or Antioch or south-east to the Yemen. Its location acquired religious significance through claims that Petra was the site of Moses' Spring and Aaron's grave, the latter high above Petra on the Jebel Haroun, 5 km west of the city and 1500 m above sea level. The unverifiable traditions about Moses and Aaron lent legendary status to Petra.

The Nabateans had migrated from Arabia and settled in Petra by the fourth century BCE (Graf, 'Nabateans'; Bowersock, *Roman Arabia*, ch. 2; Holyland, *Arabia*, 70–4), apparently pushing the earlier Edomite rivals of biblical Israel westwards in a relatively peaceful displacement. The Edomites came to be known by the Greek form of their name, 'Idumeans', and re-enter the biblical story through Herod the Great, king of Judea from 40 to 4 BCE, whose father was Idumean and his mother Nabatean; some portion of his personal wealth probably derived from his Nabatean roots (Richardson, *Herod*, ch. 3). The Nabateans never lost their affinity for the trade opportunities of the southern part of the Arabian Peninsula, though they substantially extended their territory west through the Negev to Egypt's border at the Mediterranean and north around the Decapolis into southern Syria, for a short time as far as Damascus.

Hoping to acquire direct or indirect control of Nabatea's trade routes, Augustus dispatched Aelius Gallus, governor of Egypt, on an expedition into Arabia Felix in 26/25 BCE, along with 1,000 Nabatean soldiers and 500 from Herod's bodyguard (Josephus, *Ant.* 15.317). Augustus 'conceived the purpose of winning the Arabians over to himself or of subjugating them. Another consideration was . . . that they were very wealthy, and that they sold aromatics, . . . for he expected either to deal with wealthy friends or to master wealthy enemies' (Strabo, *Geography* 16.4.22). No doubt because one of the expedition's aims was to undercut Nabatean influence over the south Arabian trade, Syllaeus (who was leading the Nabatean contingent) was accused of sabotaging the expedition, which ended in disaster (Richardson, *Herod*, 230–1; Holyland, *Arabia*, 44–5).

The necropolis

The most impressive feature of Petra's religious landscape, like Palmyra's, was the way it built for death. Petra's tombs dominated the hills around the city, the roads into the city and even the city centre. The tombs ranged from relatively simple shaft tombs with small subterranean chambers (Bikai and Perry, 'North Ridge Tombs') through façades with stereotyped decorative elements to elite royal structures, whose elements imaginatively combined a limited repertoire of rock-cut features in structures of immense size and impact. Through close study of the monumental forms and comparison with datable tombs at Hegra (Medain Saleh) a typology of the tombs has been established that permits dating the structures in Petra (McKenzie, *Architecture*; 'Keys from Egypt'). The new dates are significantly earlier than those proposed by previous scholars: it was once thought that Nabateans could not possibly have developed the creative blend of architectural elements on their own before the period of increased Roman influence after Nabatea's annexation (cf. Bowersock, *Roman Arabia*, ch. 5). In fact, the most creative structures predate that event.

In developed urban centres of Greece, Rome, Egypt, Israel and elsewhere, the necropolis was limited to areas outside the walls, because corpses were viewed as impure or defiling. In Pompeii or Athens or Jerusalem tombs ringed the city walls, so that the first impression on approaching ancient cities was reverence for the dead. In Petra, too, many tombs were on the perimeter. But it differed from most analogous cities in one important respect. A group of 'Royal Tombs' dominated the urban centre and acted as a focus, matching the focus on the temples in the city centre. Tombs were usually built during the first occupant's lifetime, so the site selection, form and expenditure were all decisions of the familial head while still alive. We can be confident, then, of deliberate intentionality in locating these Royal Tombs. The necropolis in Petra was developed into a high art form in a symbolically significant location, where the structures for death rivalled the buildings for the living. In contrast to Palmyra, however, where numerous individual loculi had identifiable portraits, few of Petra's burial monuments and none of the largest can be certainly identified, except for the tomb of Sextius Florentinus, the Roman governor (127 CE; Browning, *Petra*, 226).

Smaller tombs were clustered along the route from Bab es-Siq into the city and beyond. Most were rock-cut, relatively simple both on the interior and on the exterior, with crow-step mouldings (like the crow-step merlons at Palmyra) as a main motif. What Petra's tombs may have lacked in comparison with Palmyra's portraiture and emphasis on kinship relations, they made up for in the solidity and dignity of their simply articulated forms.

The Khasneh

The smaller tombs hardly anticipated the impact of the larger tombs. One of the largest, earliest and most perfect of Petra's tombs was the Khasneh. Its dating must be based on style probably to the reign of Obodas II (30–9 BCE) or early in Aretas IV's reign (9 BCE–40 CE). Its location, where the narrow Siq suddenly widens at the east entrance to the city proper, was especially dramatic. Rock-cut tombs were commonly found in numerous locations in the Mediterranean world, but a rock-cut tomb on the scale of the Khasneh was rare. Yet the individual architectural elements of the Khasneh feel familiar: its Corinthian order, decorated entablatures, superb detailing, tympanum, broken pediment and tholos can be paralleled in other places (in Syria, Alexandria or even Pompeii's wall paintings). The composition of the façade, however, had an unusually baroque feel, with its dramatic sense of disclosure after the constriction of the Siq, overpowering size (30 m wide by 43 m high), exuberant sculptural decoration, and bold shadow lines. Its decoration included sometimes unusual elements such as 'Nabatean/Corinthian capitals (with their complex patterns of acanthus leaves), rich entablatures and friezes, scrollwork, rosettes, and sculptured human and animal figures, including Medusae, satyrs, male equestrian figures that watch over the dead

(Dioscuri), deities, dancing Amazons, victory figures, eagles, and sphinxes or lions' (Khouri, *Petra*, 47). It was among the most memorable buildings of the Levant.

Ed-Deir

The Khasneh was bracketed on the other side of the city by ed-Deir ('the monastery'; *c.*40–70 CE). Its larger façade concentrated even more than the Khasneh on a late-Hellenistic sense of intimidating awe. Ed-Deir was situated north-west of the city centre, high above the bowl in which the city centre was set, only a few metres short of looking out over the Arabah, the long depression running south from the Dead Sea that separates Israel and Jordan. Despite its large size, it lacked the Khasneh's drama: it had no equivalent of the latter's prominent pronaos (porch), the lower register was flatter, it had Nabatean columns and a simple triglyph, and metope decoration replaced the richer vine and tendril decoration of the Khasneh's entablatures. While it retained the lively effect of the tholos between the broken pediments of the upper register, it lacked the figurative sculpture of the Khasneh that was so much a part of its impact. Coming 50 or 75 years later than the Khasneh, the shift to Nabatean capitals in place of the more traditional Corinthian capitals of the Khasneh may suggest that increasing Roman influence did not lead to the increased influence on architectural detailing. Nabatean influence seemed stronger in ed-Deir.

Royal Tombs

The most remarkable collection of monumental tombs was in the city centre on the lower slopes of al-Khubtha, though regrettably the façades are in a sad state of repair because of their greater exposure to the elements. Collectively known as the Royal Tombs, they balanced a group of religious structures at the other end of the cardo. The Royal Tombs included the Urn Tomb and Silk Tomb (both first half of the first century CE), the Corinthian Tomb (40–70 CE) and the Palace Tomb (second half of the first century CE).

The Urn Tomb had a rather plain, high, narrow but powerful

façade. It would be thought unsuccessful were it not for two elements in its composition: first, flanking colonnades of five columns with corner pilasters were carved from the rock on both sides to create a deep forecourt high above street level; second, the floor of the forecourt was supported on two tiers of (later) vaults, reached by ascending an imposing set of steps over the vaults. The engaged half-columns of the tomb façade were Nabatean, the colonnades' free-standing columns Doric. In the frieze above the architrave were four portrait busts, so badly damaged (defaced?) that it is impossible to tell if they were royal personages or gods. Burial chambers with loculi were located in the windows between the columns and above the north colonnade. Later, the interior of the Urn Tomb (18.5 m by 20.5 m) was remodelled as a church (446–7 CE; dated by a painted inscription) by inserting martyria for relics and a table into earlier recesses and adding a pulpit (ambo), chancel screen, altar, tomb and a receptacle for holy water.

The Silk Tomb (early first century CE) also was set back, though not as deeply, from the rock face. It was similar to but simpler than the Urn Tomb, with a single burial niche above the door, and crow-stepped mouldings in place of the triangular pediment, supported on a double cornice.

The Corinthian Tomb (40–70 CE), like the Khasneh and ed-Deir, combined various styles. Its tholos projected boldly between broken pediments in the upper register, with half-columns forming an octostyle façade of a mixed order on the lower register. The interior plan was unusual, with four rooms all skewed inexplicably at different angles to the façade, with doors different from each other.

Finally, the Palace Tomb, created just a few years later (late first century CE), was the most complex façade, with five storeys or registers and four rooms in plan on the ground level. The lower levels were entirely rock-cut, but since the bedrock did not rise high enough vertically to accommodate the full height of the planned façade the top storeys were built of masonry. The Nabatean columns of the lower register, which framed four large doors, gave it its dominant architectural character. The composition was interrupted by a kind of continuous plinth (almost like a podium), above which a differently designed second register had eighteen engaged columns spaced at varying intervals. There were six niches between the more widely spaced central columns – possibly added later – that further modulated this register. With the added upper storeys, the whole gave the effect of a large urban palace façade, 49 m wide by 46 m high.

This group of Royal Tombs was not designed and laid out as a single composition but developed gradually. We gain some sense of the importance and the impact of the tombs from the fact that all were built over about half or three-quarters of a century in the middle portion of the first century CE, with the tombs on the south nearest the road being built first, and the others being added roughly in the sequence in which they are now seen. At the same time, the effect of this group of monumental structures was not altogether casual and unplanned. Once the first one was built it would have seemed both natural and desirable that the others should follow in due course, precisely in order to create an overpowering sense of the splendour and prestige of Petra's royal family, if that was their social background.

It is difficult to evaluate their social and religious significance, but the architectural impact is self-evident even in their present shabby state. Prior to their construction, the great vertical rock face of al-Khubtha was essentially bare, framing the east side of the city centre. In less than a century it was transformed into a remarkable symbol of a progressive civilization and a powerful ruling dynasty. Petra's city centre was built within a limited time period, two groups of structures being created in overlapping periods of half a century or so, with the religious structures at the one end coming a little earlier than those at the other. There must have been an urban design decision to balance these two sets of components, the Royal Tombs on the east with the temples on the west. Petra's compact and speedy building activity occurred within the classical Nabatean period, when Roman influence may have been felt, but before the formal takeover of Nabatea as the Province of Arabia in 106 CE. The density and scale of the building activity implies a high degree of social organization and control, overall planning and even zoning, along with considerable individual creativity in the design of each monument.

Roman Soldier Tomb

Another element is added to the impression of variety among the tombs by the Roman Soldier Tomb (first half of the first century CE). The complex straddled two sides of the Wadi Farasa, with the tomb on one side and its triclinium (dining room) on the other. Its name refers to the fact that the figure in the central niche was dressed in typical Roman military dress, so it is supposed, not implausibly, that this was the tomb of a Roman resident in Petra who had acculturated to Nabatean ways. Not all the borrowing was one-way. Excavations have shown that a peristyle courtyard enclosing a trapezoidal garden architecturally connected the structures in the two opposing rock faces. It is difficult to gain a full impression of this complex, since many elements are now missing that were essential to its original character. The monumental façade had two Nabatean columns (distyle-in-antis), topped by an unusually low-pitched pediment. The doorway, with its Doric frieze, led up a short flight of steps into a square burial chamber with arched recesses for the burials. Across the garden court and down a few steps from the courtyard level, the triclinium (about 11 m square and 5.3 m high) was used for funeral celebrations and memorial meals. It was Petra's most impressively decorated interior, originally plastered, with fine Ionic half-columns alternating with framed niches presumably for sculpture.

Roads and bridges; dams and aqueducts

The main road that ran down the Siq and emerged at the Khasneh was eventually paved in the Roman manner. It then went north past the theatre and turned west into a colonnaded street with shops on the south side; on the north side the colonnade had only an architrave without a roof (Kanellopoulos, 'Shops', 20). Above the cardo on the south were markets, a fine garden/pool complex (paradeisos) and temple. The cardo in its earliest form may have been more nearly a processional way, but it was one that led into the city, not out of it to a nearby sanctuary as in most cases. It was about 18 m wide in its eastern portions; at a later stage the addition of more commercial space and colonnades narrowed it. In its second-century form it ended at a monumental three-arched gate at the entrance to the temenos of the Temple of Dushara. Though the monumental gate has been considered Petra's most Roman structure it was also one of the latest, perhaps Severan (193–211 CE; Kanellopoulos, 'Shops', 21). The gate functioned as if it were a formal propylaea at the entrance to a temenos.

The Nabateans were masterful in their ability to manage and control the scarce water resources of their region, skills they learned in the desert. They applied these skills in fresh ways once they adopted a sedentary way of life. A recent regional research study of the water management around Petra (led by Jaakko Frosén and Zbigniew Fiema) with a four-dimensional quick-time virtual reality model (Aaro Söderlund) has shown the great care with which the Nabateans built small dams that worked as a coordinated whole in each drainage area, so that whatever water fell would be stored and utilized for agricultural purposes, permitting more intensive farming of the terraced areas and greater agricultural produce than might otherwise be thought possible.

The main civic water supply was the spring of Ain Musa, which ran naturally through the city. Its flow had helped to shape the Siq. But this advantageous arrangement was also a disadvantage. When heavy rains in the areas above the Bab es-Siq flowed through the Siq, the extremely high walls and narrow passages (up to 103 m high and occasionally less than 2 m wide) led to a serious danger of flash floods. Tourists in the twentieth century still faced this problem; I vividly recall the deaths of German tourists trapped in the Siq by a wall of water in 1963. The Nabatean solution to this problem was to build a control dam and diversion tunnel where the Siq narrowed: the dam prevented water rushing down the Siq and the tunnel through the rock diverted the water to a nearby wadi (between 40 and 106 CE; Browning, *Petra*, 115). The combination permitted better water management and control. A monumental arch with associated niches sprang from side to side across the Siq a few yards from the dam to mark the entry point into the city (after 50 CE).

Civic water supply was of fundamental importance in ancient urban design; it was crucial to obtain a regular supply, ensure its safety and purity, get it into the city and make it readily available to everyone. Major cities had permanent sources, as well as the cisterns filled by rainwater from roofs and courtyards that were characteristic of smaller towns and villages in the Levant. Among the major installations were two aqueducts, one in an open channel and one in pottery pipes cemented together, a technique well known both in the Hellenistic and Roman worlds. Both aqueducts descended into the centre of Petra along the walls of the Siq. Two nymphaea, a semicircular one on the north side of cardo and a smaller one across the street on the south side, provided public water supplies, drawing from the aqueducts along the Siq. This was also the point where the water from the diversion channel came back into the centre of the city and met the cardo. From this point on, the collected waters of Ain Musa and other wadis ran in an open waterway parallel to the Cardo Maximus. The urban river required five bridges over the wadi to provide access to the buildings on the slope on the north side of the city centre (Kanellopoulos, 'Shops', 6, fig. 1). This was not unlike the arrangement hypothesized at Palmyra, with an earlier main street running parallel to a wadi just south of the Temple of Nebo; Perge in Pamphylia had a striking but more remote analogy: a raised water channel flowed down the centre of the cardo with small platform bridges that allowed pedestrians to cross from one side to the other.

While some of these elements of layout, design and technology were similar to and may have been borrowed from Rome, some of the major features were unusual, such as the design and location of the tombs, their integration into the civic design, the overall management of water and the unusual incorporation of the Wadi Musa into the streetscape.

Business and pleasure

There may have been two large side-by-side market areas at Petra; if so, it will be an important indication of the importance of the city's trade, parallel to Palmyra's Tariff Court and Agora. The markets at Petra were at the east end of and above the colonnaded street, on a plateau formed by cutting and filling the hill

(Kanellopoulos, 'Shops'). Some of the houses on the southern slope were demolished in the late first century BCE/early first century CE to make way for the upper market (Kolb et al., 'Excavations at az-Zantur'). A later phase included a propylaea, steps up to the raised market and a 'Trajanic arch' at the edge of the cardo (early second century CE). The shops at this point have been excavated; one of them, room 28 just west of the stairs to the upper market, functioned as a triclinium or tavern in close proximity to the nymphaeum (Kanellopoulos, 'Shops', 16). The unexcavated upper market area, however, has not yet been fully clarified. Beam sockets on the vertical eastern scarp left by the quarrying when the area was flattened indicate it had surrounding stoas, probably on all four sides (Kanellopoulos, 'Shops', 19–21), the spacing and height of whose 'pseudo-Corinthian' columns can now be established.

The city centre had a relatively early Roman theatre (first century CE) with a cavea that was almost entirely rock-cut (capacity about 7,000 to 8,000 persons). Drains and run-off channels protected the rock-cut facilities from the winter rains. The scaenae frons was decorated in imported marble and rose to the full height of the cavea; it combined a Nabatean order with typical Roman sculpture in yet another combination of cultural fashions. There was a second small theatre (capacity about 500–800 persons) in the small 'suburb' of 'Ain Sabra, about 8 km south, in which cisterns, collection facilities and other water installations were integrated with the theatre function. It was also unusual because it was designed on Hellenistic rather than on Roman principles; its date appears to be late first century CE and so slightly beyond the usual period of active Hellenistic theatre design.

A fine, well-decorated, small bath complex (first century BCE) was located near the monumental gate, with a very early example of a circular dome covering a room with semi-columns and small apses. A similar dome without the elaborate wall treatment was included a few years earlier in the famous fortified upper palace of Herodium built by Herod the Great.

Excavations began in 1998 in the so-called lower market, on the same plateau and just east of the Great Temple, revealing a previously unknown feature of the civic amenities of Petra (Bedal,

'Pool complex'). The Great Temple excavations (below) had demonstrated that the sole access to this area was through the forecourt of the Great Temple; it had long been realized that there was a small rectangular building towards the rear of the area. In fact, a monumental pool complex (Paradeisos; 53 m by 65 m) was created on the plateau that had been created by cutting the bedrock and filling the lower parts of the hillside behind a retaining wall alongside the colonnaded street. A majestic pool (43 by 23 by 2.5 m) occupied the southern rock-cut portion of the plateau, contained behind a 3 m-wide retaining wall that bisected the area. A flat-roofed pavilion (11.5 by 14.5 m) stood in the centre of the pool with doors in three or four sides; the north door was connected to the retaining wall by a vaulted bridge. The pool complex dates from late first century BCE/early first century CE and the bridge from later renovations (early second century CE).

There was an imaginative development of ornamental gardens or paradeisoi in the Hellenistic and Roman periods. One of the nearest and best analogies to the Petra pool was the pool surrounding the Tobiad palace at Araq al-Emir, west of Philadelphia (Amman), which dates from the early second century BCE (Netzer, 'Tyros'). Several Herodian complexes included pools, though all were for Herod's and his guests' pleasure: the closest analogy was the large pool with gazebo at Herodium (23–15 BCE). Bedal suggests that Herodium, though larger (garden: 105 m by 125 m; pool: 72 m by 46 m), had a virtually identical plan, though this is not quite correct. Both Petra – if one includes the adjacent Great Temple – and Herodium had complex facilities: peristyle courtyard, pool, gardens, gazebo, bath, exedras, monumental building. Not all of Herod's private palaces had monumental swimming pools, as Bedal claims: Alexandreion, Machaerus and Cypros, to name three, did not, though they may have had swimming facilities and certainly had baths. Bedal, however, is entirely correct when she points to the 'exchange of ideas and innovations between the two cultures' (Bedal, 'Pool complex', 37).

An eastern tradition of paradeisoi in association with royal palaces stretched back to the third millennium BCE. The civic and perhaps religious nature of the Petra pool complex, however, varies from the royal pattern, as the entrance from the Great

Temple's east colonnade implies. In this respect it may have been slightly similar to Vespasian's later Temple of Peace in Rome (*c.*75 CE), which combined civic and religious garden elements with a museum. Whatever the precise character of the Petra pool complex, it was an imaginative addition to the city centre, which drew its inspiration from eastern paradeisoi traditions.

Religion

Nabatean religion took a number of forms: djinn blocks and god blocks that were more or less aniconic (Holyland, *Arabia*, 168; Wenning, 'Betyls'); niches; statuary; worship of traditional gods, especially Dushara ('he of Sharra') and al-'Uzza ('the mighty goddess'). '[I]n the idolatrous temple at Petra . . . they praise the virgin with hymns in the Arabic language and call her khabu (*ka'ba*?) . . . in Arabic; and the child who is born of her they call Dusares' (Epiphanius, *Panarion* 51.22, cited in Holyland, *Arabia*, 252 n. 1; see also pp. 183–7). A number of the god blocks show a large and a small block side by side, and some niches, now empty, referred to both deities: 'These are the baetyls of al-'Uzza and the Lord of the House, made by Wahballahi, the caravan-leader, son of Zaidan'; 'These are al-'Uzza and the Lord of the House, which were made by 'Oqbar, son of Fahim, and Hagay, the artisans' (Wenning, 'Betyls', 80–1, 83). Such representations were found along the roads into the city, so that religious devotion was present in a muted way before reaching the city centre. The use of abstract 'eye-Baetyls' and 'the non-figurative representations of the gods among the Nabateans and other[s] . . . determined a non-figurative course for the art of Islamic monotheism' (Holyland, *Arabia*, 168). Petra's religion balanced highly visible tombs, temples and altars with other subtle representations of deities. Specifically religious sites included the large group of tombs noted above, which was matched by a central cluster of important temples at the west end of the cardo. And the whole was surrounded with sacrificial high places on the plateau around the bowl that contained the city.

Planning considerations

The central sites included the Great Temple (possibly to Dushara) with its pool complex, the Qasr al-Bint or Temple of Dushara, the Temple of the Winged Lions (probably to al-'Uzza) and other minor temples, all arranged around the cardo and constituting the city's focus. The primary cult temple, to Dushara, was at the end of the main street, which may have acted as a processional way before it was developed into a colonnaded cardo. The retaining walls of the Wadi Musa and five bridges over the wadi, which give access to the northern slope, imply that the street's alignment was originally more informal, with several minor bends. These were later straightened out when the colonnaded street was built (second century CE), the opposite of the situation at Palmyra.

After the cardo's formalization with columns and shops, the present monumental arch was constructed where an earlier gate had also been located (second century CE, perhaps late). The monumental gate at the entrance to the temenos postdates the paving of the cardo; twin towers flanked it. The line took a slight bend at the temenos gate, so that the axis of Dushara's temenos was slightly north-west from the axis of the cardo. Dushara's precise orientation was repeated though reversed on the north side of the wadi in the orientation of the Temple of the Winged Lions, across a bridge just outside the monumental gate. The same orientation was also reflected in another smaller temple south-west of the arch; the adjacent bath's orientation was almost the same. Other buildings south of the street, however, followed a different orientation. Like the markets farther east, the Great Temple and Pool Complex, which lay just outside the gate, were at 90 degrees to the orientation of the cardo. The unidentified building in area W, east of the Temple of the Winged Lions, follows neither orientation, and seems to derive its axis from the earlier street line.

The clustering of four or more religious sites in a single composition stands out; on a much smaller scale, the Nabatean temples at Si'a (to Ba'al Shamim, to Dushara, and a third temple) were slightly similar. Petra's orderly design relationships and tight chronological span imply that the planning decisions were coordinated. Was it accidental that the axis of the Great Temple went through the centre of the holy place of al-'Uzza's temple? Why did the axis of a still unexplored area W ('Royal Palace'?) bisect the gazebo in the pool complex? Was it accidental that the mass of al-'Uzza matched the mass of the Great Temple, with their rear walls being roughly the same distance from the centre of the cardo? Whatever the rationale, the architectural result was that the Great Temple and the Temple of the Winged Lions had a balanced but curiously unstable relationship to each other. At the same time they created a sense of anticipation in the approach to the Temple of Dushara. These relationships, seen easily in plan, are consistent with studies of late-Hellenism elsewhere in the eastern Mediterranean that have shown that such relationships were consciously designed, so deliberate design decisions may be presumed. The monumental arch, whose axis bisected the angle of the other two axes, completed the scheme (Browning, *Petra*, 152–6).

Temple of Dushara

The Temple of Dushara (Qasr al-Bint) refers to the god Dushara, 'he of Sharra', alluding to the mountain rising north of Petra. The classic portrayal of Dushara was an aniconic or nearly aniconic god-block, with little modulation or definition. He came to be assimilated to Zeus in the Roman period. The Temple of Dushara was built in the reign of Obodas II (30–9 BCE) or a few years later. This would make it slightly earlier than the Temple of Bel in Palmyra and almost contemporaneous with the Temple in Jerusalem. The temenos (first century CE) and the monumental gate (second century CE) were laid out on a long east–west axis at the end of the colonnaded street. The axis of the naos was at right angles to the temenos axis, so the temple façade in fact faced north, an unusual orientation for a religious building in antiquity. While the constraints of the site may have imposed this orientation on the temple, it seems likelier that it faced north to bind the sanctuary explicitly to the mountain Sharra; such orientation to features of the landscape was not uncommon in antiquity (Scully, *Architecture*, chs 2–3).

Axes laid out at right angles to each other have already been seen in a different form in the Temple of Bel at Palmyra (above, Chapter 2), and will be noted again in the Jerusalem Temple (Chapter 6, below). At Palmyra locating the door on the propylaea's axis satisfactorily solved the visual ambiguity of the crossed axes. But that meant that the two holy places (Bel had a double adyton) were unrelated to the axis of the temenos. The visual problem at Petra was more difficult, and the change of axis was not altogether satisfactorily resolved architecturally. The vista was closed by an exedra in the west wall of the temenos, the mass of the altar, the sight of ascending steps into the temple on the left and even – or especially – the mass of the rock face of el-Habis behind; these focused visitors' attention to the left onto the naos of the temple. It was an uneasy and not especially well-resolved transition, but it did permit the axis of the adyton to be aligned with the axis of the façade and altar.

The naos was square and on a podium in typical Nabatean fashion, with a porch or pronaos of four columns with projecting side-walls (antae), tetrastyle-in-antis to use the Roman description. Inside the naos, a central adyton or holy of holies was flanked by two other two-storey holy places, with stairs on either side mounting to the second floors and then to the roof above, parallel to the arrangements at Palmyra and Jerusalem. The central adyton held either a god block or a statue, either abstract or sculptural. Since a clenched hand from a statue that would have stood about 7 m high was found on the podium, it must have been a statue in the final stages of the building's occupation, but earlier probably a god block. The interior was decorated with painted plaster and lit by windows, another design decision that was found at Palmyra both in the Temple of Ba'al Shamim and in the Temple of Bel. The exterior decoration includes a number of imported motifs (some from Rome such as Pompeian-style frescoes, some from Greece and Macedonia such as the triglyph and metope frieze).

A high altar stood in front of and on axis with the Qasr al-Bint (13.4 m by 11.8 m and almost 3 m high), with steps ascending from the south. It was set near the centre of a square plaza that extended to the edge of the wadi. The north-west portion of the temenos was never paved; whether the unpaved area was filled with a garden or was used to tether animals is not clear (Browning, *Petra*, 164). The exedra in the west peribolos wall was located at the centre point between the porch of the Qasr and the north wall of the temenos, though without a discernible relationship to the temenos gate or the temenos itself. The long south wall of the temenos had a bench and two small platforms, possibly reflecting Nabatean temples to Dushara that had benches in the temenos (Si'a and others). A small temple and other structures were located above the south wall, reached through a monumental doorway.

Temple of the Winged Lions/al-'Uzza

North-east of the Temple of Dushara was the Temple of the Winged Lions (Aretas IV's reign, 9 BCE–40 CE), probably dedicated to al-'Uzza, a fertility goddess, like Attargatis of Syria, Isis or Aphrodite (Bowersock, *Roman Arabia*, 86–7). The temenos was reached from the cardo by a monumental stair and bridge across the Wadi Musa, on a slight angle to the street but on the same orientation as the Temple of Dushara. The temple façade faced south towards the hill of es-Zantur and the wadi that led to Sabra. The Temples of Dushara and al-'Uzza were built within a generation of each other and were part of the same urban composition. Al-'Uzza was a strongly symmetrical composition in its public areas, with a large forecourt, middle court and naos. Its porch or pronaos was uncharacteristically small, enclosed and entered through doors on either side. The square holy place contained an altar pedestal surrounded by free-standing columns forming a three-sided interior colonnade; the inside face of the outer walls was decorated with engaged columns and alternating niches. Like the Temple of Dushara and the Great Temple, it was surrounded by a corridor, within which the main structure seemed to float. The building was remodelled in the mid-first century CE and then partly destroyed by fire in the early second century CE, following which it had only casual use. Possibly connected with rebuilding work after its partial destruction, various workshops (paint, metal and sculpture) have been excavated west of the temple.

Great Temple

South of the Temple of al-'Uzza was the Great Temple, perhaps also a Temple of Dushara, under excavation since 1993. It was built in the last quarter of the first century BCE, with a large forecourt (28 m by 42 m) being added in the mid-first century CE (Joukowsky, *Petra Great Temple*; Joukowsky and Basile, 'More pieces'). The rigidly symmetrical complex was entered from the cardo up monumental stairs between shops (like the later instances at Gerasa; see Chapter 4 below). On the first terrace was a large peristyle courtyard with hexagonal limestone paving, surrounded by double colonnades 20 m high; stunningly designed Indian elephant-headed capitals, of which two complete examples and some 328 fragments have been found, topped the columns. The two side colonnades had large exedras on the south ends, with a partial cryptoporticus under the west side. The walls of the peristyle were decorated with Pompeian-style frescoes.

Stairways rose from the forecourt to the main or upper level, where there was a large pronaos or porch (like the Temple of Dushara, tetrastyle-in-antis) that in turn led to the naos, surrounded by a walkway. Inside through another large opening (distyle-in-antis) was a theatral area (first century CE) that made this the most unusual building in Petra. Theatral areas are known in other religious structures of the same period or earlier: Dushara at Si'a, Demeter at Pergamon, Demeter at Corinth, and the Telesterion at Eleusis, to mention a few varied arrangements. But the formalism and assurance in the design of the Great Temple are remarkable, and especially noteworthy is the fact that the theatral area was located inside the naos in a kind of bouleutêrion arrangement, seating about 500–600 persons and facing towards the entrance. Its function is unclear, but Joukowsky insists on a religious function, a kind of 'sacred' or 'ritual' theatre (in part following Segal, *Theatres*). The excavators seem still puzzled by what they have discovered, and the excavations of the monumental pool next door have complicated the problem further.

Its function is wrapped up with the interpretation of two fragmentary inscriptions found in the Petra church on the other side of the wadi (Joukowsky and Basile, 'More pieces'; Jones, 'Nabatean inscriptions', 346–9, with note by Bowersock). The inscription has been reconstructed to read, '[This is the . . . ,] which Halpa'la, [son of . . . ,] made, and these are the theatron to Dushara [and the . . .], in the month of Tebet in the year eleven of Haretat (Aretas), king of the Nabateans, who loved his people.' The final clause is the standard description of Aretas IV. If the 'theatron' of the inscription was the 'theatron' of the Great Temple, it means (1) that the theatron was built relatively early in the construction history of the Great Temple and (2) that the Great Temple was also dedicated to Dushara. If this were the case, all four of the major structures or sanctuaries forming the focus of the west end of the city (Qasr al-Bint, Temple of the Winged Lions, Great Temple, and the Garden–Pool complex) were devoted to only two deities: Dushara and al-'Uzza.

High Places

Surrounding the central area of Petra, 200 m above the central areas, were a number of rock-cut High Places (the best-known is the high place on the Attuf Ridge; first century CE), presumably for animal sacrifice. Close by were two obelisks that were left standing when the surrounding rock was carved away in a major quarrying effort, perhaps for an adjacent fort. They may represent the two same two leading deities of Nabatean religion, Dushara and al-'Uzza, who figured in the temples below. While the Temple of Dushara had its own sacrificial altar, the Great Temple and the Temple of the Winged Lions had minor altars or none at all. So the high places supplement sacrifice in the city centre. In function and design they offer insights into the way in which animal sacrifice worked in antiquity. Located between rock and heaven, the experience of worshipping at such locations, looking out over the rest of the city, must have been awesome. A sunken seating area provides for worshippers, whose attention was focused on a low platform in the centre and a higher altar with steps in a central position behind it on the west side, beside a circular ritual installation also with steps that was connected to a basin.

Later periods

Petra declined in the middle/late Roman periods, during which some of the main structures were destroyed or seriously modified. The city was reinvigorated when Christianity arrived. The vitality resulted both in newly constructed churches and in the adaptation of other existing structures. The main structure adapted to ecclesiastical purposes in the city centre was the Urn Tomb (446–7 CE), effected through a relatively simple set of alterations that included altars, chancel screen and other bits of furnishing. Three new buildings were built in the city centre: the Central or Papyrus Church, the Ridge Church and the Blue Chapel, all three fifth century CE. On top of Jebel Haroun there was yet another Christian structure (also fifth century CE). The Petra Church has become extremely important because of the finding of an archive of papyrus documents, now being painstakingly restored despite their having been burned in antiquity. They will shed almost unique light on the social, economic and familial circumstances of the Christian community in Petra during the Byzantine period.

City with a focus

Petra was laid out originally along a sacred processional way leading into the city – to the Temple of Dushara. This approach with its dramatic entry through the Siq gave a sense of gradual disclosure, perhaps more than any other city of antiquity. 'One point is key: the model upon which urban space is organized differs from that of the traditional cities of the Mediterranean and Near East' (Augé and Dentzer, *Petra*, 56). As the city developed, the processional way became a more typical colonnaded cardo, with amplified facilities for the convenience of citizens and visitors. In this later period, the route led from outer areas with water works and monumental arch, past a considerable number of tombs, the civic theatre and two nymphaea, to the commercial areas and then ultimately to the religious focus of the whole. Religion was not the only cultural feature to receive careful attention; indeed, the number of religious buildings was smaller than in some comparable cities. But the religious structures gave shape and form to the central area in a way peculiar to Petra.

The formal architectural elements, though sometimes late Hellenistic or Roman in details, were joined with other indigenous influences (e.g. Assyrian, Hittite, Persian and Parthian) in such a way that its buildings were uniquely Petra's own. That special quality was expressed in the tombs, which visually dominated Petra, but it could be found in all the major structures, as recent discoveries have shown. Two close observers of Petra a generation apart put matters aptly: 'The architecture [of the Qasr al-Bint and the temenos gate] shows clearly that, for all the presence of Rome, the Nabateans never wholly deserted their native style, which kept reasserting itself in new pseudo-classical guises' (Browning, *Petra*, 154). 'The result of this combination of eastern and Classical features [in capital design] by the sculptors at Petra is unique to Nabataean architecture, giving it distinctive features not previously identified as such' (McKenzie, 'Keys from Egypt', 102). Petra's architecture and urban design show a creative blend of Mediterranean and native Arabian elements.

The baroque developments in the architecture of Petra were more vivid and unusual than in Palmyra. The experimental elements at Petra – the elephant-headed capitals, a theatral area in a temple and civic adaptation of a paradeisos complex – cannot be matched at Palmyra. These were mixed with other exuberant elements, such as broken pediment, bracketed tholos in the second register and Syrian arch. Even the more prosaic elements that established so much of its character (extensive use of Nabatean capitals, austerity of the simple tombs, grandeur of the royal tombs, use of water) were sometimes not typical of other parts of the Roman Empire. So the baroque impression of the whole had a more exotic and less familiar tone. The art, too, showed similar multiple influences (Zayadine, 'Sculpture', 55–8).

If Palmyra fell somewhere between Rome and the desert, Petra fell between Alexandria and the desert. The one was influenced in detail if not in conception by Roman architectural design; the other was influenced in detail and to some extent in conception by late-Hellenistic design. It is neatly consistent with this architectural analysis that Petra rose to prominence and then peaked a century or so earlier than Palmyra, and that Palmyra took over Petra's influential trading role when trade routes shifted to the Euphrates route.

More important is what ties Petra and Palmyra together. Both superficially appeared to be cities rooted in Greece or in Rome, with details to support such an impression. On closer inspection both retained strong and decisive elements from their Arabian roots. Both resisted – that is, did not fully include – the full range of Hellenistic and Roman features. To the Roman or Greek traveller in antiquity, both must have seemed 'oriental'. The degree of Romanization in the architecture and urban design was limited in both cases. It can hardly be denied that in a number of details, technological areas and building types, such as bath, nymphaeum and theatre, Roman influence was strong. Yet both Petra and Palmyra diverged strongly from Roman models in religious and funerary architecture – as one might expect, since civilizations are usually conservative in matters of death and worship – and also, I would claim, in their overall urban design. When we get to Jerusalem, these same kinds of factors will again play a significant role. In the next two chapters we consider Gerasa and Caesarea Maritima, cities with more pervasive late-Hellenistic and Roman influences yet still with local influences.

Table 3.1 Petra chronology

Before 106 CE

Khasneh	1st c. BCE
Great Temple	1st c. BCE
Pool and gazebo	late 1st c. BCE (or early 1st c. CE?)
Qasr al Bint	before 1st c. CE
Baths	1st c. BCE
Winged Lions	first quarter 1st c. CE or earlier
Urn Tomb	first half 1st c. CE (converted to church 446–7) CE)
Silk Tomb	(first half 1st c. CE)
Tomb of Roman Soldier	first half 1st c. CE (also triclinium)

Bab es Siq arch	after 50 CE
Corinthian Tomb	40–70 CE
Bab es Siq triclinium	40–70 CE
Obelisk Tomb	40–70 CE
Ed-Deir	possibly 40–70 CE (second half 1st c. CE)
Dam and tunnel	*c.*40–106 CE
Theatre	1st c. CE
High Place	1st c. CE
Temenos	1st c. CE
Palace Tomb	second half 1st c. CE
Main street redesign	late 1st/early 2nd c. CE
Sabra theatre	late 1st c. CE?

106–313 CE

Trajanic arch at market	early 2nd c. CE
Main street revisions	2nd c. CE
Temenos Gate	2nd c. CE (perhaps Severan?)
Nymphaeum	2nd c. CE

After Constantine

Church – Urn Tomb	446–7 CE
Papyrus Church	5th c. CE
Blue Chapel	5th c. CE
Ridge Church	5th c. CE
Monastery, Jebel Haroun	5th c. CE

[Most dates are from Judith MacKenzie, *Architecture of Petra*.]

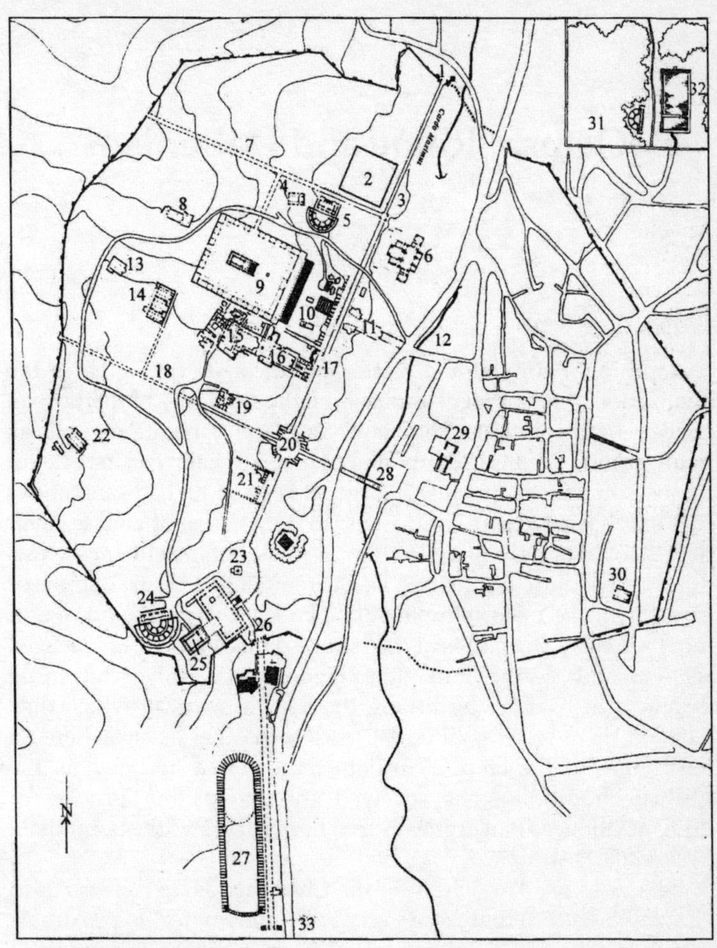

Figure 37 Plan of Jerash (After Pillen). 1: North Gate. 2: Agora? 3: North Tetrapylon. 4: Church of Bishop Isiah. 5: North Theatre. 6: West Baths. 7: North Decumanus. 8: Synagogue Church. 9: Artemis Propylaeum. 10: Temple of Artemis. 11: Artemis Processional Way. 12: North Bridge. 13: Church of Bishop Genesius. 14: Church of St John Complex. 15: Church of St Theodore. 16: Cathedral. 17: Nymphaeum. 18: South Decumanus. 19: Ummayyad houses. 20: South Tetrapylon. 21: Macellum. 22: Church of SS Peter and Paul. 23: Oval Plaza. 24: South Theatre. 25: Temple of Zeus. 26: South Gate. 27: Hippodrome. 28: South Bridge. 29: East Baths. 30: Church of Procopius. 31: Festival Theatre. 32: Tanks. 33: Arch of Hadrian.

Plan of Gerasa

4

Gerasa: Rome and Hellenism

Introduction

Juxtaposing Palmyra and Petra, products of two great Arab civilizations, encouraged emphasis on the similarity of their urban concerns and solutions. Both gave very careful attention to burial, in tower tombs, temple tombs and hypogea at Palmyra, in rock-cut tombs, sometimes immensely large, at Petra. Both had sanctuaries that emphasized their Arab roots; in both cases, of course, their deities could be assimilated to Roman gods, but in neither case was this emphasized. Both cities had a remodelled central street or cardo with the major temple at one end of the street and one or more funerary structures at the other, so that both cities balanced religion and death. Both cities blended classical architectural details with Arabian traditions, though the ways in which they blended them were as different from each other as elsewhere on the fringes of the empire. In both there was a 'tenacity' in the Arabian traditions that survived throughout the process of Romanization, as Ball argues even if he exaggerates the point (Ball, *Rome in the East*, 396).

Gerasa – or Antiocheia-on-the-Chrysorhoas as it was also known – was different from Petra and Palmyra, for its proximate roots were not in Arab culture, though it did have numerous earlier phases back to the Neolithic, but rather in the conditions following Alexander the Great's conquest and re-founding of the cities of the region. It continued to retain a connection with Macedonian Hellenism through subsequent periods. Since that Hellenism was ultimately Greek-inspired, and since Rome also drew heavily on Greek and Hellenistic traditions, the character of

Gerasa was naturally overlaid with a stronger indebtedness to Rome than was true at either Petra or Palmyra. Gerasa gave a strong sense of its dual Hellenistic and Roman inheritance.

All the cities of the Decapolis, a loose confederation of cities mainly in northern Jordan and southern Syria (S. Thomas Parker, 'Decapolis', *OEANE* 2.127–30, with bibliography), were weighted more heavily to late-Hellenistic and Roman conventions than either Petra or Palmyra was. This was also true of cities on the Mediterranean coastline (Tyre, Sidon, Ptolemais, Dor, Strato's Tower, later to become Caesarea Maritima; Chapter 5 below). In one sense the raison d'être of both the coastal cities and the inland cities in the pre-Roman period was precisely to be cultural centres of Hellenism, from which that inheritance might influence the surrounding areas. They were usually treated by Rome after 63 BCE as separate from the surrounding states, because they were visibly and culturally different from Judea or Nabatea or even Syria, their nearest neighbours, though several fell under Herod's rule for varying periods; on his death all were restored to their independence (Richardson, *Herod*, 88–91). A Hippodamian or gridiron plan was incorporated into the plans of a number of them (Hippos, Gadara, Gerasa, Damascus, Caesarea Maritima), typical of many Roman provincial cities of this type, but in other cases such a plan was very difficult for site-related reasons (Beth Shean, Pella, Philadelphia, Abila, Tyre). The public facilities with which such cities were endowed were typical of Roman cities elsewhere, especially those with a tradition of self-governance.

In the Greek and Hellenistic world, such a self-governing city was a polis (pl. poleis) or 'city-state', with a high degree of autonomy and cohesiveness, including the minting of its own coinage. It had the typical cultural and administrative structures of a Greek city (gymnasium or xystos, theatre, stadium, bouleutêrion and so on) and was surrounded by its own territory (its chôra) that made agricultural self-sufficiency possible. The Decapolis cities through the first century CE were similarly self-governing, even if they fell under the ultimate control of the Governor of Syria, a status they lost with the creation of the Province of Arabia.

Gerasa's location on a permanent river, the Chrysorhoas ('golden river'), accounted for its having been settled from the

Neolithic and early Bronze periods. It took form in the Seleucid period (from about 200 BCE onwards); its name, Antioch-on-the-Chrysorhoas, reflected the determinative role of either Antiochus III, the Great (223–187 BCE), or Antiochus IV Epiphanes (175–164 BCE). Gerasa came under Jewish control late in the reign of Alexander Jannaeus (103–76 BCE), following the successful Hasmonean revolt against Syrian rule and Judea's subsequent expansion. With Pompey's conquest of the region and his newly imposed political arrangements, Gerasa became an independent city loosely attached to the Province of Syria. Its coins and inscriptions date from the Pompeian period (in this case from 62 BCE). Jewish revolutionaries attacked it during the Jewish Revolt (Josephus, *War* 2.450); despite that, Josephus says that 'the people of Gerasa not only abstained from maltreating the Jews who remained with them, but escorted to the frontiers any who chose to emigrate' (*War* 2.458). It lost its independence and became part of the Province of Arabia from 106 CE (on most of these points see Schürer, 2.149–55).

Gerasa showed much the same baroque architectural flair as Petra and Palmyra, when it was dramatically transformed from a small Hellenistic city, originally confined to the southern part of the later city, to one of the dominant cities of the Decapolis. Religiously it was different from both cities. Its temples did not honour Arab deities but were dedicated instead to the Olympian pantheon. Its small but perhaps influential Jewish community during the early period was later superseded by a fast-growing Christian community. There seem to have been fewer religious influences from the other parts of the Near East than we might have expected in such a pluralistic city. While there were lots of signs of a thriving city, there are not a lot of material signs of international caravan trade, as at Palmyra and Petra.

Gerasa reflected better than its neighbours close attachment to Greco-Roman religious and civic experience. As an inland city, and so without the directness of contacts with Rome that coastal cities enjoyed, most of its architectural details and planning were Roman in character. This should not be altogether surprising, for Gerasa owed its independence, after a period under Jewish control in the first century BCE, to Rome, which had made it a polis again. Given the commitments of its citizens, its cultural role and its developmental history, therefore, we should expect it to be significantly different from Petra and Palmyra, with their Arab roots, indigenous cultural roles, and longer independence, even though Gerasa's location put it almost exactly midway between Petra and Palmyra.

Greek and Roman religion

Temple of Zeus

The earliest sanctuary in Gerasa was to Zeus (the Seleucids' official religious cult), which was located just inside and west of the south city gate on a rising hill that faced the original settlement on an adjacent small hill. Much of the sanctuary has survived or been reconstructed, the lower temenos in its first-century CE form, the upper naos in its second-century CE form, after it had been expanded to reflect the new wealth of the city. It is best to examine it initially in its first-century form. The lower temenos was a simple but aesthetically pleasing monumental altar, a large box open to the air in an ancient Semitic style that originally seems to have been entered from the south-east, judging from a door found in the later city wall. Because of the sloping ground, it was built on a vaulted substructure of boldly bossed ashlars. Enclosed colonnades surrounded the courtyard, with its large altar towards the north-west end. These nicely modulated inner colonnades, closed rather than open, were its most attractive feature, providing a roofed and protected walkway around the temenos. The highly simplified form may have owed something to indigenous Nabatean influences. Similarly simple walled religious structures without the enclosed colonnades could be found in two first-century BCE structures in Judea, at Hebron and Mamre, both by Herod the Great and both dedicated to Abraham, in the case of Hebron with the other patriarchs and matriarchs. More remote parallels, particularly to the overall composition, could be cited at major Hellenistic sites such as Lindos and Cos, but the lower temenos at Gerasa was more likely to be indebted to eastern traditions.

Browning conjectures that originally the lower temenos was the complete sanctuary (Browning, *Jerash*, 39, fig. 5), but this seems unlikely. There may have been an earlier temple on the upper level. In any case, it was rebuilt at about the same time as the city expanded, and its extension had to fit into the new overall form of the city. This posed a major urban design problem. The late-Hellenistic town (second to first century BCE) was laid out generally in a north-west–south-east orientation, accommodating the slopes of two hills in the south part of the city, though the Hellenistic street pattern is not known precisely. This conclusion seems inescapable from several factors: the layout of the Zeus temenos, the orientation of the south theatre beside it, the orientation of the south gate, the alignment of the street in front of the Zeus temenos and the orientation of streets in the south end of the modern city of Jerash. Certainly the layout of the later Roman city was radically different from that of the Hellenistic city. Following its first-century CE replanning the city followed the general line of the river: a north–south gridiron plan was imposed on the city, altering substantially how the city fitted the landscape. The cardo, as was normal, ran from a North Gate to a South Gate (about 800 m), though both gates were skewed from the cardo's orientation. It connected with major interurban roads from its gates, north-west to Pella, Scythopolis and the Mediterranean coastline, north to other Decapolis cities and south to Philadelphia and the Red Sea. The slightly later Via Nova Traiana (106–11 CE) passed east of Gerasa (Graf, 'Via Nova Traiana').

In this substantial reorganization, the cardo took a dog's leg to the east at the south end of the city so that it slid past the Sanctuary of Zeus and emerged through the south gate. We have already noted how a similar reorientation of Palmyra and its cardo was necessitated by urban design considerations; during that work, the Temple of Nebo's temenos was truncated and the bends in the cardo were resolved by building a monumental arch and a tetrakionion. At Gerasa the difficult design problem was solved brilliantly by the creation of an elliptical piazza at the point of intersection (80 m by 90 m), so that the curve on the west side blended into the face of the Zeus temenos, and the curve on the east met the Temple of Zeus at right angles exactly at its new monumental steps. The 'Oval Piazza' was later embellished with the Ionic

1 The central section of Palmyra's Cardo Maximus, looking east to the Monumental Arch and, beyond it on the right, the Temple of Bel. Note the unpaved street, the consoles on the columns and the decorative architectural elements.

2 Looking east through Palmyra's Tetrakionion towards the Monumental Arch. Sixteen imported pink granite columns (these are modern reproductions) sat on four bases, which in turn sat on a single base within an ovoid plaza.

3 Palmyra's Funerary Temple, to the north-east. In the foreground is the south anta with its fine decoration and behind it the columns of the east façade.

4 The naos of the Temple of Bel, to the northeast. In the foreground is the ablution pool. The monumental doorway to the naos faced the Propylaea; one of the rear columns of the peristyle can be seen. Note the reconstructed crow-step merlons at the eave and parts of two decorated beams, now at ground level, right of the doorway.

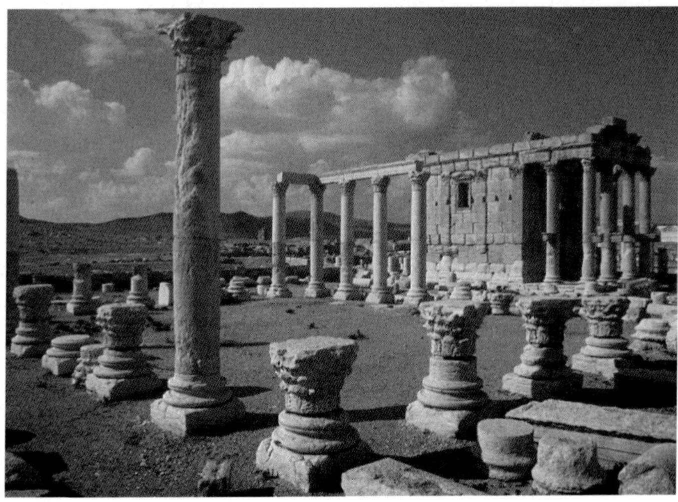

5 View to the north of the south court of the Temple of Ba`al Shamim. The small naos was windowed, like the Temple of Bel, lighting a delightfully baroque interior.

6 Façade of the Khasneh, with its rich details, Nabatean/Corinthian capitals, tholos in the upper register and 'baroque' design approach.

7 The Khasneh, as one emerges from the Siq, looking west. Note the boldly defined porch on the first level and the broken pediment on the second level, with sculpture between the columns on both levels.

8 Petra's Royal Tombs acted as a focus of the city on the east; the Urn Tomb had a relatively plain façade but boldly rock-cut stoas on two sides of a courtyard supported by two levels of vaulting. A stair approached on the right from the south.

9 Ed-Deir, the largest of the tombs (note the figure in the doorway), with its bold upper register, flat lower register and Nabatean capitals. The conical roof of the tholos contains a kind of viewing platform.

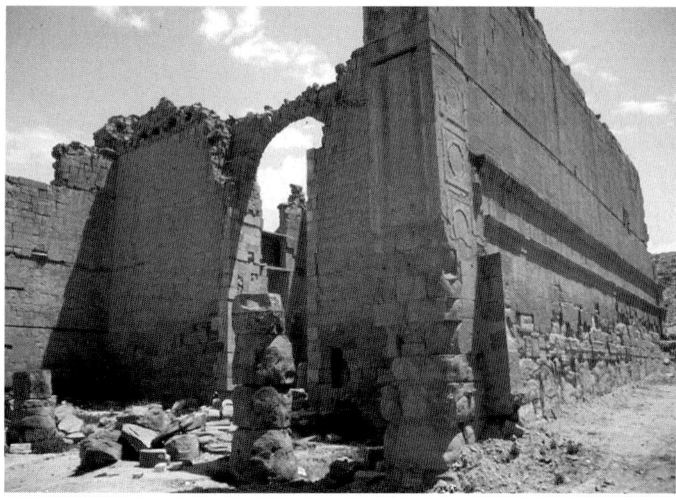

10 View to the south-east of the naos of the Temple of Dushara. The columns of the pronaos (porch) are in the foreground with the arch over the main door behind. The rich plaster details on the exterior are visible just right of centre on the anta.

11 The Temple of the Winged Lions (Temple of Allat) at Petra, looking south across the Wadi Musa and the Cardo to the sites of the Great Temple and the Monumental Pool Complex (at the time of the photo neither yet was excavated).

12 Gerasa to the north, from the porch of the upper Temple of Zeus. In the foreground is the lower temenos of Zeus, behind it the Oval Piazza, and running into the distance the Cardo Maximus. The South Decumanus is in the left middle distance and behind it the columns of the Temple of Artemis.

13 The curve of the Oval Piazza meets the lower temenos of Zeus at the main steps. The naos has an axial relationship to the steps but also to the Cardo Maximus, creating a dynamic web of relationships in the southern section of the city.

14 Gerasa's main sanctuary was the Temple of Artemis, approached up a monumental flight of steps through its baroque-feeling propylaea, with a massive central door and flanking side doors. In antiquity the upper temenos wall would have obscured the columns of the naos porch, which are just barely visible here (looking west).

15 The Artemis propylaea, monumental steps and columns of the naos, looking west through the columns (on the left) of the Propylaea Plaza, which created an important part of the processional way. The Propylaea Plaza was later converted into a church.

16 Gerasa's richly decorated Nymphaeum still gives a strong sense of the play of light and shade. Originally the basin was covered with a semi-dome, the niches were filled with sculpture and water poured into the basin from the lower statuary.

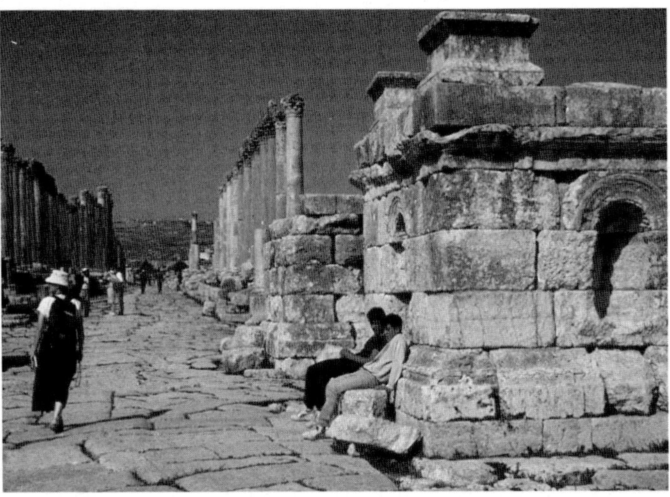

17 North up the Cardo; in the foreground is the base of Gerasa's Tetrakionion, which sat in a circular plaza. In contrast to the design at Palmyra, the road went straight through the base. In the background the higher columns distinguished the Nymphaeum and the Artemis Propylaea.

18 Looking south across some of the piers of Caesarea's inner harbour toward the crusader fortifications. On the left are the substructures of the platform for the Temple of Roma and Augustus.

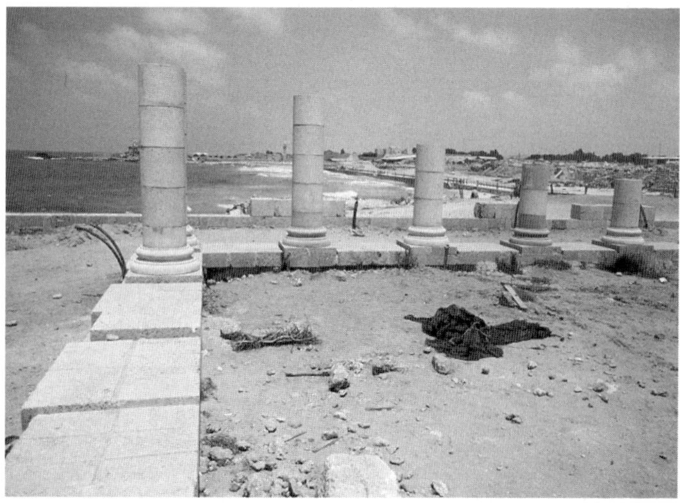

19 Looking north from the peristyle of the upper level of the Promontory Palace (the columns are modern reproductions). In the distance on the left are the remains of the harbour; in the middle distance on the right is the hippodrome.

20 Looking west across the lower level of the Promontory Palace, with its central pool and reception rooms. Just below the wall in the foreground was a small bath, similar to those in other Herodian palaces.

21 A complex of small shrines set into the east side of the hippodrome/amphitheatre for the religious needs of the participants. A number of votive offerings were excavated in this area.

22 Vaulted substructure under the Temple of Roma and Augustus, from the south-west, after landscaping covered parts of the inner harbour. Just left of centre was a monumental stair up from the harbour.

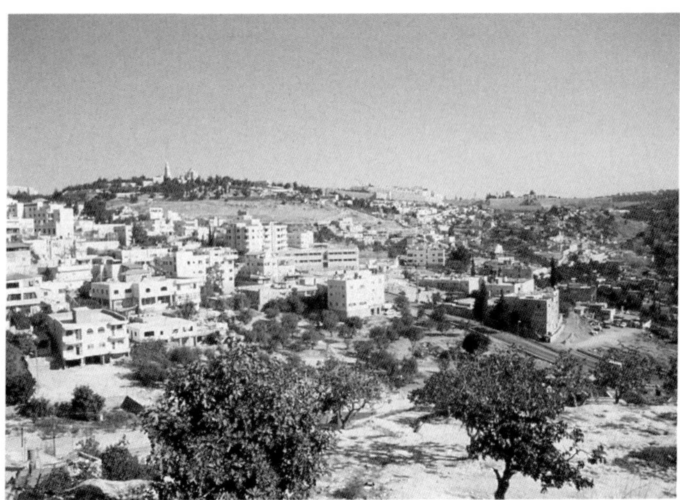

23 Jerusalem, looking north from the site of Herod's theatre: the Kidron Valley is on the right, the Tyropoeon Valley just right of centre, Mount Zion between it and the Hinnom Valley on the left. The City of David is on the ridge between the Kidron and Tyropoeon Valleys, with the Dome of the Rock immediately above it.

24 Seam on the east wall of the Temple Mount: the masonry of the Hasmonean extension is on the right (north); the Herodian extension is on the left (south), with the projecting stones of the springing of an arch that carried an exit stair on the upper left.

25 Herodian capital, still in situ at north end of street running alongside the new west retaining wall of the Temple Mount, perhaps the oldest colonnaded street of which there is direct evidence.

26 The Haram al-Sharif to the south from the Al-Omariyah School (the site of the Antonia Fortress). The Dome of the Rock, roughly on the site of the naos, sits on a raised platform; the present colonnade on the right gives a somewhat similar effect to that of the Herodian colonnades around the temenos. The Dome of Al-Aqsa Mosque to the right of the Dome of the Rock marks the southern limit of the temenos.

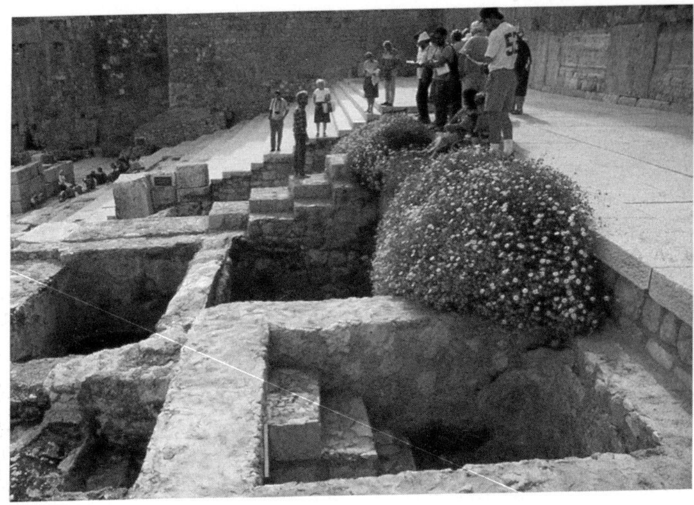

27 The plaza and monumental stairs leading to the Huldah Gates, from the east. The south wall and gates are on the right, a group of ritual bathing pools (*mikvaoth*) in the foreground.

28 The stair in the foreground, just in front of Al-Aqsa Mosque, is in the location of one of the stairs emerging from the tunnels under the Royal Basilica and conveys a sense of the entrance from the Huldah Gates. The Dome of the Rock is roughly on the site of the naos.

29 A small fragment of one of the monolithic ceiling slabs of the Huldah Gates, now located in the Citadel Museum.

colonnade of 160 columns that partially survives. The creativeness of this solution as a vital visual component of Gerasa's city plan can hardly be exaggerated; it was a stroke of sheer genius, as is clear from comparison with the oval piazza on the west decumanus at Palmyra a century later, whose purpose was unclear and whose execution was timid. Gerasa's Oval Piazza put more emphasis on Zeus, using typically Greek oblique views, than might have been possible with the city's earlier orientation.

The rebuilt Zeus temple of the second century (161 CE) involved a massive flight of steps up the hill with a new peripteral temple (eight columns by twelve) at the top, not unlike the Hadrianic Temple of Zeus Hypsistos at Neapolis. In overall conception, the design approach of the expansion seems as much Hellenistic as Roman, especially in its utilization of changes of level with new vistas as one approached the sanctuary. The drama of changing vistas began from a point up the cardo, and would have been especially striking from the monumental gate (in a Corinthian order) between the cardo and the plaza. The planners contrived to have the façade of the naos of the upper Temple of Zeus on the axis of the cardo as one walked south. This visual connection does not mean, however, that the cardo functioned as a processional way (as Ball claims, *Rome in the East*, 256–8); it was a true cardo and not a processional way like those at Palmyra or Petra (or Miletus or Ephesus), a major purpose of which was to lead directly into the main sanctuary. Nevertheless, the expansion of Zeus together with the change of orientation of the streets and the creation of the elliptical plaza permitted an aesthetically pleasing change of axis, which in turn resulted in a dynamic sense of space that had much in common with Hellenistic design. It was an almost perfect solution to a difficult problem.

The upper naos of Zeus had well-carved Corinthian columns (15 m high) and an elaborate cornice dominating the building's façade, as it overlooked Gerasa from the upper temenos (28 m by 40 m). The whole was beautifully constructed, both outside and inside. By contrast the earlier lower temenos had been rather crudely carved, suggesting a substantial difference in status between first- and second-century Gerasa. The exterior walls of the naos had arched semicircular niches matching each inter-columniation on the sides and front, with two niches on the rear. The interior side-walls were modulated with five pilasters on each side.

Temple of Dionysus

Halfway along the cardo was a second major religious sanctuary. The site was so overbuilt in the Byzantine period that it is impossible to say for certain to whom the cult was dedicated or much about the details, but it is likeliest that it was a temple to Dionysus. Recent evidence suggests the temple was built in the early second century CE (Brenk, Jäggi and Meier, 'Neue Forschungen'), but its history was more complicated than that, for earlier excavations revealed evidence of Nabatean influences (crow-step designs, a bilingual Nabatean and Greek inscription, and an inscription to the 'Arabian god'). There may have been a Temple of Dushara on the site of the Temple of Dionysus, for in some places the two were identified with each other. This may in turn suggest Nabatean/Gerasene religious and cultural and trade connections at an early period, connections that had faded by the end of the first century CE.

The Temple of Dionysus was about the same size as the Zeus temple; its major design difficulty derived from its location to one side of and above the cardo. The builders solved the problem of access that arose from this location differently from the more prominent site occupied by Zeus. In the case of the Temple of Dionysus the shops behind the cardo's colonnade (originally mid-first century CE) were interrupted to permit creation of a gateway or propylaea; the temple was up a monumental stair and within a temenos at the top. This arrangement lacked the dramatic open setting of Zeus, behind and above the lower temenos with its altar. What was worse, in the period after the cardo's rebuilding (second century CE), the Temple of Dionysus had difficulty making its presence felt. While it would have been more visible and better integrated into the urban fabric in the earlier form of the cardo with its smaller Ionic columns (first century CE), the Sanctuary of Dionysus may have seemed cramped and almost invisible. It could only be appreciated properly from the hill itself or from a distance, across the river on the eastern hill.

Temple of Artemis

The section of the cardo between the two decumani was the setting for the majority of public buildings in the second century CE. Along its west side were the Temple of Dionysus and immediately beside it the nymphaeum (190–1 CE). Farther north on the east side of the cardo, almost at the North Decumanus, were the West Baths (second century CE). Fronting on the North Decumanus, at the same point as the West Baths but to the west of the cardo, was the North Theatre. Within this concentration of civic buildings, much the most important was the Temple of Artemis (dedicated 150 CE), the largest of the temples in Gerasa. It occupied a central place at almost the highest point of the western hill, between the Nymphaeum and the North Theatre, stretching for almost 120 m along the cardo, including the thirteen columns on either side of the propylaea. Both the Nymphaeum and the Temple of Artemis were signalled to pedestrians on the cardo by distinctive columns, those of the nymphaeum higher than those of the colonnaded street, and those of the propylaea of the Temple of Artemis still higher (about 16 m).

Its overall plan had design features in common with the Temple of Dionysus: the builders interrupted the cardo colonnade, created a gate or propylaea, built monumental steps up the hill, and created a temenos on the flat area at the top. The similarities were deceptive, for the architectural character of the Sanctuary of Artemis was rather different from Dionysus: larger, richer, more complex and more sophisticated. In scale, it was several times the size of Dionysus and about half the size of the Sanctuary of Bel in Palmyra. Its importance was signified, not only by its larger footprint within the city plan, but also by the size of the individual elements and their decoration. The propylaea was a major focus in the composition of the cardo, with its stupendous roofed gateway fronted by four massive free-standing columns supporting a richly embellished broken-pediment with Syrian arch in the middle spanning the larger central opening (Browning, *Jerash*, figs 31, 87). The central door (9 m high, 5 m wide) with two smaller side doors – the side doors topped by semicircular niches – created a sense of monumentality and scale unmatched in Palmyra. The whole was richly decorated. Inside the door all one saw from street level was a carefully contrived broad ascent of stairs and landings, culminating in another wider terrace at the top with an altar, which ultimately led into the sanctuary itself.

Focus on religion

The three main traditional cults of Gerasa – to Zeus, Dionysus and Artemis – dominated the western hillside of the city. From the housing areas on the eastern side of the city (covered today by the modern town of Jerash) their silhouettes overlooked the rest of the city. All three were built within a hundred years: Zeus, from about 22 to 69 CE; Dionysus, late first century CE; Artemis, about 150 CE; expansion of Zeus, 161 CE. It might be argued from the first stages of Zeus and Dionysus that urban design considerations were not paramount in the first century CE as the city was beginning to develop. This would be too rash a view, however, for it was precisely in the late first century that the city plan was being reconfigured and the line of the new cardo being laid out. It was from the structures of the early-Roman period at the south end that the city's design developed. The most important element was the design of the Oval Piazza, which provided a centre for urban life. The location of the lower temenos of Zeus at the end of the cardo, beautifully integrated into the elliptical layout of the piazza, was a major element in that design, even before its upper level was completed; the raised temenos of Dionysus would have balanced the city's religious character farther north.

Sanctuary of Zeus expansion

Around the mid-second century CE the role of religion was expanded and the monumentalization of its expression within the urban setting was emphasized. The Sanctuaries of both Zeus and Artemis received special attention, located on either side of the recently built Temple of Dionysus. Both were carefully integrated into the city's new axes following its replanning and orthogonal layout, though only Zeus was easily visible from the southern portion of the cardo. The major rebuilding of the upper naos and temenos of Zeus beside the South Theatre had enhanced its importance. In a remarkable tour de force, the centre of the façade of the naos coincided with the axis of the cardo. Whether this relationship between upper temple's façade and the cardo was already anticipated in the first-century redesign of the street layout is not clear. But when in the second century CE (the highpoint of Gerasa's development) the cardo was embellished in two stages and the Temple of Zeus made more monumentally impressive, the effect on the citizen or traveller walking south down the cardo would have been intense.

At that stage the relationship between the lower temenos and the Oval Piazza was not a happy accident but a deliberately integrated design decision, and it may be that the effect of the various parts of the architectural composition were anticipated earlier. The carefully considered spaces made this area much the most dynamic part of the city: the linear volume of the cardo, the oval space of the piazza, the open rectangular area of the lower temenos of Zeus, skewed to the cardo but integrated with one side of the Oval Piazza, the stairs integrated with the other side of the Oval Piazza and the effective use of changes in gradient all deserve notice. This grand scheme made the south end of the city – the original location of the city in the Hellenistic period – a continuing major element in the later urban design. The fact that there was an altar in the middle of the Oval Piazza makes this civic space of even greater significance.

Procession to the Temple of Artemis

If the Temple of Zeus was the most brilliant achievement of Gerasa's urban designers, their subtlest achievement, despite – and partly because of – its monumental size and grandeur, was the axial treatment of the Temple of Artemis. The city's main axis was north–south, established by the north–south course of the river and by the major routes in and out of the city. The decision to lay out the Temple of Artemis on an east–west axis, even though this was the traditional orientation of temples, created some architectural and planning difficulties. The solution for the Artemis sanctuary was found in creating a processional way (500 m long by 14 m wide) that crossed the cardo and intersected with it.

This processional way began on the east side of the river and is still visible today in the remains of a bridge on the west side of the river; the route over the bridge led to a flight of steps and through a triple-arched outer propylaea, thence into a long narrow colonnaded rectangle now known as the Propylaea Church (see below). At the end of that colonnade steps went up into an area known as the Propylaea Plaza, a splayed or wedge-shaped symmetrical open space (whose features were at eccentric angles to each other), enclosed within walls decorated with pilasters and columns. The wedge-shaped plaza led into and prepared the worshipper for the next steps in the sequence. Each side of the wedge had an aedicula, probably with fountain; the plaza in turn opened out onto the east side of the cardo. Below the Propylaea Plaza's paving were found remains of a street (from about 50 CE) on the axis of the present bridge, possibly evidence of an earlier Temple of Artemis.

The volume of the colonnaded rectangle and then of the plaza led towards the much greater volume of the propylaea itself, with its very high columns. From the plaza the processional route went down four steps onto the cardo, crossed the cardo, then rose back up the same number of steps through the main propylaea, the sanctuary's formal entrance. The design problem created by a processional way that crossed the cardo was difficult, but the care given to the intersection made the solution especially successful and dramatic. The opening from the Propylaea Plaza on the east side exactly matched both the width of the propylaea's colonnaded entrance court to the east and the propylaea proper to the west on the other side of the cardo, creating a rectangular space that effectively solved the visual and dynamic problem of crossing the cardo. Such careful attention to the details of axial and volumetric relationships in the processional way underscores both the skill of the urban designers and the increasing importance of religion in the city. Its dynamic and baroque character is seen in the series of entrances, wedge-shaped plaza, gradually increasing heights, arches, exedrae, fountains, floral decorations and so on.

Attidius Cornelianus, legate under Antoninus Pius, built the propylaea proper on an immense scale. Its effect was enhanced by its height (more than 20 m) and depth (about 15 m). The propylaea broke the pattern of two-storey shops, which abutted a 14 m-high retaining wall, along the cardo, allowing the doorway façade to be further recessed. Only at the triple door to the sanctuary were the monumental steps (19.35 m wide) up the hill readily apparent. The staircase comprised seven flights of seven steps, with minor landings between the flights. At the top a large U-shaped terrace – a kind of outer temenos – more than 100 m wide focused on an altar. There was yet another set of steps, the full width of that terrace, to the east peribolos wall of the temenos. This free-standing colonnaded wall probably had a Syrian arch in the centre matching the Syrian arch in the propylaea, with towers at the two ends, creating a strong impression of a powerful enclosed space. Inside the peribolos wall a peristyle defined the temenos (121 m north to south by 160 m east to west; the courtyard's open space was 88 m by 124 m). The colonnades on the south, west and north sides were 14.2 m wide by 7.5 m. high; a row of small rooms alternated with rectangular recesses behind a continuous row of Corinthian columns.

Finally the visitor to the Sanctuary of Artemis got a view of the naos, which had been hidden until one entered through the temenos wall. The naos was set on a high podium (22 m by 40 m by 4.3 m high) with frontal steps just behind another altar, arranged in two flights of seven steps. The column arrangement was six by eleven columns (13.2 m high), free-standing, with a double-width pronaos. Its interior was panelled in marble. Its floor was supported on a barrel-vaulted substructure, whose height rose as the floor of the naos rose to the holy place (adyton) with Artemis's statue. A relieving arch over a flat arch still marks the place.

It is impossible not to be enormously impressed both by the powerful drama and by the subtleties built into this route. The symmetrical axiality could have been forced and prosaic, even static, but in fact there was a grand sense of motion, with widenings, narrowings and changes in height as one proceeded towards the desired goal, worship at the Temple of Artemis. No similar eastern Mediterranean approach to a sanctuary from the Roman period is as dramatic, though the design and scale of the Temples of Jupiter at both Baalbek and Damascus had features in common. Within the Hellenistic world, the Temple of Athena at Lindos and the Asklepieion at Cos shared some of the same dramatic use of levels, as did the Temple of Zeus at Gerasa. The effect of the Sanctuary of Artemis, though it did not have the lightness of those others, was in a class by itself in terms of its scale and dominance.

Maioumas

One other religious space should be mentioned briefly: the cult of Maioumas, beside the Birketein ('double pool'), was situated outside the north city walls. An inscription makes the identification certain. It was an erotic and esoteric cult, not very well known, centred on water-related activities that became rather notorious by the Christian period. The very large double pool, which survives intact (43.5 by 88.5 m and 3 m deep), also acted as a reservoir for the city. On the west side at the south end a small theatre – one of the few structures of the third century CE – has survived in fairly good condition, though the upper level of the cavea is missing. A colonnade (209 CE) framed the west side of the pool. Near this sanctuary was the Temple of Zeus the Fruit-Bearer, though little is known about it except that Germanus son of Molpon built it; his tetrastyle prostyle temple-tomb, three Corinthian columns of which still have their beams, was further along the road to the north (Browning, *Jerash*, 216).

The religious structures of Gerasa can be viewed together as a group. Its urban design was focused on a set of major religious structures, all on the west side of the city, that were related almost like beads on a string along the central axis of the city: Zeus, Dionysus, the Nymphaeum, Artemis, Maioumas, Zeus Fruit-Bearer. The linearity of this layout of the urban fabric is more pronounced than is usual in standard Roman urban design, though not unknown. It was, however, substantially different from the clustering of sanctuaries at Petra and the distribution of sanctuaries at Palmyra. Even in this most Roman of cities of the

Levant there were differentiating elements both in the urban design and in the exciting features of individual buildings.

Synagogues and churches

During its most vigorous days in the second century Gerasa seems not to have absorbed Near Eastern cults or mystery religions with much enthusiasm, though the cult of Maioumas and a Nabatean temple broaden the repertoire. An exception to this generalization was Judaism. Gerasa was under Jewish rule for roughly a generation in the early first century BCE as a result of Alexander Jannaeus's conquests in the Decapolis in about 83–80 BCE (Schürer, 1.226; cf. Josephus, *War* 1.104; *Ant.* 13.393). There may have been a Jewish community in Gerasa from then onwards. Jewish control ended with Pompey's campaigns in 64/63 BCE, when self-government was restored. There is little direct evidence of relations between Jews and Gerasenes. The one sure indication occurred in 66 CE when Jews attacked Gerasa during the early stages of the Revolt (Josephus, *War* 1.458); Gerasa was the only city not to initiate reprisals against its Jewish inhabitants (*War* 2.480).

It is conceivable that there was a relatively early synagogue in Gerasa; architectural fragments identified as from a synagogue were found in fill for Hadrian's arch (130 CE). By the fourth century CE at the latest, a synagogue was centrally located on a prominent and advantageous site overlooking the Temple of Artemis. It was an attractive and well decorated building, if small and simple, with an atrium on the east, nicely designed Corinthian capitals, cushion-type bases, and an unusual mosaic floor whose main motif was Noah's Ark (Kraeling, *Gerasa*, 234–42, 318–24). Greek inscriptions mention Shem and Japheth (and presumably Ham), the sons of Noah; another is addressed 'To the most holy place, Amen, Selah. Peace upon the congregation.' A Hebrew inscription wishes 'Peace upon all Israel, Amen, Amen, Selah' (similar to the phraseology of Paul's wish in Galatians 6.16). The synagogue was taken over and converted to a church in 530/1 CE, when the building's orientation was reversed by constructing a new apse on the east over the original doorway, making the atrium almost useless. The social and religious background of the takeover is not known: whether violent, officially sanctioned, a gradual process of dwindling numbers or conversion from Judaism to Christianity is now unclear.

What is unmistakably clear, however, is that there was an explosion of churches in Gerasa in the early Byzantine period as there was in some other towns and cities east of the Jordan. Gerasa had at least sixteen churches, including the following (brief descriptions of most in Applebaum and Segal, 'Gerasa', 2.474–8).

- The Cathedral Church (about 350–75 CE) was built on the site of the demolished Temple of Dionysus, utilizing its old approach from the cardo.
- On a higher terrace to the west and partially integrated with it was the Church of St Theodore (464–6 CE).
- The Church of the Prophets, Apostles and Martyrs (464–5 CE) was located near the North Gate.
- On the east was Procopius's Church (526–7 CE).
- West of the Cathedral there was a triple church; the centrally focused middle church was dedicated to St John the Baptist (529–33 CE).
- Flanking it to the south was a church dedicated to St George (529–33 CE).
- Flanking it to the north was a church dedicated to Sts Cosmas and Damian (also 529–33 CE).
- The so-called Synagogue Church (530–1 CE) usurped the existing synagogue.
- Bishop Isaiah's Church was west of the small theatre (540–611 CE).
- Sts Peter and Paul were memorialized in a church with an additional small chapel (540 CE) in the south-west area of the city beside the Mortuary Church.
- The Propylaea Church was created by roofing over the Propylaea Plaza that led from the bridge towards the Temple of Artemis (probably about 565 CE).
- Bishop Marianos's Church was built just inside the monumental gate, south of the city beside the hippodrome (570 CE).
- In the south-west between Sts Peter and Paul and the city walls was a Mortuary Church (sixth century CE).

- Bishop Genesius's Church was located west of the triple church (611 CE).
- There was a church on the altar terrace of the Temple of Artemis above the monumental stair.
- There was a church in the temenos of the Temple of Zeus.

The question of interest here – apart from all the obvious things one might say about the effects of Christianity upon the cultural, economic and spiritual life of the city – is the impact of these religious structures on the built form of the city, its circulation and its dynamics. How did this flurry of church-building and adaptation of existing spaces change Gerasa's urban character? The churches were scattered around the city, but it is significant that with only one exception all were within the walls. Further, to a large extent the Christian community was clustered in the centre around the Temple of Artemis, just as religion had been focused earlier in this part of the city: there were two churches in parts of the Temple of Artemis, one just west of it, one in the Temple of Dionysus, one immediately beside it, three just west of it, and one more west of those, for a total of ten churches in the immediate central area. This grouping of churches was not organized like beads on a string, as the sanctuaries were in the city's earlier form, but rather as a clump. The city underwent a substantial reshaping from the mid-Roman to the mid-Byzantine period.

The circulation pattern must have changed substantially at the same time. Kraeling has argued cogently for the destruction of the North Bridge leading to the Artemis Propylaea in the earthquake of 551–4 CE, making the rectangular colonnaded area (which was probably also destroyed at the same time) available for rebuilding as a church a short time later. With one of the city's major east–west streets interrupted both by the bridge's destruction and by the presence of the Propylaea Church, we must conjecture some reshaping of the city as Christian builders altered old foci and established new ones within the central area of the city. The South Bridge on the South Decumanus became the only route across the River Chrysorhoas; that street led directly to the eastern edge of the city where Procopius's Church was near the wall. On the west side of the city, where most of the churches were clustered, the north–south road west of the Sanctuary of Artemis provided easy access to at least seven churches (Mortuary Church, Sts Peter and Paul, St George, St John the Baptist, Sts Cosmas and Damian, Bishop Genesius's Church and the Synagogue Church). That street may have come to rival the earlier cardo in importance. Thus, the orientation and circulation patterns of the city probably altered substantially after the fifth and sixth centuries.

There was high enthusiasm for the new Christian religion at several sites in Jordan, among which Gerasa with its sixteen churches was the largest. Patrons and bishops and clergy showered religious buildings on the region. Umm al-Jimal, north-east of Gerasa, had fifteen, nearby Khirbet es-Samra had eight, Madaba had fourteen, Umm er-Rasas had fifteen. None of these were large cities and some were only towns or villages; in these instances the new religion built itself into a highly visible and dominant role that cohered with its new political position following Constantine. It did so without major pilgrimage sites in the region. This built form for Christianity in Provincia Arabia was almost unparalleled, except in larger pilgrimage cities. The socio-religious conditions that prompted such a burst of building are not clear, but the evidence shows the considerable importance of Arabia east of the Jordan for Christianity. The 'Christianization' of the area was mainly a takeover from 'pagan religion', but perhaps partly also from its sibling Judaism, as the paucity of synagogues suggests in general and the Gerasa Synagogue Church implies specifically.

One curious instance in Gerasa underscores the general trend. An annual ceremony was celebrated in the Fountain Court – the atrium of the Gerasa Cathedral – that recalled the water-to-wine incident at Cana in Galilee (John 2.1–11; Richardson, 'What has Cana'; Finegan, *Archeology*, 123). Epiphanius (*Panarion Haereseis* 51.30.1–2) refers to 'a *martyrium* and miraculous fountain in Gerasa, where every year the spring ran with wine on the anniversary of the miracle at Cana, which was also the feast of the Epiphany'. This 'Feast of the Miracle of Cana' at Gerasa took place where the Temple of Dionysus (and still earlier the site of a Nabatean temple, perhaps to Dushara) had stood. It was not unknown that there were celebrations of water being turned to wine at Temples of Dionysus. It seems plausible that Gerasa was one of those; if so, Christians took the old pagan site and converted the celebration to a comparable Christian celebration, recalling an incident from Cana in Galilee. The Christian ritual was predicated not on an indigenous pilgrim site but on associations with a known site that were given local meaning through an earlier pagan tradition associated with Dionysus, and behind that Dushara.

Entertainment, commerce and civic facilities

Religion was spread widely throughout the city in entertainment, cultural and administrative structures – all located on the western hill – as well as in sanctuaries. Theatres, hippodrome, baths all had religious activities such as prayers, offerings and the like that added to the presence of religion in the city.

The theatre associated with the Maioumas sanctuary north of the city was rather small (capacity about 1,000). There were two other theatres in Gerasa, a larger South Theatre (capacity over 3,000) and a mid-size North Theatre (capacity about 1,600). The South Theatre was begun during the Flavian period (last quarter of the first century CE) and finished soon after the creation of the Province of Arabia in 106 CE, of which Gerasa became a part; some remains under the stage imply that it may have had an earlier phase, possibly establishing the later orientation. The theatre was richly decorated; Browning remarks on the *scaenae frons*, describing what I have been calling the 'baroque' elements of this eastern architecture:

> above the main columns there was an entablature which followed exactly the line of the podium below, breaking forward over the pairs of pillars and sweeping back in to the oval recesses . . . It is probable that the whole arrangement was repeated on a second tier giving the effect of a forest of pillars undulating across the curved and rectangular wall at two levels . . . [T]his was a striking design with a marked sense of 'movement'. The constant breaking forward of the entablature, the change from rectangular to curved space, the strong vertical and

horizontal emphases, all amount to a piece of great visual excitement.

(Browning, *Jerash*, 129)

The theatre's location encroached slightly upon the Upper Temenos of the Temple of Zeus; it was oriented differently from most of the rest of the city, differently even from the Temple of Zeus, suggesting an earlier more informal plan of the city at the time when the theatre's location was originally set. The fact that the rites of the 'Sacred Guild of the ecumenical, victorious, crowned artists in the service of Dionysus and of our Lord' were held in the theatre (Browning, *Jerash*, 126) emphasizes that religion was not limited to the explicitly religious buildings.

The mid-size theatre (160s CE) was just north of the Temple of Artemis, fronting on the North Decumanus. It was a fine example of a smaller theatre, probably to be understood as an odeion, since there is good evidence that it was roofed: the length of the primary beams, reaching from the inner corners of the stage to the back of cavea was about 25 m; the secondary beams (about 1.6 m wide) have left their imprints on the top of the cavea (the small theatre at Pompeii was similar). The North Decumanus widened between the scaenae frons and the street and also on the other side of the street to create a small urban plaza, marking the location of the North Theatre and providing a crush space for crowds.

Gerasa also had a major hippodrome or circus (begun second or third quarter of the second century CE), between the south city gate and the arch that memorialized Hadrian's visit to the city in 130 CE. Despite the fact that the city's new orientation had been set by this period, the hippodrome had a different axis from the Temple of Zeus, the theatre and the cardo, no doubt set by the route of the main road as it headed towards Philadelphia through Hadrian's arch.

In addition, there were three public baths, two to the west and one to the east of the river. The large and impressive West Baths (50 m by 75 m) was constructed in the second century CE between the cardo and the river, near the North Decumanus. The smaller Baths of Flaccus, north of the Fountain Court, were built in 454–5 CE, and restored in 584 CE. The much larger East Baths were on the other side of the river between the two decumani, and may have been built in the early third century.

The most important of the public facilities was, of course, the Nymphaeum (190–1 CE), providing a pause on the Cardo Maximus, a public 'watering spot' and a necessary supply of water for the bulk of the population. Higher columns along the colonnaded cardo marked its position. This was the most baroque structure in Gerasa among a number of playful, dynamic spatial experiences. A broken pediment with a Syrian arch dominated its façade and identified it in the streetscape. The semicircular public fountain (11 m in diameter) was topped by a half dome; free-standing columns in the semicircle stood between alternating rectangular and semicircular niches on two levels, with broken pediments over the semicircular upper niches. The lower of the two rows of statues in the niches acted as fountains, pouring water into the main basin and thence into the red granite basin on the sidewalk level. The nymphaeum's façade penetrated the commercial shopfronts and interrupted the cardo's linear movement, creating an additional dynamic compositional element and establishing a spatial pause along the street. Marble and frescoed finishes, together with the play of sun and shadow and the movement of water, made this a gem of Gerasa's architecture, matching the impression of the theatre's scaenae frons and the Artemis Propylaea.

Like Palmyra, the intersections of cardo and decumanus were marked with a tetrapylon and a tetrakionion. The North Tetrapylon looks as if it should be earlier: at this point the cardo retained its original, relatively narrow form, utilizing an Ionic colonnade. In fact, the North Tetrapylon dated from the late second or more likely early third century CE, when the city began to decline as a result of the uncertainties of that century. It was stolid, massive, impressive in its own way with a domed interior, but lacking the graceful weightlessness of its sister to the south. Its main virtue was that it satisfactorily resolved the difficulty of the two different widths of the cardo to its north and south. The South Tetrakionion was constructed at the intersection of the South Decumanus and the cardo, a little after the widening of the south half of the cardo (mid-second century CE); it was surrounded by shops and set in a circular plaza, almost 44 m in diameter (time of Diocletian, 284–305 CE). Unlike the similar structure at Palmyra, the South Tetrakionion with its four sets of four columns did not sit on a unified base; rather, each set of four columns had its own base, so that the streets moved straight through the monument without interruption. The tetrakionion was associated with a new sewer that was installed under the cardo, when the colonnades were heightened and topped with Corinthian capitals in place of the earlier Ionic capitals. Some were in barber-pole design, known also from Apamea and other locations in the Levant.

Shops were built into the colonnaded streets, mostly utilitarian two-storey shops, where the mezzanine level was used for living quarters, storage or production, as was standard for commerce in ancient cities. Especially pleasant was the delightful octagonal Macellum or meat market (second century CE), with shops around its perimeter and a beautifully designed octagonal fountain in the centre providing a water supply (Uscatescu and Martin-Bueno, '*Macellum* of Gerasa'). Shops were also integrated into the supports for the hippodrome seating (capacity 15,000) that opened onto the main route from the south through Hadrian's arch. Gerasa was a strongly commercial city, with more provision for ordinary consumer goods than for international trade and commerce; no agora or caravanserai, for example, has been discovered, though there must have been one, perhaps near the North Tetrapylon. While it used to be thought that the Oval Piazza functioned as the forum, that now seems unlikely.

The North Gate (115 CE) of the city might be mentioned briefly, since it was a little like the monumental arch in Palmyra that was noted in Chapter 2. The two faces were at an angle to each other so that each side independently was at right angles to the line of approach, accommodating the different line of the road leading towards Pella.

Conclusion

By contrast with Palmyra and Petra, with their obvious indigenous and eastern influences that gave a more exotic, less Roman, character to the cities, an explicit late-Hellenistic and Roman character marked Gerasa. Petra and Palmyra retained their traditional gods, even if as time went on they gradually became assimilated to Roman deities; the cult centres were not rebuilt in the light of newly appreciated Roman ideals and Roman canons of building, though in the embellishing of the cities they absorbed details and the trappings of Roman taste and refinement. In Palmyra, though the city 'feels' familiar, it is still a caravan city only lightly Romanized. Petra seems less familiar, and if one thinks only of Roman or Hellenistic conventions one never feels quite at home when faced with the monumental tomb façades, for example.

Petra and Palmyra were closer to their Arabian roots, the desert and the source of their wealth in long-distance trade, than Gerasa was. Given Gerasa's beautiful setting in a fertile valley with one of the region's few permanent streams, it is hard to realize that it was not far from the desert and close to major trade connections. Its potential as a caravan city, however, was outweighed by its re-founding as a centre of Hellenistic culture in the Seleucid period. Its inclusion among the Decapolis cities following Pompey's conquest of the region and his re-establishing of its independence meant that it was a harbinger of Roman civilization, along with its sister cities such as Scythopolis/Beth Shean, Gadara/Umm Qeis, Pella/Tabghat Fahil, Hippos/Susita, among others. Gerasa never ceased looking westwards during this period of turmoil and changes in political fortunes, when Roman influences were extensive and widespread. When it was integrated into the Province of Arabia (106 CE) and fell even more directly under direct Roman influence, it achieved a degree of development and refinement that made it one of the great cities of the Near East, a beacon of the Roman world and what it offered. It is in fact possible to argue, as Parapetti does, that 'such a remarkably organic urban achievement . . . belongs to and is the expression of a new eastern architectural school, to which we are indebted for the last inventions of the ancient world . . . . Gerasa can be considered the center best qualified to improve our knowledge of the achievements of architecture and town planning of Roman times' (Parapetti, 'Architectural significance', 257, 259).

While there were still indigenous influences in Gerasa, there were not as many as in Palmyra and Petra. These three dramatic cities of the eastern Empire were different. The extensive excavations in all three provide enough information, both general and detailed, to assess their overall urban design and the individual structures and civic amenities that made them up. Their different origins, different developments and different relationships to their Roman masters were reflected in the surviving structures. They also differed in the ways in which they absorbed religious change; none seems to have had a very wide range of new cults from farther east or even from the eastern Mediterranean. Gerasa may have had the fewest. Only Palmyra appears to have had an imperial cult building – a modest one – suggesting something important about relations with Rome. Both Palmyra and Gerasa had synagogues, nurturing the local Jewish community, though in both cases the Jewish communities eventually disappeared. Christianity was accepted early and enthusiastically in the region, especially in Provincia Arabia.

The remains of churches are not especially impressive in either Petra or Palmyra, though the main church at Petra had an extremely important archive of burned papyrus documents. But the region in and near the Decapolis should be ranked as one of the most important centres of early Christianity, to judge from the extent, size and quality of the material evidence. The two earliest 'complete' physical remains of churches have been found in Jordan and Syria. At Aila (Aqaba), south of Petra, the archaeological team believes it has uncovered the earliest purpose-built church yet discovered (*c.*290 CE). And in Dura Europus, on the Euphrates, a very early house-church (*c.*230 CE) was excavated.

In one marked respect, at least, Gerasa, Petra and Palmyra were similar throughout their history prior to the Byzantine period. They all had a marked preference for a pantheon of deities that gave character and form to the city's urban design, shaping the attitudes to death and burial and providing a focus for the city's religious activities. The other two cities considered here – Jerusalem and Caesarea Maritima – permit analysis of how cities developed that had essentially one religious centre. How did monotheism affect the built form and the special characteristics of those cities?

Table 4.1 Gerasa chronology

As a Decapolis city

Temple of Zeus: lower temenos	22–69 CE
City walls and gates	completed 75–6 CE
Cardo, south section (Ionic order)	39–76 CE
South Theatre	late 1st c. CE
Oval Piazza	end 1st c. CE
Cardo, northern section (Ionic order)	late 1st (early 2nd?) c. CE
South Synagogue, near Hadrian's Arch (?)	(?)

Incorporated in Province of Arabia (106 CE)

North Gate	rebuilt 115 CE
Hadrian's Arch	129/30 CE
Temple of Dionysus (?)	early 2nd c. CE
Macellum	early 2nd c. CE
Hippodrome	2nd quarter 2nd c. to early 3rd c. CE
South Gate	129/30 CE
Temple of Artemis (including propylaea)	dedicated 150 CE
Temple of Zeus renovations and expansions	163 CE
North Theatre	165/6 CE
Cardo, south section (Corinthian order)	last half 2nd c. CE
South Tetrakionion	last half 2nd c. CE
Monumental arch at Oval Piazza	late 2nd c. CE
Nymphaeum	190/1 CE
South Tetrapylon	2nd c. CE
Tomb of Germanicus (inscription)	2nd c. CE

West Baths	late 2nd c. CE
North Tetrapylon	early 3rd c. CE
East Baths	early 3rd c. CE
Birketein reservoir	early 3rd c. CE
Birketein theatre	later than reservoir
Circular Piazza	Diocletian (284–305 CE)

Constantine and later

Central Synagogue	4th c. CE
Shops at South Tetrakionion	early 4th c. CE
North Theatre	rebuilt 320 CE
Cathedral	late 4th c. CE
Baths of Flaccus	454–5 CE; restored 584 CE
Cathedral fountain court	remodelled 464/6 CE
Church of Prophets, Apostles and Martyrs	464/6 CE
St Theodore	494/6 CE
Procopius Church	526–7 CE
Sts Cosmas and Damian	529–33 CE
St George	529–33 CE
Synagogue Church	530–1 CE
St John the Baptist	531 CE
Sts Peter and Paul	540 CE
Church of Bishop Isaiah	between 540 and 611 CE (?)
Propylaea Church	May 565 CE (inscription)
Church of Bishop Marianos	570 CE
Bishop Genesius Church	611 CE
Cathedral Chapel (south side)	6th c. CE
Mortuary Church	6th c. CE

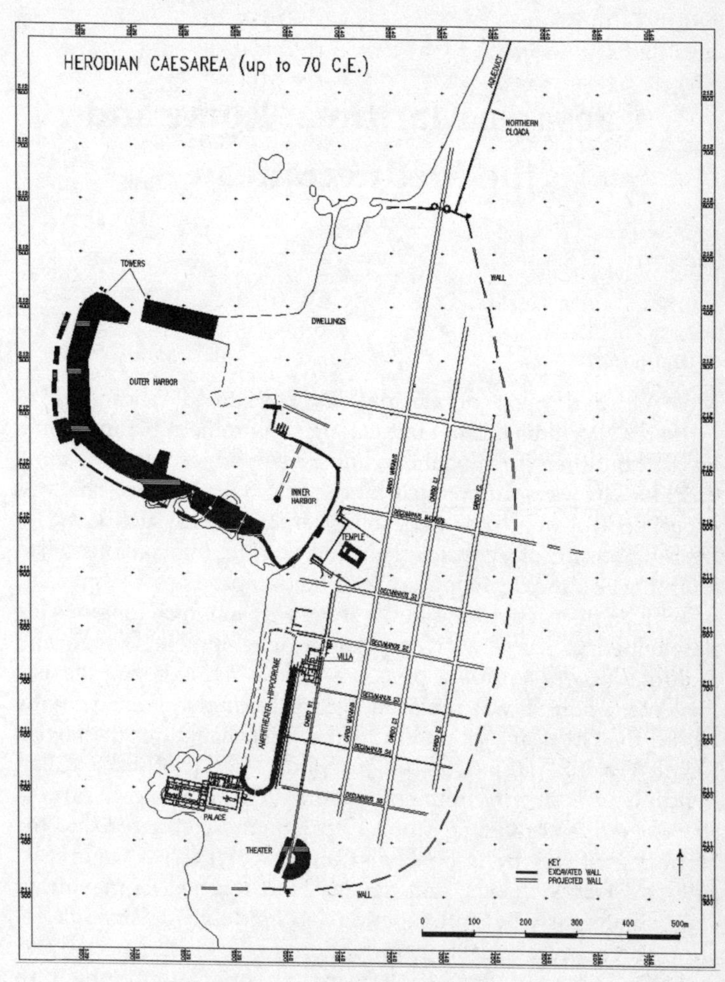

Plan of Caesarea Maritima, © Anna Iamim, Caesarea Graphics Archive

5

Caesarea Maritima: Rome and the Mediterranean

Introduction[1]

Most cities develop organically. Even planned cities such as Caesarea Maritima did not in the long view remain planned cities throughout their functional life, but developed – sometimes fairly quickly – in ways unintended by the original planners. This was especially true of provision for religious activities in such a city, for the religious life of a city, in all its official and unofficial forms, had an impact on the developing urban landscape. Caesarea presents us with an instructive case study of the way in which religious life has helped to shape a city's organic development (Raban and Holum, *Caesarea Maritima*, pp. xxvii–lxiv). Having begun life as a Hellenistic polis, it was replaced with a strikingly planned city by Herod the Great. It was refounded by Vespasian after the Jewish Revolt (Tacitus, *History* 2.80.1; Josephus, *War* 4.588–629; Millar, *Roman Near East*, 73), commemorated by Trajan on a coin of 115–17 CE, commemorated again by Hadrian, and converted into the Metropolis of Syria by Trebonianus Gallus (251–3 CE; see Holum et al., *Herod's Dream*, 113, 124, and figs 69, 8). It reached its maximum extent in the early Byzantine period and gradually declined thereafter. There were radical transformations in the Muslim period and in the Crusader period, when there was a 'reorientation of the Arab world away from the sea toward the desert . . .' (Levine and Netzer, *Excavations*, 179). Since its destruction in 1265 its history has been largely desolate. In the period covered by this chapter, roughly from the city's founding as Strato's Tower to about 200 CE, with the emphasis on the first centuries BCE and CE, there is one sharp break – between the Hellenistic polis and the planned city of Herod – and longer periods of gradual change. My major concerns are the planned city and how this planned city moved away from the original planners' vision (Richardson, *Herod*, ch. 8). One key to weighing these changes is the evidence of religion and cult.

Herod signalled the religious character of the city in its name (Holum et al., *Herod's Dream*, 11–16, 113, and figs 2–6, 68). This Caesarea, like others named Caesarea at about the same time, honoured Augustus, and the harbour was separately named Sebastos, the Greek equivalent of the name Augustus that was bestowed on Octavian in 27 BCE (Barag, 'Sebastos', 609–14). Both constructions pointed to Herod's debt to Octavian, who, along with Mark Antony, had persuaded the Senate to name Herod King of Judea in late 40 BCE. Herod had missed being on the losing side at Actium because Antony wanted him to engage the Nabateans; in late winter or early spring (30 BCE), he went to Rhodes to offer Octavian the same loyalty he had shown Antony. Octavian accepted, and unexpectedly gave Herod new territories to add to his royal domain, including Strato's Tower. Herod never wavered from total loyalty to Octavian's and Rome's interests.

He expressed his obligation to Octavian in the enormously costly conversion of a small late-Hellenistic seaport into a showpiece of Roman urban design and maritime engineering, beginning five years after Octavian became Augustus. The project occupied the years 22 to 10 BCE (alternatively 21 to 9 BCE; Fritsch, *Studies*, 1), and was formally dedicated in the 192nd Olympiad (10/9 BCE) with flamboyant celebrations paying tribute to Augustus. Its exciting urbanism can be seen in the archaeology and sensed in Josephus's long descriptions that rely on first-hand observations and on descriptions by Nicolas of Damascus, Herod's historian.

History of settlement

Strato's Tower

Strato's Tower was founded (possibly by Strato I of Sidon in the fourth century BCE) as a southern outpost of the Phoenician city, an ancillary harbour for ships needing shelter or provisions, and a centre for exports, particularly grain from the Sharon Plain (Levine, *Roman Caesarea*, 3; Holum et al., 'Caesarea Maritima'; Stieglitz, 'Stratonos'; Raban, 'Inner harbor'). It appears in the historical record first when Zenon, assistant to Egypt's treasurer under Ptolemy II (285–246 BCE), visited it in 259 BCE, alluding to the anchorage and the food. About 103 BCE, during Hasmonean expansionism, the city was acquired by Alexander Janneus, ousting the local tyrant, Zoilus. When Pompey intervened in Hasmonean affairs (63 BCE) – as he had in Syria a year earlier, in both cases because of dynastic in-fighting – he gave Strato's Tower autonomy (Josephus, *Ant.* 14.76). A generation later Octavian handed the city with its territory to Herod; this gift was crucial for Herod's economic programme, for it gave him a port, not very large or important but one that, with vision and resources, could be expanded. Caesarea remained Herodian territory until 6 CE, then became a part of the Province of Judea throughout the Roman period.

Thus Caesarea was first a Hellenistic city spun off from an originally Phoenician city, Sidon; then under Egyptian control, Syrian control and Jewish control; then an autonomous city from 63 BCE, then part of the Judean homeland under Herod and Archelaus and finally the centre of Roman rule in Judea/Palestine from 6 CE onwards. To reduce the ethnic complexity to Greek/Syrian and Jewish, related to events at the onset of the First Revolt (Josephus, *Ant.* 20.173; *War* 2.266), cannot be adequate (Tcherikover, *Hellenistic Civilization*, 105–16; Millar, *Roman Near East*, 337–86). The chequered history shows through in the archaeological record to some extent, though two closely related facts limit the evidence severely: first, the underlying city of Strato's Tower has not been a primary focus of the excavations, and, second, Herod's planned city of Caesarea has obliterated some of what might have remained for examination.

The site offered relatively little to set it apart as a harbour. Three small hills rose above the general level of the dunes, and a few rocky promontories gave barely enough shelter for a harbour. Significant remains of installations associated with the harbours of Strato's Tower have been identified at two locations: a northern harbour close to the point where the city wall met the shoreline (a quay, evidence of industrial or commercial activity), and a southern harbour below the inner harbour of Herod's Sebastos (a quay, a mooring stone, foundations of a round tower; Raban et al., *Combined Caesarea Expeditions*, 7). These two harbours anchor the relatively modest Hellenistic city to the area between them. It was a small fraction of Herod's city (Holum et al., *Herod's Dream*, 43; Raban and Holum, *Retrospective*, 105–20; Raban et al., *Combined Caesarea Expeditions*, 1.53).

The walls and extent of Strato's Tower are still disputed. Two competing views are held by the archaeologists. One group holds that Strato's Tower was walled in such a way as to embrace both north and south harbours; the other holds that Strato's Tower was unwalled and that Herod fortified the city (contrast Holum et al., *Herod's Dream*, 44, 49–50, with Frova et al., *Scavi*, 247–92). The solution to this problem is important for understanding urban developments. If the former view is correct, as I think likelier, Strato's Tower was a well-defined small city that had not yet expanded into all the areas within its walls, as the absence of occupation evidence in its southern and north-eastern sections suggests. The negligible pre-Roman evidence under the temple platform area would support this, since most of that platform was outside Strato's Tower, as conjectured by CAHEP. For our purposes, the importance is that – attractive as the idea may be – there was probably no earlier temple on the site of Herod's Temple of Roma and Augustus.

Earlier excavations found synagogue remains north of the Crusader wall, sitting on remains of a Hellenistic house, confirming the early occupancy of that area (Avi-Yonah, 'Caesarea', 278–9). It is unclear how far back the synagogue occupancy went, but it was not early enough to attest a Jewish community within Strato's Tower. The connections between the later strata, the pre-70 CE stratum, and the Hellenistic house have not been clarified:

it remains an intriguing possibility – but only a possibility – that the late-Hellenistic house was the origin of the synagogue.

Caesarea under Herod

'Filled with enthusiasm for all things Roman, Herod brought Roman entertainment, Roman gods, and even Roman concrete into his kingdom' (Holum et al., *Herod's Dream*, 105). He deliberately shifted 'the religious and cultural focus of the town, from Greece to Rome' (Stieglitz, 'Stratonos', 394). His plans for Caesarea showcased better than any other project his commitment to Rome, and in some respects he outdid Rome – in the size and embellishments of the harbour, technological advances, commercial provisions, drama of his royal palace, planning of the southern quarter and impact of the imperial cult building. Excavations to date have demonstrated that Josephus's description is not over-enthusiastic (*War* 1.408–15; *Ant.* 15.331–41) – indeed in some respects it is exceeded by the findings – though at the same time the excavations have tended to reduce the amount of construction attributed to Herod (fewer warehouses, less housing, no amphitheatre).

Herod laid the city out with insulae on a Hippodamian plan (modified in the areas around the temple platform). There was ample provision for Herod's own needs (especially the Promontory Palace); for the amenities that citizens would expect, such as structures for municipal administration, support for commerce and trade, recreation facilities (a theatre, capacity about 3,500; a hippodrome about 51 m by 290 m; an amphitheatre probably from the first century CE), temples, running water and sewers, streets, walls and gates, territory around it for food production; and for a substantial population of about 50,000 Greeks, Romans (including demobilized veterans), Jews and Samaritans (Holum et al., *Herod's Dream*, 74–5). The Temple of Roma and Augustus, which tied harbour and city together, was the main cult centre of the polis; the dedication of the city to Augustus and the attention to the imperial family in the city's main temple was reflected at the harbour mouth with statues of family members, notably Drusus, who died in 9 BCE. The Drusion tower probably functioned as the lighthouse, and may have contained royal apartments, like several of Herod's other towers.

The city's south end was occupied by three related structures: the Promontory Palace, hippodrome and theatre (Netzer, 'Palace'; Gleason, 'Ruler and spectacle'; Burrell, 'Palace to praetorium'). They constituted a secondary urban focus in the design of Caesarea, emphasizing Rome's athletic and cultural influence through the combined structures that revolved around the residence of the client king of Judea. Precisely why Herod decided to locate these facilities in one place cannot be known; Gleason has conjectured, perhaps correctly, that he was influenced by the examples of his friends Augustus and Marcus Agrippa, and particularly by their architectural projects in Rome, seen in his visits of 40 and 17 BCE (Gleason, 'Ruler and spectacle', 208–9; Roller, *Building Program*, chs 1–3). She suggests that much of this influence came from Agrippa, and precisely in the period during which Caesarea and other important projects were under construction. There was a calculated effect – in part an axial relationship – among the buildings, felt as one moved from palace to hippodrome through gardens or sat in the theatre's cavea focused on the palace.

> But none of these buildings individually is remarkable within Herod's larger development program. Rather, the greater contribution to our understanding of Caesarea lies in assessing Herod's creation of a quarter of the city devoted to those buildings that in the Hellenistic traditions had expressed the fruits of peace and empire within palace districts . . . Yet in the larger context of Judaea, many such Hellenistic structures and activities were unwelcome and represent Herod's attempt to balance his Hellenizing ambitions with his desire to rule his country independently . . . Herod was not simply following the models of the Hasmonaeans or of the Romans . . .
>
> (Gleason, 'Ruler and spectacle', 224)

Apart from the harbour Sebastos, the areas of Herod's Caesarea that are best known now are the temple platform in the centre (about 90 m by 105 m) and the southern quarter of the city. Of the rest of the city proper, the indications are still scant. It is clear that Herod walled the city, perhaps utilizing some of the earlier walls of Strato's Tower, along the line of the so-called 'inner wall'. There was an agora, though it has not yet been found, and a tetrapylon. There may have been other religious structures, though that is unclear (see below). Some areas of the city, especially the south-east quarter, were unoccupied. Nevertheless, Herod's Caesarea has become over the last decade his best-known city and one of the best-excavated cities of the ancient Mediterranean world.

Caesarea Maritima in the early Roman period

Following Herod, the city continued to receive imperial attention and patronage, especially as a result of the city's new role as the capital of Judea from 6 CE onwards. Not only was it the centre of trade and commerce, it was now the centre of power and authority. Jerusalem retained its role within the religious sphere until 70 CE, but even for the period 6–70 CE it had been effectively sidelined. Herod's Promontory Palace became the Roman praetorium, a role it played from 6 CE until the seventh century; modest modifications were made, most notably introducing an apse into the triclinium (Burrell, 'Palace to praetorium', 228–30). In the early first century CE, Caesarea's still empty south-east area was built over, utilizing fill that brought its level up to the top of the east cavea of the hippodrome (Porath, 'Evolution', 110–11) and a new amphitheatre was added in the north-east part of the city (62 m by 95 m). At a later point the temple platform was modified by adding a nymphaeum and additional warehouses. In the second century there was a new demand for games, and a new hippodrome built farther to the east (Humphrey, '"Amphitheatrical" Hippo-Stadia', 121–9), so that the original hippodrome became partially unused and was altered into something like an amphitheatre. The theatre was regularly improved, altered and adapted, with a major change to its scaenae frons in the Severan period and the inclusion of numerous statue bases for decorative effect.

Caesarea also continued to develop religiously. In addition to the original cult centre dedicated to Roma and Augustus, Pontius

Pilate dedicated a Tiberieum to Augustus's adopted son Tiberius. Later still, a Hadrianeum was built (*c.*130 CE), the cult statue of which may have been the impressive porphyry statue found in a reused Byzantine setting in 1951. An undated inscription to Marcus Flavius Agrippa notes his roles as *duumvir*, *pontifex* and orator, roles that related directly to the imperial cult and the city. Tyche continued to be worshipped in Caesarea; two statues of a Fortuna-type Tyche have been found, in addition to Tyche of an Amazon-type, and it seems likely that numismatic representations of Tyche between columns of a temple reflected that she had a temple of her own in Caesarea (Fischer, 'Marble', 257). In the late first or early second century CE the Mithraist community was sufficiently self-confident that it acquired property for its communal needs, about the same time that Christians were becoming organized, though no archaeological evidence for their early years exists. Jews were strongly represented, and by the third to fourth centuries at the latest a synagogue was built.

The city's refinement appears from the introduction of marble decorative elements, beginning perhaps in the first century CE but expanding considerably from the second century CE, architectural components and sculpture being the two most obvious visible elements. For example, some of the city's streets were given colonnades and sidewalks in the late second century, as the city continued to develop through the Roman period.

Religion

Despite the fact that the archaeological investigation of Caesarea continues at an impressive rate, the evidence for religion in Caesarea is not as extensive as might have been expected from comparable cities (Gersht, 'Representations'): only one temple was certainly included in Herod's planned city (Roma and Augustus), and only three other religious sites have been certainly identified, none part of Herod's original plan (Mithra; shrine in the hippodrome; synagogue). Religious adherence of other kinds is attested from the archaeology, but in most cases they appear to be later developments for which provision may have been made in some formal, informal or adaptive way. A brief check list (drawn from several sources) of known or possible religious activities in Caesarea shows a typical balance between Roman and eastern deities: Roma and Augustus, Tyche, Aphrodite (Gersht, 'Sculptural pieces'), Apollo, Asklepius, Hygieia, Athena, Zeus (?; see Frova et al., *Scavi*, inscription 9), Dionysus, Jupiter, Demeter and Kore, Hecate, Isis, Sarapis, Cybele (Nemesis?), Jupiter Dolichenus, Ephesian Artemis, the Dioscuri, Mithra, Samaritan worship focused on Mount Gerizim, Jewish worship focused on Jerusalem, Christian worship focused on Jesus. The list is not unusual or unexpected, but the paucity of architectural information on religious sites associated with these religious activities is noteworthy, especially the complete absence of evidence about other sanctuaries in Herod's initial plan.

Temple of Roma and Augustus

Given the practical significance of the city as the gateway of Judea and its symbolic significance for Herod's patron and mentor, it is no surprise that the most significant religious building in Caesarea Maritima was the Temple of Roma and Augustus (Fischer, 'Marble', 259–60). The temple was located on a mostly artificial platform, being studied in detail, in the centre of the city facing the harbour (cf. Vitruvius, *Ten Books*, 4.5.1, 9; 1.7.1). The podium's core was a small natural hill that was extended artificially in all directions (Kahn, 'Temple'). The platform, which comprised the temenos, was approached from all four sides; Byzantine stairs on the west and the south have been identified and show their grandiose character. The Herodian temenos had two projecting wings on the west side, creating a lower plaza in front of the inner harbour; this was later covered with vaults and the temenos extended westwards.

There was, however, one unusual feature of the temenos and the structures upon it. Instead of being laid out on the same orientation as the rest of the city, the temple was skewed from the city's axial regularity, striking an odd note in a planned city (Porath, 'Evolution', 109). Relatively few cities with a Hippodamian plan provide analogies to this curious feature in Caesarea; most carry the rectilinear design through with considerable regularity. Two possible explanations suggest themselves. The angling of the central religious structure of the city might have been determined by some earlier structure on the same site, or it could have been the direct result of planning considerations that were deemed more important than following the gridiron scheme. No previous structure that underlay the Temple of Roma and Augustus has been discovered, though some have surmised that a late-Hellenistic temple was located on the small natural rise. While Herod might have chosen an existing religious site as the location for the imperial cult, and while comparison with other cities with similar construction histories makes this plausible, in fact it appears that the majority of the platform was outside Strato's Tower and thus unlikely to have been occupied by a major temple in the late-Hellenistic period (cf. the Temples of Zeus, Dionysus and Artemis at Gerasa). Still, in the previous period the line of the southern harbour was on the same line as Herod's temple; and this reinforces the other possible rationale, the relationship between the harbour and the temple. The angle of the temenos that follows the line of the Hellenistic harbour focuses on the geographic centre of the Herodian harbour, creating a more striking visual impact than perfect rectangularity would. Since the harbour was named Sebastos and was the way by which all important visitors entered Judea, the visual linking of the harbour and the temple reinforced the impression of Caesar's city; from the harbour visitors were confronted by the full frontal façade of the Temple of Roma and Augustus. In the end, both previous and current design considerations prompted the eccentric orientation of the temenos.

From 1992 onwards, in situ evidence of the temple has been found, including remains of foundation walls and of the naos. The foundations discovered in 1995 had been revised for a later church (the sixth-century octagonal church) utilizing Herod's foundations. When linked with fragments of column, capital, base and architrave, which were discovered in the excavations, a reasonably sophisticated effort can now be made to visualize this important temple as hexastyle (about 31 m by 54 m by 25–30 m high), with Corinthian columns 20.5 m high (Kahn, 'Temple', 138–45, figs 2–8). We are less well informed of the temenos wall and whether stoas surrounded the temenos, though in scale and treatment the whole complex must have been rather similar to the nearly contemporary Temple of Augustus and Livia in Nemausus (Nîmes) in Southern France (the Maison Carré) or the slightly later Temple of Claudius in Camulodunum (Colchester) in England, both of which fitted neatly into their regulated street plan without dominating the city in the same way. It might also be compared to Mars Ultor in Rome (Kahn, 'Temple', 141–2).

From Josephus we learn that the cult statues inside the temple were modelled on famous classical statues, Augustus on the staggeringly large representation of Zeus at Olympia, and Roma on the statue of Hera at Argos. Whether Josephus intended to suggest that their size was also replicated is not clear, but he certainly meant his readers to be impressed with the significance and religious correctness of these models. So the religious impact of the temple complex as a whole – judged from its orientation, size, elevation, connections with the harbour and the city, overall character and furnishings – was deliberately and impressively dominant. While all Temples of Roma and Augustus made a 'statement', this one in particular commented powerfully on Herod's relationship to Octavian and his willingness to court unpopularity within his own realm in order to honour his patron, at a time when there were relatively few imperial cult temples in this part of the Roman east. Without doubt, this was the focus of Herod's city.

Tiberieum and Hadrianeum

One of the most heralded early finds in Caesarea's theatre was a reused inscription referring to Pontius Pilate's dedication of a Tiberieum, probably a minor religious site dedicated specifically to Tiberius. Why the inscription should have been found in the theatre is unclear, though the most economical explanation is that the Tiberieum was somewhere in the southern sector of the city near the theatre.

What kind of structure was it? The modest size of the inscription, despite the importance of a dedication to the Emperor, implies a small structure – neither a free-standing naos within a self-contained temenos nor the rededication to Tiberius of the original imperial cult building, for the inscription would be inadequate for such an occasion. The notion of a rededication would be incorrect in any case, since the one imperial cult centre would have included all those who were deemed worthy of the honour and were a part of the imperial family. From later emperors' lifetimes, a few well-known examples might reasonably be adduced: at Side, a delightful small shrine, dedicated to Titus and Vespasian (dated 74 CE) and later modified as a nymphaeum; at Ephesus, two structures on the main street, one dedicated to Trajan and one to Hadrian (the latter, dedicated in 118 CE to Hadrian, Artemis and the people of Ephesus; the former, a nymphaeum dedicated to Trajan in 114 CE). These types of structures, integrated into the streetscape, with relatively little in the way of space or facilities, but with sufficient decoration to meet the needs of piety appropriate to a provincial *praefectus*, seem a better understanding of the Tiberieum than either a piece of paving or a self-standing cult-centre. Obviously, Pilate wished to show proper piety towards Tiberius, perhaps a special concern after the fall of Sejanus, Pilate's patron, in the year 32 CE. A modest street-oriented structure, somewhere in the region of the palace (now that the Promontory Palace was the Praetorium) and close to the theatre and hippodrome where many civic functions would have taken place, would have been highly appropriate.

The Hadrianeum is known only from much later evidence, and nothing can be said about it other than that such a structure existed. It probably followed the same pattern just sketched out, and was consistent with the Hadrianeum at Ephesus.

Civic religion

A considerable number of civic structures – forum, bouleutêrion, prytaneion, stadium, theatre, amphitheatre, basilica, bath, gymnasium – had religious functions regularly or occasionally: a brief religious service prior to games in the stadium or amphitheatre, prior to the meetings of the town council in the bouleutêrion, or prior to the sitting of magistrates in the basilica. Much of civic life was imbued with numerous religious activities. Herod's hippodrome was modified to segregate a 12 m-wide section from the rest of the east cavea by balustrades and stairs, underneath which lay a shrine with three small rooms with niches cut into bedrock, approached from the arena through the podium wall. Inscriptions and other objects were found there, notably seven votives of sandalled and bare feet (Porath, 'Herod's "Amphiteatre" '; Gersht, 'Representations', 306–11). This minor religious shrine was developed to serve charioteers or gladiators who entered it from the arena, no doubt to pay their religious obligations either before or after an event (Weiss, 'Jews'). Weiss argues strongly that at least at a later period Jews participated in games, not only as spectators but as athletes, charioteers and gladiators, and such an argument broadens the issues related to this curious little shrine under the hippodrome's east cavea.

Frova's excavations at the theatre unearthed important statuary that must have decorated the theatre, two of which showed scenes of sacrifice (Frova et al., *Scavi*, figs 230–61, here 239–40). But the most important evidence of religion from the theatre is the cult-statue of Artemis of Ephesus, perhaps also from the time of Hadrian. What role exactly the statue played and where is uncertain, though it may be evidence of the presence of her cult in Caesarea. Another inconclusive piece of evidence is a rectangular building that may have been a religious sanctuary west of the piazza behind the scaenae frons (Frova et al., *Scavi*, 159–60). Nothing can be said of the amphitheatre; exploratory trenches have shown how thoroughly plundered it was. An apparently public late-first-century bath was found north-east of Caesarea (most contemporary baths were attached to palaces), supporting the assumption that there must have been a public bath in the city proper from early on in its history (Hirschfeld, 'Ramat Hanadiv').

As noted above, the juxtaposition of theatre, hippodrome and palace at the southern end of the city was unusual. The linkage of these civic buildings (the palace, the south end of the hippodrome and the theatre were unusually closely linked) leads to the conclusion that these three structures played interrelated roles in the dynamic of the city, not only in the later period when Rome ruled directly, but especially in the original phase, when Herod laid them out in this way. This suggests some particular fascination on Herod's part with entertainment and spectacle, and perhaps with their religious aspects.

Jewish synagogue

A synagogue in Caesarea, located near the Hellenistic north harbour, is well attested but has received inadequate attention, no doubt because it is an old excavation (1940s to 1960s) that is poorly published. Five strata stretched from the Hellenistic period to sometime beyond the fifth century CE; three superimposed synagogues emerged, though without the clarity of plan and detail needed for a full discussion. The excavators found evidence of ashlar walls from the early-Roman period (Stratum II, possibly an adaptation of the Hellenistic house found in Stratum I, identified by the excavators as a synagogue), then a gap (Stratum III), then a third-century synagogue (Stratum IV, incorporating the ashlar walls of Stratum II, with the important inscription that refers to priestly courses) that was destroyed in the fourth century, then a mid-fifth-century synagogue built on those ruins (Stratum V, with three important inscriptions, one of which dates that particular structure to 459 CE; see Avi-Yonah, 'Caesarea', 278–80). The literary record of religious hostility at Caesarea might correlate with the archaeological record. The Stratum II structure was destroyed (first century CE, possibly in 66–74 CE) and replaced by a cistern, with a lengthy gap from first to third centuries. The synagogue site remained available for the Jewish community to reuse again many years later. It was again destroyed, not in war but by other forces – perhaps Christian persecution – in the fourth century, after which there was a second gap from the mid-fourth to mid-fifth centuries. Throughout this period, despite the long gaps, the site of the synagogue remained fixed; it was not occupied by another major user who might have prevented the site being reused; all this suggests that the Jewish community may have weathered these reverses resiliently. Herod the Great would not have incorporated provision for a synagogue in his plans for Caesarea, for he was not particularly interested in synagogues (Richardson, *Herod*, 265–9; Richardson, 'Augustan-era synagogues'). So evidence of a synagogue is an indication of the ways in which even this showcase city developed organically from its 'fully' planned condition to its gradual adaptation to fit the religious needs of the various religious communities living within its boundaries.

Mithraeum

The city's Mithraeum was located from the late first through the late third centuries CE in a horreum just south of the Crusader walls (Blakely, *Pottery and Dating*, 58, 103, 149–50). The adaptation of a previously commercial site for a Mithraeum, buried indistinguishably in a warehouse complex at an important junction in the city but not in a highly visible location, emphasizes how, in their formative years, new religious movements were not prominently visible. Like many Mithraea, the building incorporated appropriate symbolic values: a dark vaulted space suggesting a cave, a modest size accommodating only a small group, a shape focusing on one end, inclusion of benches, extensive fresco decoration with a white plaster floor, and a roof that allowed the opening of holes to permit sunlight to enter. The Mithraist community in Caesarea adapted an existing space to meet their religious needs, providing another instance of the organic development of the city and its changing religious needs. In this case, it found an unobtrusive location close to the centre.

Samaritan synagogue

There are no building remains showing the presence of Samaritans in Caesarea. An inscription from Mount Gerizim says: 'I, Zosimos the cook from Caesarea, have made [this] as a vow for [my] sister Rebecca. Three solidi.' Leah di Segni argues persuasively that he must have been a Samaritan, making the gift on either his own or his sister's behalf in the period before the Christian church replaced the Samaritan temple. The dating is uncertain. But clearly the Samaritan community was large, at least at some periods, for within the lamp assemblage from Caesarea, a noteworthy subset derived from the Byzantine Samaritan community, with Samaritan legends and motifs; they were found widely distributed throughout the whole city (Sussman, 'Lamps', 356–7). The literary evidence also speaks strongly for a vigorous Samaritan presence in Caesarea at earlier periods, and for some tension between the Jewish and Samaritan religious communities. Again we must visualize some later adaptation to meet the community's needs.

Christianity

There is good literary evidence of the early development of Christianity in Caesarea, but none of the archaeological remains falls within the early period. Caesarea shared with other major cities in Constantine's triumphalism, though even after that period we still have to rely on literary evidence for some time. The pattern of house-church would have been the likely solution to meeting its early needs.

Other Cults

Archaeological evidence for religion at Caesarea includes statues, coins, lamps, inscriptions, votives and literary descriptions. While not a lot, it is enough to establish the multi-cultic character of the city, which by the early-Roman period must have gone well beyond the few architectural remains now known to be associated with buildings for religion. The most likely cult centres, beyond Augustus and Roma, Mithra, and Tyche, were Isis and Sarapis, Demeter and Kore, Asklepios and Hygieia, Apollo, Hecate and Dionysus; to these might conceivably have been added Athena, Aphrodite, Ephesian Artemis, Cybele or Nemesis, and the Dioscuri. Those that had cult-sites will, in most cases, have developed them long after Herod's planning of the city, though we should not exclude the possibility that one or two might have originated right at the beginning and have been included in his plan. This review of religious evidence shows how important the growth and spread of religious affiliations was in the life of a city and how common it must have been for the needs of religious communities, whether old or new, to be met informally.

Relationship to other eastern cities

Comparison with other cities in the eastern part of the Roman Empire helps to shed light on the particular urban character of Caesarea. I will limit the comparisons to the other four cities in this volume – Gerasa, Palmyra, Petra and Jerusalem – not to argue that Caesarea was precisely the same as any of them or that it was *sui generis*, but rather to suggest how attentiveness both to unusual and to common elements in a city helps us to understand it better.

Urban development over several periods

All five cities developed over many hundreds of years, and in the four other cases something of the inherited religious arrangements continued to influence the shape of the early Roman city. This permanence of location of religious sanctuaries was often one of the defining features of a city, seen obviously in Jerusalem, where the only sanctuary remained fixed on the Temple Mount for well over a millennium, almost as clearly in Gerasa, where the Temple of Zeus remained settled from the Hellenistic period and helped to influence significantly the Roman-period plan, in Palmyra, where the Temple of Bel continued in its original location and orientation despite important changes to the city's plan, and to a lesser extent in Petra, where there is less evidence of longitudinal occupation of specific sites for different cults. The urban plans of all of these cities were substantially revised in the periods on which this volume focuses, in the case of Gerasa, Palmyra and Jerusalem, dramatically so, yet in no case did the city obliterate the earlier religious precincts. Indeed, in most cases, it would seem, the plan adapted to those earlier sites. In the case of Palmyra it resulted in a contorted solution, as the Cardo Maximus wound past the Temple of Nebo and truncated the original temenos. In the case of Gerasa it resulted in a brilliant civic structure, the Oval Piazza, that accommodated the new Hippodamian plan to the original location of the lower temenos of the Temple of Zeus.

In Caesarea, then, despite the imposition of Herod's new city plan, we might expect that prior temples would be respected in their locations if not in the cult itself. It is this that makes especially interesting the still-undecided issue of a precursor temple below the Temple of Roma and Augustus and that makes the orientation of the later temenos an intriguing clue, and the evidence of the inner harbour's orientation especially suggestive. The general issue also bears on the question of the presence of other religious activities in the earlier city – other temples, perhaps, or even a possible synagogue – though until evidence is forthcoming, there is little room for speculation. The least we should say, however, is that even in the case of newly planned cities, there was some continuity in the elements of the plan, perhaps especially with respect to traditional religious commitments.

Focus on central sanctuary

Caesarea was noteworthy for its forceful focus on one central sanctuary, beside which we can compare Gerasa, with a carefully contrived focus on the Temple of Artemis, or Palmyra with its focus on the Temple of Bel, and to some extent Jerusalem, with its central sanctuary off to one side of the city. In the case of Gerasa's Artemis Temple, great care was taken with the ways in which form was given to this centrality: its location in the centre on a hill was the most obvious; its identification with taller columns along the cardo at the propylaea; its almost overpowering stairs; but especially its carefully managed approach from the eastern side of the city across a bridge and through a beautifully articulated Propylaea Court. Despite the presence of other temenoi, there can be little doubt that Artemis was the central cult. The case of Petra's focus is complicated, for it seems rather that the focus was not so much on a single sanctuary as on a cluster of sanctuaries at one end of the cardo.

Caesarea (along with Sebaste as well) gave central position to a Temple of Roma and Augustus, emphasizing its role by location, elevation, embellishment and size. Nothing at Caesarea detracted from the position of the cult dedicated to Augustus, especially in the Herodian period. It is thus likely that Herod intended Caesarea to be viewed as a one-cult city in somewhat the same way as he intended Jerusalem to be viewed as revolving around the demands of one Lord. If this was the case, Caesarea was the litmus test of Herod's loyalty to Augustus, the place where no other cult had a significant role to play – maybe no role at all. It appears from the excavations to date that his plan in this most planned of cities made no room for other cult centres, and it may be that his plan deliberately swallowed up a Hellenistic temple site, though that is not yet clear. It is noteworthy that some cities (e.g. Gerasa, Petra) seem to have thought the presence of the imperial cult unimportant.

Balance among several cult centres

Most Greek and Roman cities deliberately created a balance among the various religious precincts, reflecting importance, historical development, religious needs and so on. Gerasa, Petra and Palmyra, in quite different ways, show aspects of this juxtaposition. Gerasa, for example, had the Temple of Artemis as its focus, but that centrality was balanced by the beautiful, older and important Temple of Zeus, in its prominent location on a hill on the axis of the Cardo Maximus, fronted by the Oval Piazza, created to solve the change in axis introduced with the new Hippodamian plan of the city. It was also balanced by the Temple of Dionysus, on the slope of the same hill on which Artemis sat, but without the same attention given to its place in the city.

Petra, I have argued, deliberately clustered three major cult sites plus paradeisos (and perhaps another minor site) in a carefully contrived conjunction at one end of the cardo, balanced at the opposite end by an equally impressive cluster of Royal Tombs, which visually dominated the central space of the city. When the monumental arch was built, the three became an almost unified composition around that focus.

By contrast, Palmyra achieved its balance in a quite different fashion, without a true centre among its religious sites. The main cult site and premier temenos in Palmyra was, of course, Bel's, but this was at one end of the cardo, on its traditional site and with its traditional orientation, unaffected (except in its enlargement) by the new city plan. It was balanced at the other end of the cardo with the cult of Allat, not a large precinct but an important one. In between, along the cardo, was the Temple of Nebo, and a little later a modest imperial cult site. To one side was the beautifully articulated Temple of Ba'al Shamim. Palmyra thus had a less obvious but more dynamic balance among the religious parts. I need to observe only that Caesarea did not have this traditional juxtaposition of one temenos with another. Its focus remained entirely on the one temple, as was true in Jerusalem.

Provision for new religious cults

As cities developed provision was usually made somehow for new religious activities. Jerusalem, as it was rebuilt after the devastating destruction of the Great Revolt, incorporated temples to Aphrodite, Jupiter and Asklepius, not to mention the early development of the Christian house-church. But this was an unusual situation, where the city had to rise from the ashes. In the case of Gerasa, a similar process can be seen in the custom-building of a synagogue for the Jewish community in a remarkably central location immediately behind the Temple of Artemis; it is worth noting that the evidence for other new religions in Gerasa is relatively thin. In Palmyra, one can trace the same process in the inclusion, again in a prominent location beside the theatre, of the imperial cult, with a possible development of a synagogue in what was originally a house.

Evidence at Caesarea showed something of the same features as elsewhere: unpredictable locations, such as the central location for Mithra, unpredictable continuity, as in the case of the synagogue, incorporation of a shrine in the hippodrome, and the development of other cults in unspecified locations.

Competition and coexistence

This raises the question of the relationships among these religions and their adherents in such an urban setting. Was there religious rivalry in the first century? This notion of rivalry is to a large extent a Christian (and perhaps a Jewish and Muslim) construct, impelled by the monotheism that lies at the heart of these religions of the book. Indeed, rivalry is a peculiarly apposite notion specifically when discussing the relationship between sibling religions, as the material evidence occasionally shows. The Synagogue Church in Gerasa was a telling instance of a Jewish synagogue that was taken over by Christians and then reconstructed for the Christian community's use by reversing the orientation and adapting the rest of the structure. A related instance worth noting was the takeover of the Samaritan holy place on Mount Gerizim as the site of a church dedicated to Mary Theotokos. More frequently the Christian community took over a 'pagan' site, as happened in Gerasa at the Temples of Dionysus, Zeus and Artemis, each in different ways, and these instances could be multiplied almost endlessly, not least in the case of the octagonal church that occupied the site of the Temple of Roma and Augustus in Caesarea. There obviously was rivalry in the ancient world, but most of it was a later phenomenon, the description of which is conditioned by pervasive Christian assumptions about how religions work and relate to each other.

A consideration of the urban fabric of ancient cities – and this seems equally true of Roman as of Hellenistic and Greek cities – reminds us that for much of antiquity the proper model is not so much rivalry as competition. And perhaps even that overstates matters. With a plethora of divinities and cults, with the possibility of supporting many or few but only rarely one, there was no need to insist on some kind of competitive confrontation with other cults. Usually coexistence was the normal expectation. While the city had its major deity, that deity, except in the unique case of Jerusalem, did not demand unconditional allegiance. It was clear from the layout and the design decisions, the size and the degree of embellishment, coins and inscriptions, who was the city's main deity, and no visitor would be long in doubt. But almost all cities made provision for the worship of other gods and heroes, and even gods that were exclusive – such as the God of the Jews or the Samaritans or the Christians – could be permitted a cult site in a city such as Gerasa or Palmyra. The converse was, of course, not equally true. Other gods could hardly be given a place in Jerusalem, as long as Jerusalem remained the capital city of Judea and was under Jewish control.

Organic growth, urban design and religion

Caesarea Maritima provides an excellent example of a planned city, created not de novo but on the site of an earlier foundation. At its founding it insisted on the importance of one cult – the imperial cult – the relatively new form of piety focused on Octavian and his family in Rome. The city grew and developed much beyond that newly founded city, accommodating other religious activities within its walls, thus reshaping the character of the built-form of the religious presence in the city, though we have little that points to the ways in which this reshaping might have taken place. At the point of its greatest extension in the Byzantine period Caesarea had almost reverted to one religion, with Christianity now being the occupant of the temple platform that had accommodated the Temple of Roma and Augustus.

As more evidence accumulates, it will be possible to say more in detail about the balance among the religious activities of Caesarea, their competitiveness and their coexistence. At the moment, the most we can affirm is (1) that there certainly were other cults in the city that have left slim remains, though not enough in most cases to be sure that they in fact occupied their own cult-sites. Through the Roman period, probably beginning in the first century CE, these other cults began to proliferate, and the proliferation continued through the third or fourth century. It seems likely (2) that among the other cults that had a place in the urban configuration, some of the most successful and earliest were four that would be rivals for a long while, Judaism, Samaritanism, Mithraism and Christianity. The evidence for the presence of three of these is fairly good, though the archaeological evidence is best for Mithraism at an early period. This particular combination, given Caesarea's setting in the east, is not surprising, though the paucity of evidence for Judaism and Samaritanism is unexpected in such a location. It is also not surprising, given the political history of the Roman Empire, (3) that Christianity would come to triumph in Caesarea as elsewhere, and that it would occupy the temple platform that had been the centre of the religious life of the city for over half a millennium. Here the one really clear case of religious rivalry comes into sharp focus, as the excavations show the Christian takeover of the traditional central religious site, reusing the foundations of the Temple of Roma and Augustus. Though such takeovers were common, this took place unusually slowly, for the octagonal church that replaced the temple was not built until the early sixth century CE, implying that the temple and its site had lain unused for almost 200 years. I argue, finally, (4) that Herod's city had only two religious foci, one explicit and one implicit, both of which worked to exactly the same end: promoting Rome and her interests. Both the Temple of Roma and Augustus and the civic religion associated with the hippodrome, theatre and royal palace in the southern sector were intended to remind the population of the benefits Rome brought to Judea, and to demonstrate unmistakably Herod's dependability as client to Augustus. Not only did he demonstrate this in the unusually large construction project, Sebastos-Caesarea, in which both halves reflected the role of Augustus, but he made it brilliantly clear in his structure for the imperial cult and in his combined facilities for the people. Herod seemed quite content to have no other religions but worship of the imperial family practised in the city.

Table 5.1 Caesarea chronology

Zoilus ousted from city by Jannaeus	103 BCE
Independence granted by Pompey	63 BCE
Strato's Tower ceded to Herod by Octavian	31/30 BCE
Herodian period	
New design of city and harbour	23/22 BCE
Temple of Roma and Augustus	22–12 BCE
Promontory Palace	22–12 BCE
Theatre	22–12 BCE
Hippodrome/Stadium	22–12 BCE
Warehouses and commercial buildings	22–12 BCE
Walls	22–12 BCE
North Gates	22–12 BCE
High level aqueduct	22–12 BCE
Roman period	
Promontory Palace converted to Praetorium	about 6 CE
Southern part of city reconfigured	early 1st c. CE
Amphitheatre	early 1st c. CE
Tiberieum	26–36 CE
Nymphaeum added to temple podium	late 1st c. CE
Mithraeum	late 1st/early 2nd c. CE
Hadrianeum	about 130 CE
Second high level aqueduct	about 130 CE
Hippodrome altered to amphitheatre	2nd c. CE
New hippodrome	1st half 2nd c. CE
Renovation of theatre	2nd c. CE
Alterations to scaenae frons	late 2nd c. CE
Colonnading of some streets	late 2nd c. CE
Semi-circular platform behind theatre	3rd c. CE
Conversion of orchestra to pool	3rd–4th c. CE
Archives building	about 300 CE
Synagogue	3rd or 4th (?) c. CE

Byzantine period

Harbour submerged	4th c. CE
Low level aqueduct	4th c. CE
Byzantine walls	late 4th/early 5th c. CE
Synagogue alterations	459 CE
St Procopius Church burned by Samaritans	484 CE
Octagonal Church	early 6th c. CE
Theatre converted to fortress	6th c. CE
Byzantine colonnaded street	6th c. CE
Samaritan Revolt	529–30 CE
North Bath	550 CE
Churches burned	555 CE

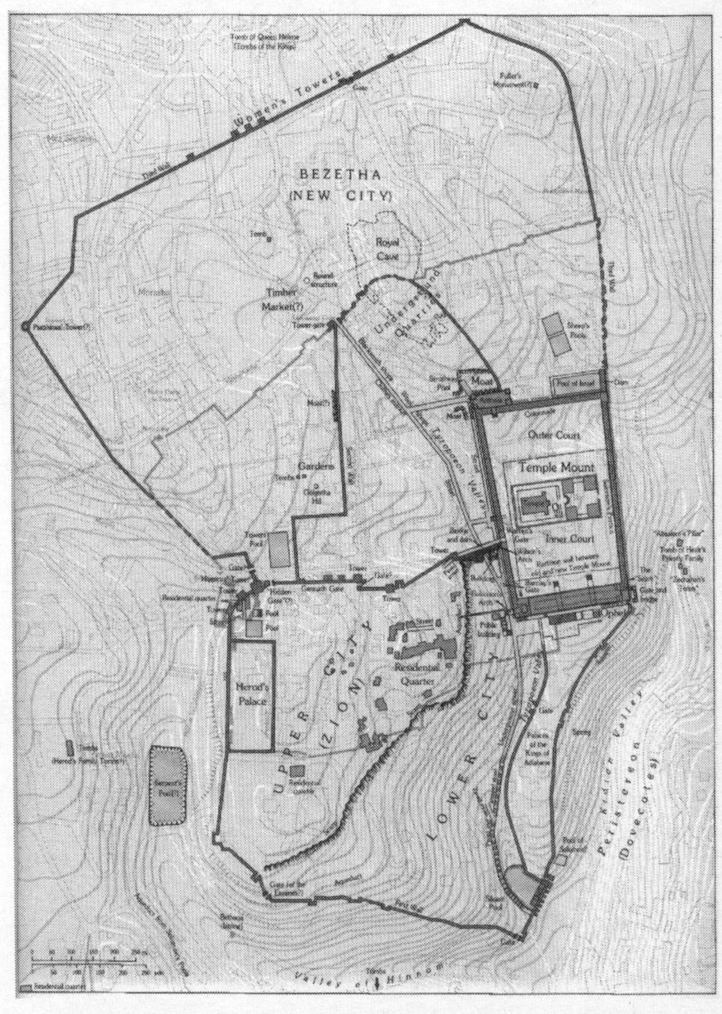

Plan of Jerusalem, © Carta, the Israel Map and Publishing Company Ltd.

6

Jerusalem: Rome and Monotheism

Historical background

Jerusalem had been the centre of Jewish life and worship from about 1000 BCE. For much of the first millennium the city had occupied mainly the eastern ridge, with the temple and royal palace higher up the ridge to the north and the city proper, the so-called City of David, below it near the permanent water supply. Babylon destroyed the city in 586 BCE, and though the city was rebuilt in the Persian period (see Ezra and Nehemiah), it was a relatively poor, minor administrative centre for Persia's province of Yehud (Levine, *Jerusalem*, ch. 2). When Alexander the Great died in Babylon as he returned from his extensive conquests (323 BCE), the area of ancient Israel was held first by Ptolemy I. For much of the third century BCE it was fought over by the two main successor empires, the Ptolemies of Egypt and the Seleucids of Syria. With Antiochus III's victory over Ptolemy V at Panias in 200 BCE, most of ancient Israel (Judea, Samaria, Galilee) fell to the Seleucids, with their capital at Antioch (Levine, *Jerusalem*, ch. 3). Repressive measures against Jews and Jewish religion by Antiochus IV Epiphanes (175–164 BCE) led to a surprisingly successful, religiously motivated freedom movement under the leadership of a family of minor priests, the Hasmoneans (167–142 BCE). Descendants of the family assumed both political and religious leadership of the country for just over a century, until Rome intervened directly (Levine, *Jerusalem*, ch. 4; Schürer 1.137–232).

Rome's interest in the region intensified substantially during the Hasmonean period, first of all through treaties between the Hasmoneans and Rome. The amicable relationship changed in

64/63 BCE when Pompey the Great used dynastic quarrels both in Syria and in Judea as a pretext for his intervention. The internecine Hasmonean dynastic in-fighting involved the brothers Hyrcanus II and Aristobulus II; the latter had Pompey's support. His legendary – or notorious – approach to Jerusalem in 63 BCE is recorded in the *Psalms of Solomon* (Richardson, *Herod*, 73–80; Schürer 1.233–80); 'someone' in line 1 is clearly Pompey and 'the leaders' in line 3 are Hyrcanus II and his followers:

> [God] brought someone from the end of the earth, one who attacks in strength;
> he declared war against Jerusalem, and her land.
> The leaders of the country met him with joy. They said to him,
> 'May your way be blessed. Come, enter in peace.'
> They guarded the rough roads before his coming;
> they opened the gates to Jerusalem, they crowned her city walls.
> He entered in peace as a father enters his son's house;
> he sets his feet securely.
> He captured the fortified towers and the wall of Jerusalem,
> for God led him in securely while they wavered.
> (*Psalms of Solomon* 8.15–19)

Pompey's political ascendancy in Rome had created a long period of uncertainty and civil unrest in the Roman world: he was murdered (48 BCE); Caesar was assassinated (44 BCE); a 'second triumvirate' was formed by Mark Antony, Octavian and Lepidus (43 BCE); Cassius and Brutus fled to the east and were defeated at Philippi (42 BCE); Mark Antony's and Octavian's subsequent power struggle culminated in Octavian's victory at the Actium (31 BCE), following which Antony and Cleopatra died by their own hands in Egypt.

The east, where much of this action took place, shared in the general malaise and the need to take sides in these world-shaping events. Judean events in the 40s paralleled Roman events, with familial conflict between Antigonus, son of Aristobulus II, and Hyrcanus II, with his allies Antipater and his sons, Herod being the most prominent: Antipater was poisoned, Hyrcanus executed.

Octavian in the one setting and Herod in the other were victors or survivors. At the urging of Mark Antony and Octavian the Roman Senate named Herod King of Judea in 40 BCE, aiming to pacify the area and stymie Parthian ambitions. Still, Herod had to fight for two and a half years to work his way up to Jerusalem, then in 37 BCE had to take it by siege (Richardson, *Herod*, ch. 7). Jerusalem suffered badly from the above events, especially the sieges of Pompey and Herod only 25 years apart. When Herod gained effective control, the city and the temple were functional but there had been much damage to the fabric of the city that needed more than just repair. He did some essential repairs in the 30s, but it was not until the 20s BCE that Herod gave concentrated attention to rebuilding Jerusalem, slightly earlier than the similar extensive building activities already considered in Petra, Palmyra, Gerasa and Caesarea Maritima. His early concerns were to strengthen the walls, to restore the Baris and to make the Hasmonean palace usable again.

After Octavian brought stability to Rome (31 BCE) the newly established security permitted him to give attention to rebuilding the city of Rome and the rest of his growing empire. When he confirmed Herod in his position at Rhodes (30 BCE), Herod too was able to turn his attention to larger projects within Jerusalem. The often-quoted remark that Octavian found Rome a city of brick and left it a city of marble accurately reflects the general optimism of the period throughout much of the Roman Empire, not least in Judea.

Topography and urban plan

Jerusalem's plan has always been influenced by its difficult topography. The city sat on two ridges, bisected by the steep Tyropoeon Valley; it was surrounded on the west and south sides by the Hinnom Valley and on the east side by the extremely deep Kidron Valley. Originally the city had occupied only the north–south ridge bounded by the Kidron and the Tyropoeon Valleys, with the main urban area in the City of David at the south end of the eastern ridge and the sanctuary higher up to the north. In fact, the city expanded and contracted in various periods, sometimes occupying only the eastern ridge and at other times occupying both eastern and western hills. The three parallel valleys constricted the city. Because of the steepness of the Wadi Kidron on the east, making access from the east difficult, the city did not expand in that direction. Access was easier from the west, from the north easier still. When the city was small and contained on the eastern ridge, the temple impeded access from the north. When the city was relatively large, as it was in the first century, the focus tended to move west, because the newer elite housing was on the western hill and the city's approaches shifted to the easier routes from north and west where the slopes were less steep.

The Tyropoeon Valley was the central feature. Its slopes became quite steep on both east and west sides as one moved south, so that east–west circulation required either stepped streets or streets angled across the contours. North–south streets could be more direct, but mostly followed the contours. An east–west street, possibly from the Hasmonean period, led from today's Jaffa Gate across a bridge over the Tyropoeon Valley to the temple. Areas south of this line had been reoccupied in the Hasmonean period, though during the Herodian period many of the older buildings were rebuilt. The area north of this line on the western hill was outside the city during the Hasmonean period. Parts of it were incorporated into the city between the late first century BCE and the late first century CE (Kenyon, *Digging up Jerusalem*, chs 12–13); these areas may have been planned, laid out on orthogonal lines as much as possible (so Wilkinson, *Jerusalem*, 62). The city thus had several neighbourhoods: elite housing on the south-west hill (today's Jewish Quarter), poorer housing on the hillsides and in the valleys, older housing in the City of David (given new status in the 40s CE by Queen Helena of Adiabene's palaces; Josephus, *War* 5.253; 6.355) and a kind of 'suburban' housing, both in the central north (period of Herod the Great, part of today's Christian Quarter) and north-east (Bezatha, planned under Agrippa I, today's Muslim Quarter). The city walls were altered to include those areas, including a 'third wall' on the north (mid-first century CE), where the city was especially open to attack.

The street system can be partly reconstructed for the first century CE. After the inclusion of the new north-western area there were probably two main roads going south, from near today's Damascus Gate, one along the eastern floor of the Tyropoeon Valley, the other along its western upper edge. These roads at about a 40-degree angle to each other were formalized later, and continued to dominate the street pattern until the present. As excavations tunnelled under the Muslim Quarter have shown, there was a minor Herodian colonnaded street in the first century BCE along the base of the temple mount, two columns of which are still in situ. There was also a more major Herodian street on the present line up the Tyropoeon Valley. Excavations have also disclosed streets and stairs across the valley, in addition to the bridge, that eased traffic between the temple and the western hill (Ben-Dov, *Shadow*, ch. 6).

The temple on Mount Moriah, the eastern ridge, dominated the city from the time of David or Solomon through to the destruction of the temple in 70 CE. Its role was crucial, especially during the Iron Age when the city was small and mostly confined to the eastern ridge (tenth and ninth centuries BCE); there was some occupation of the western hill during the eighth and seventh centuries prior to the city's destruction in 586 BCE. The Persian period city, when the city was being rebuilt from 538 BCE onwards, was confined once again to the eastern ridge. Though the temple was still the focus of the city, for most of the following period it was a relatively poor structure, completed about 516 or 515 BCE (Haggai and Zechariah).

Little is known about how the temple may have been altered and remodelled during the next four centuries. There was major expansion during the Hasmonean period, which may still have been relatively utilitarian, though it included at least expansion of the temenos and undoubtedly improvement of the surrounding areas. Herod's almost total rebuilding of the temple followed along the path the Hasmoneans had sketched, including larger extensions of the temenos, additional entrances and gates and rebuilding of the temple's naos.

Roman rebuilding following the destructions in 70 and 135 CE was not very extensive. They continued to use the temple area for a Temple of Jupiter, but how much building took place there cannot be determined. The importance of that site was balanced by construction of a new Temple of Aphrodite on the western hill, in a location that would come to be important as the site of the Church of the Holy Sepulchre. Rebuilding in the post-Constantinian development of Jerusalem was focused on the putative sites of Jesus' death, burial and resurrection at the site on the western hill developed first by the Romans. The original temple mount was left empty. Outside the city, the Mount of Olives became a second major Byzantine area. The centre of gravity of the city thus shifted decisively westwards during the Roman and Byzantine periods away from the traditional centre. With the Muslim period the centre shifted back to the eastern ridge and especially to the huge temenos associated with Herod's temple. The revitalization of the Haram al-Sharif in that period included both the magnificent Dome of the Rock and the larger but more utilitarian al-Aqsa Mosque. The city thus swung back and forth in its main urban focus as a result of changing religious dominance.

Hasmonean and Herodian periods

Hasmonean building activity in Jerusalem had been concerned primarily with defence; they rebuilt and realigned the city's walls in several stages in the mid- to late second century BCE, incorporating parts of earlier walls. The Hasmonean-period expansion to the western hill reoccupied areas that had been settled in the First Temple period but not resettled after the exile (summary in Bahat, 'Jerusalem', 227–9; Levine, *Jerusalem*, ch. 4). The Hasmonean walls also enclosed the temple mount and the old City of David, altogether more than doubling the area within the walls (Bahat, *Atlas*, 34–40; Kenyon, *Digging up Jerusalem*, ch. 11); a major challenge was the city's northern defences.

The city's major source of water was historically the Gihon spring down in the Kidron Valley. This was inconvenient for the new shape of the city, so a new (lower) aqueduct system was built during the Hasmonean period coming from Solomon's Pool, but with a collection area that extended to the Wadi 'Arub; the main aqueduct was 24 km long, its total length was 61 km (Avigad and Geva, 'Jerusalem', 746–7; map in Shanks, *Jerusalem*, 127). The roughly parallel high-level aqueduct dates from Herod's reign or later. There were also major reservoirs outside the walls, some arranged to serve the higher built-up areas not served by the aqueducts.

The Hasmoneans extended the temenos of the temple beyond its First Temple extent, mainly on the east and the north, and probably also on the south towards the area known as the Ophel. They created a partly natural and partly man-made fosse to the north of the temple and then reconstructed the earlier fortress (the 'Baris') outside that northern wall (Josephus, *Ant.* 15.403; 18.91–2; *War* 5.238). Some of this work may have been done under Jonathan, especially the retaining wall on the east (161–143 BCE; 1 Macc. 10.10–11). They also no doubt undertook some alterations or renovations to the temple, but exactly how much is disputed.

Jerusalem's character as a city of one God created civic and urban design problems. An impressive processional way leading to the sanctuary, for example, might have been expected, but there is little evidence of such an effort, only a few installations between the sanctuary and the City of David to the south. According to Josephus, the Hasmoneans worked in other parts of the city, including a bouleutêrion or council chamber, which is sometimes identified with a very fine room (the 'Chamber of Hewn Stone', though the use of that term for this room may not be correct) that has survived almost completely intact below the bridge across the Tyropoeon Valley (Bahat, *Atlas*, 36). The room was finely finished, with a carefully constructed ashlar wall decorated with delicate pilasters set on a carefully moulded base around the perimeter. The Hasmoneans built a substantial palace on the east slope of the western hill near an earlier – and religiously controversial – gymnasium, or to be more precise xystos, a colonnaded area attached to the gymnasium (Josephus, *Ant.* 20.189, concerning Agrippa II's extension of the earlier Hasmonean palace); Levine argues for the xystos being between the City of David and the temple. No remains of either of xystos or Hasmonean palace have been found, but the chamber just described shows that very fine structures were built in the Hasmonean period.

Herod the Great (40–4 BCE) responded to the intense challenges posed by Jerusalem with careful attention to individual buildings and overall urban design (generally, Levine, *Jerusalem*, chs 6, 10). Herod's building efforts were more concentrated and were completed sooner than the similar efforts at Palmya, Petra and Gerasa; surprisingly, work was going forward on both Jerusalem and Caesarea Maritima at the same time (Caesarea, 22–12 BCE; Jerusalem temple, mainly 23–15 BCE). In general planning, the reconstruction of Jerusalem was more similar to the situation at Palmyra and Petra, neither of which had been fundamentally altered with a new plan, whereas Caesarea Maritima and Gerasa both had new overall plans imposed on them. The influences and limitations in Jerusalem were dauntingly different, however, because of its historic monotheistic role. Herod completely – and brilliantly – rebuilt the temple. The construction work he began continued for 75 years under his grandson and great-grandson. The later rabbis, hardly fans of Herod, said: 'He who has not seen Jerusalem has not seen a beautiful city.'

The civic projects included rebuilding and expansion of the fortress (Baris) that was renamed 'Antonia' in honour of Mark Antony (30s BCE), a new palace on the western hill named in honour of Augustus and Caesar (20s BCE), new streets and aqueducts and reservoirs, a theatre and a stadium, general improvement in commerce and shops and such a boost in the finances of the city that there was an outburst of private building, especially houses and tombs. Herod must inevitably have altered the street pattern, as already noted; it has been argued that he even imposed a kind of Hippodamian layout on parts of it, within the limitations of the topography, though the limited evidence may apply better to Aelia Capitolina (Wilkinson, *Jerusalem*, 53–65; cf. map, Geva, 'Jerusalem', 758).

The late first century BCE through the middle of the first century CE was a golden period in Jerusalem's architectural history, if not in its political history. We have already seen that the four other cities considered here also had golden periods; a comparison is suggestive: Jerusalem, last third of the first century BCE; Caesarea, last quarter of the first century BCE – first century CE; Petra, late first century BCE – early first century CE; Palmyra, first – second centuries CE; Gerasa, late first century – second century CE. This pattern of periods implies that those with the strongest indigenous influences were the earliest to flower as strong and influential urban centres and were also the least Romanized.

Jerusalem's impressive beauty in the Herodian period was in stark contrast to its condition after the destruction of the city during the Jewish Revolt of 66–74 CE against Imperial Rome. A second major revolt, the Bar Kochba Revolt of 132–5 CE, though shorter and less successful, was followed by an even more thorough destruction. It took several hundred years for Jerusalem to rise out of the ashes; only in the Byzantine period and again in the subsequent Muslim period did it become a major centre again, rivalling its brilliance in the earlier periods (Asali, *Jerusalem in History*, ch. 4).

Temple

Josephus says that Herod claimed, on the occasion when he announced his intention to rebuild the temple (probably 23/22 BCE), that although the Persian/Hasmonean temple was much smaller than Solomon's temple 'no one should condemn our fathers for neglecting their pious duty, for it was not their fault that the temple is smaller. Rather it was Cyrus and Darius . . . who prescribed these dimensions for building . . . our fathers . . . had no opportunity to restore this first archetype of piety to its former size' (*Ant.* 15.386). So Herod 'restored the temple and, by erecting new foundation-walls, enlarged the surrounding area to double its former extent' (*War* 1.401). In Herod's rebuilding – or as Josephus would have it 'restoration' – the brilliant new temple was clearly the city's most distinguished structure.

He enlarged the site substantially in several ways to mark its importance for all Jews everywhere. Just as the southern ridge at Petra was quarried and filled to create room for the Great Temple, the Paradeisos and the Upper Market, so a large portion of the rising bedrock on the north was cut away in Jerusalem, leaving a high vertical scarp as the base for the Antonia fortress. Like Petra's Upper Market, the scarp shows beam supports that permit deductions about the size of the stoa at that point. The builders filled a transverse valley and the fosse that were part of the Hasmonean city's northern defences. They built a massive new retaining wall on the west, today's Western Wall, dropping into the Tyropoeon Valley; because of the slope, the farther out the walls were moved the higher they had to be built. This was an acute problem on the south, where the height of the wall increased to dangerous proportions. Had a retaining wall with fill behind been used here, the outward pressure would have been so great that it would probably have eventually given way. Instead, multiple arches and vaults were built in the south-eastern portion of the temenos to lighten the structure, solving the problem of the 43 m difference in height between bedrock and platform. The Hasmonean eastern wall continued to be utilized, but it was extended both north and south to enclose the newly added areas. The difference in construction techniques is easily visible today, particularly the southerly 'seam' between the Hasmonean and Herodian walls, 32 m north of the south-east corner. This work resulted in a flat temenos for the sanctuary of roughly 14 hectares (315 m on the north, 470 m on the east, 280 m on the south and 485 m on the west). It was the largest sanctuary in the Roman world.

The ancient southern approach to the temple site was awkward because of the site's steepness. There is no evidence of a formal route through the City of David, though this southern approach was the main pilgrim approach in most periods. Perhaps because the ridge was constrained and the area heavily built-up, site conditions made a processional way impossible, unlike Petra and Palmyra. Two other urban factors should be noted. First, for the last century or so of the temple's existence, the nearest equivalent of a cardo, the north–south street down the Tyropoeon Valley, slid beside the temple and almost ignored it. Second, possibly as early as the Hasmonean period there was an east–west bridge across the Tyropoeon Valley, which led into the temenos, though it was not on the axis of the naos. It was a curiosity of Jerusalem's temple that though it had a number of entrances the city was not laid out so as to lead worshippers inevitably and directly to the temple. It had only indirect and minor entrances from the adjacent main street near the western wall; the major entrances were on the south or south-west, and across the bridge. Unlike Caesarea Maritima, which also put all the emphasis on one central sanctuary, the street pattern did not focus on the temple. So pilgrim progress towards the sanctuary was less a matter of moving along a processional way than a movement towards the sanctuary from wherever in the city or outside it one began one's approach.

Yet Jerusalem's pilgrim approach was still impressive, especially once one gained the southern plaza. It compared to anything one might find elsewhere in the Roman world, including the Near East. While the structures were austere, their effect was not. From the plaza the mass of the temenos wall rose above and in front, almost 50 m above ground level at its highest point at the south-eastern corner. The retaining wall enclosing the temenos had two registers; the lower portion (up to temenos level) was constructed of massive ashlars in uniform courses 1.1 m high, with some stones being up to 10 m long (the longest was 12.1 m long) and 2.5 m wide, among the largest building stones of antiquity; the walls' thickness was 4.6 m. In this lower register, each stone had a well-defined recessed border 10 to 20 cm wide with the chisels' tooth-marks carefully at right angles to the edge. The central panel (or boss) had a lightly pebbled pattern that contrasted subtly with the borders. Each course of ashlars was set slightly (1–2 cm) behind the previous course, so that the whole wall had a very slight inward slope or batter. The stones were set without mortar, using metal anchors to minimize movement. The upper register, the peribolos wall of the temenos, was modulated with pilasters and recesses, constructed from smaller ashlars than the lower register. This gave a contrasting effect to the two registers, the lower essentially horizontal in character and the upper strongly vertical. That the contrast was a basic design decision is clear, for it was also used in almost identical fashion in the Haram al-Khalil in Hebron – the Tomb of the Patriarchs and Matriarchs – and in a form without the lower register in the Memorial to Abraham at Mamre, both Herodian structures; this claim has no firm support, but the similarities leave most scholars in no doubt of their common origins.

Because of the importance of purity in the temple cult, mikvaoth (ritual bathing pools) were set into the plaza at the top of the broad set of steps south of the temenos wall, along with shops and other structures. The plaza and stairs assisted in handling the large crowds on major festival days. The foundation wall on the south was punctured by two sets of large doors, the Huldah Gates, which led into finely decorated tunnels, whose ceilings were constructed with monolithic stone slabs, domed and decorated, not unlike the ceilings of the double adyton in the Temple of Bel in Palmyra. Fragments may be found in several museums (drawings and photographs in Shanks, *Jerusalem*, 144–5). The tunnels had no natural light; they ran level under the Royal Basilica and then rose up to the temenos by monumental stairs.

When this dramatic approach emerged in the temenos, the first thing one saw was the side elevation of the naos. This was similar to the first impression on entering the main temenos in Petra or in Palmyra. The Jerusalem naos was, however, less obvious than those. In the Sanctuary of Bel at Palmyra one saw the naos itself with its peripteral columns and monumental doorway, and in front of it on one side the altar and dining room, on the other the pool, In the Sanctuary of Dushara at Petra one saw the great altar and a portion of the naos. In Jerusalem one saw a barrier, steps and walls of the inner courtyards, and above and behind those the largely undecorated walls of the naos. The main elements were still hidden.

The temenos was surrounded with a peristyle, like the sanctuaries of Bel and Nebo at Palmyra, Artemis in Gerasa, the Great Temple and (in a different form) Dushara at Petra. Like some of those others, it was double width with a central line of columns on three sides. The Jerusalem sanctuary differed, however, in that the south side of the temenos was occupied by the Royal Basilica, the largest basilica in the Roman world, with 162 columns supporting a clerestory roof over a building about 250 m long (Josephus, *War* 5.184–227; cf. *Ant.* 15.380–425 on the sanctuary as a whole). Its main activities are debatable and details of its design are uncertain. Its north wall may have been open to complete the peristyle (*Ant.* 15.411–16), which might then have implications for how it was used. Of its immense size and quality there is little doubt, to judge from the literary accounts and a few fragments that may have survived, some from the Nea Church, south-west of the temple mount. It has been suggested that the layout and spacing of the columns in the Islamic Museum in the Haram al-Sharif correspond so closely to the column layout of the Royal Basilica (that is, they stand on foundations from the Royal Basilica) that, when extended across the temenos, they would show the pattern for the whole 162 columns.

The architectural character of the sanctuary as a whole was mixed: the peristyle and the Royal Basilica were strongly Roman, while the central naos and its appurtenances together with the effect of the exterior retaining walls and peribolos wall were typically Near Eastern. The composition of the elements was complex: a very high and austere naos rose above subordinate elements within a colonnade that surrounded a very large temenos; the massive volume of the Royal Basilica on the south was balanced on the north by the higher but less massive Antonia Fortress with its four towers. If these impressionistic comments, which depend upon literary descriptions of the structures, are correct, the whole sanctuary created a more dynamic balance than the static arrangements inside the sanctuaries of Bel at Palmyra and Artemis at Gerasa; in both the latter the most dynamic elements were found in the processional ways. Without a true processional way, Jerusalem's greatest sense of excitement was inside the temenos.

Traffic flowed in a variety of directions from the ten gates or entrances, with most traffic oriented to the holy place. The Jerusalem temple differed significantly from most other sanctuaries, which were usually entered formally from the front. A few, though, had entrances from other directions: the Temple of Jupiter in Damascus had four main entrances with two concentric courtyards, the Temple of Roma and Augustus at Caesarea could be approached from four directions, the Temple of Nebo had several minor doors. The Jerusalem temple was approachable from all sides with more than one gate from three sides.

Only the north wall had one entrance. The east wall had two, one at temenos level in the south-east corner and the Golden Gate, which may have connected with a bridge across the Kidron Valley. The most heavily used approaches would have been from west and south, where the city lay. The south wall had the two double Huldah Gates at the plaza. The west wall had five entrances: three at street level and two at temenos level; the most commonly used approach was probably the bridge across the Tyropoeon Valley from the elite houses and Royal Palace on the western hill, which carried an aqueduct bringing water for the needs of the sacrificial cult, as well. This route also served as the main ceremonial entrance for visitors (Richardson, *Herod*, 15–18). High vaulted overpasses at the two southern corners were visually bolder than the bridge. They brought visitors and pilgrims out of the temenos and down monumental stairs to the level of the streets below. These various entrances and exits reflected the amount of traffic from each direction and imply how people actually approached the sanctuary, but they were also symbolic of the temple's approachability, standing at the metaphorical centre of Jerusalem and of the world Jewish community. The Mishnah's description gives the sense but is not accurate archaeologically:

> There were five gates to the Temple Mount: the two Huldah Gates on the south, that served for coming in and for going out; the Kiponius Gate on the west, that served for coming in and going out; the Tadi Gate on the north, which was not used at all; the Eastern Gate, on which was portrayed the Palace of Shushan. Through this the High Priest that burned the [Red] Heifer, and the heifer, and all that aided him went forth to the Mount of Olives. (*Mishnah Middoth* 1.3)

The rock of Mount Moriah (traditionally where Abraham was to sacrifice Isaac) poked through the temenos in the centre. Constructing a smaller and higher plaza for the naos minimized the problem but did not solve it completely, for the highest point of the rock protruded as it still does in the Dome of the Rock. How exactly this was handled in the temple's design is disputed, with three main solutions proposed: the rock (1) was under the Holy of Holies, (2) was under the altar or (3) simply stuck out south of the naos. Each solution demands a different proposed siting of the naos with its related structures. Whatever the correct solution, the effect of the naos on a raised platform within a large temenos raised high above the surrounding landscape was impressive and awe-inspiring. It must have been unforgettable.

There was another site-related difficulty. The temenos axis was north–south, consistent with a southern entry from the City of David and the stairs from the Huldah Gates. But the holy place – the naos with its attached structures – was on an east–west axis, with the main door facing east in traditional fashion. None of the gates into the temenos were on the axis of the naos, regardless of which solution is adopted to the problem noted in the previous paragraph. The Golden Gate in the east wall was north of the axis; the gate at the bridge on the west (Wilson's arch) was south of the axis. No gate gave an axial view of the naos; the oblique views from all gates were late Hellenistic in geometry and design.

The multiplicity of entrances into the temenos was mirrored by a multiplicity of gates (the Mishnah says thirteen) through another barrier, the soreg. This barrier combined a low wall with steps up to the higher plaza. Each gate in the wall had a sign that warned non-Jews to stay within the outer courtyard, the Court of Gentiles: 'Foreigner, do not enter within the grille and the partition surrounding the temple. He who is caught will have only himself to blame for his death.' One complete and one partial inscription have been discovered.

Once through the soreg, the next level of holiness was the Court of Women, surrounded by high walls. The functional problem of two conflicting axes had to be resolved architecturally, and the literary descriptions of the Court of Women, which suggest it was bilaterally symmetrical, imply that this was where attention was redirected towards the approach to the altar and the holy place at the west of the naos. Nicanor's Gate – the eastern doorway into the women's court – was particularly important; it had Corinthian cast bronze doors, the delivery of which (by boat) eventually attracted legends. This may have been a preferred entrance door for males bringing sacrifices, but possibly all doors might be used. In any case, Nicanor's Gate (even with its architectural, visual and legendary emphasis) was not a satisfying solution to the transition from one axis to another. These architectural issues paralleled those at Palmyra and Petra; Jerusalem's solution was no more successful. In fact, the ambiguity was more acute from the bridge entrance, for it required a 180-degree turn.

There was yet another rise in level up to the Court of Israel, reserved for Jewish males. Only at this point did the sacrificial structures become visible. The altar to the left and the laver to the right were arranged as in the Temple of Bel at Palmyra (though Bel's were visible from everywhere in the temenos), and Jerusalem had no similar provision for leading sacrificial animals to the altar. Maybe no ramp was needed, since worshippers brought their own sacrificial victims with them. Nineteenth-century explorations below the surface recorded a tunnel in the bedrock on a diagonal from the Tadi Gate on the north to the Court of the Priests. Its purpose is unclear, but it is not likely that it was a route for sacrificial animals. These underground features, especially those with an architectural character, incidentally, bear on the question of the location of the naos and its design.

The naos was a somewhat prosaic structure architecturally, except for its height and its severe geometry. It is known only from texts and later depictions on coins, mosaics, frescoes and architectural fragments (and perhaps also ossuaries). The earliest and most directly relevant are representations of the naos on coins of the Bar Kochba Revolt; while their relevance and accuracy is debated they suggest that the façade of the temple was tetrastyle, with four columns across its porch, like the Great Temple and the Temple of Dushara at Petra. Frescoes at Dura Europos and mosaics in synagogues are later and less reliable. The front elevation was made wider by wings extending beyond the side-walls of the naos. Like both Palmyrene and Petran structures, it was probably adorned with crow-step merlons around the eaves. Like them also, it had a flat roof, whose purpose is uncertain though there is a coherent Near Eastern tradition of access to the roof by stairs contained within the walls. The naos was richly embellished, according to the literary accounts partly in gold.

The sequence of cultic spaces was carefully thought out. Seven areas were architecturally defined, though the architectural and functional definitions of the spaces did not always correspond: the Court of Gentiles, the soreg/parapet, the Court of Women, the Court of Israel, the Court of Priests, the Holy Place and the Holy of Holies. The ancient texts mandated most of these, but the Court of Women and the Court of Gentiles seem to have been innovations by Herod. These innovations may be important indicators of Herod's response to changes in Jewish society in the first century BCE. It is easy to see how the Court of Gentiles responded to the large numbers of non-Jews interested in Judaism; it is less easy to understand the social realities behind the Court of Women.

Despite reports of fine finishes, the temple's overall effect was architecturally restrained. Its dramatic effect was created mainly by its site, scale, size of the elements – especially the extremely large stones that were used in its construction – and quality of its interior finishes. Yet for all its openness to pilgrims and visitors it may still have had a somewhat dour aspect when compared with the variety of effects in Artemis's approach, the richness of Bel's Propylaea set within its temenos wall, the impact of the landscaped paradeisos beside the Great Temple at Petra (there was no landscaping in the Jerusalem temple) or various baroque elements noted earlier.

Though religiously the centre of the city, in fact the temple was off to one side. It was visible from virtually anywhere in the city, not because it lay at the end of a cardo but by its sheer bulk and height. There were no rivals for religious attention in this monotheistic city, so that even though it was not at the highest point of the city, at the end of a processional way or even at the centre of the street pattern, it still was the singular religious focus of the city, to which everything else was subordinated.

Other civic structures

Antonia Fortress

Despite this last comment Jerusalem had two other minor foci; the Antonia Fortress north of the temple emphasized the military, and Herod's palace emphasized kingship (as did the Royal Basilica). The fortress was among Herod's earliest works (mid-30s BCE), since it could not have been so named after Mark Antony's defeat and death. The remains are paltry: a cistern, a few architectural pieces and perhaps parts of its wall in the south wall of the al-Omariyah School overlooking the Haram al-Sharif. Josephus's description (*War* 5.238–46) does not settle debates over its size and exact location. He describes it as a hollow square with towers marking each corner, the south-eastern tower being the highest. It may have been an intentional part of the composition of the temple that pilgrims entering the temenos through the Huldah Gates saw this tower rising above and behind the naos of the temple.

Josephus emphasizes that the Antonia fortress was connected directly to the temple so that soldiers could enter the temple courtyard from the Antonia via stairs to the colonnades.

Palace

The third monumental focus in the city was Herod's palace, with twin wings named after Caesar Augustus and Marcus Agrippa (perhaps 130 m by 330 m), on the west side of town where there were other elite houses. Only a few remains survive in the Armenian Gardens and the Citadel (Tushingham, *Excavations*, passim): subterranean vaults visible in the courtyard of the Citadel and the lines of some walls, but not enough for even a sketchy reconstruction. It was memorable, according to Josephus's glittering description (*War* 5.156–83), for its gardens, colonnades and pools, as well as for its reception rooms, guest rooms and banqueting halls. It may have been that functional and ceremonial demands created by the new palace prompted a major east–west street just inside the walls parallel to the line of today's David Street, which served as a formal way to the temple for dignitaries, dropping slowly down towards the Tyropoeon Valley as David Street still does today and then linking up with the bridge over the valley that led into the temple courtyard.

There were three large towers, near but independent of earlier Hasmonean towers at the present Citadel and Jaffa Gate. In their Hasmonean guise they were primarily for defence; in their Herodian form they were partly defensive and partly, as Josephus emphasizes, to provide living quarters that were incorporated into the upper levels, similar to Herodian towers in other locations, such as the east tower in the Palace-Villa at Herodium. From the top of the tallest – the solid base of which Titus allowed to remain standing at the time of the city's destruction in 70 CE as a kind of 'memorial' – there would have been a spectacular view of the city, especially the temple and the Antonia fortress, and of the countryside south of Jerusalem.

Theatre and hippodrome

Herod built two (or possibly three) buildings for entertainment, probably a theatre and a hippodrome (Richardson, *Herod*, 186–9), neither inside the city. The location of the theatre (Josephus, *Ant.* 15.268–91), though largely forgotten, was established in the nineteenth century a little more than a kilometre south of the southern wall of the city; its cavea faced north, taking advantage of a broad view of the city's skyline. This location reduced objections among observant Jews. The hippodrome (Josephus, *Ant* 15.268; cf. *War* 2.44; *Ant.* 17.255) was located south-west of the city for the same reasons, but its location – probably just beyond the railway station – has never been found. These structures normally had religious implications and associations; Jewish authorities thought that Herod had offended against religious dictates simply by their presence and their decoration, though Josephus suggests that nothing was religiously offensive.

Water

Water supply was always an issue. The main aqueduct to the city (which came in at too low a level to supply Herod's palace) originated at Solomon's Pools, between Bethlehem and Hebron. The aqueduct was a complex system – tunnel, open channel, covered channel and raised channel – that followed in large part the contours. When it reached Jerusalem it came around the sides of the Hinnom Valley, the south end of the western hill, the west side of the Tyropoeon Valley and then across the bridge into the temple temenos. There is neither textual nor archaeological evidence of a nymphaeum, possibly because of pagan associations of 'nymphs'. There were also a number of major reservoirs around the city's perimeter, among which the Serpent's Pool, the Mamillah Pool, Hezekiah's Pool, the Sheep Pool, the Pool of Israel, and the Siloam Pool were the most important. All but the last were collection reservoirs; only the Siloam pool had a supply of fresh running water.

Housing

Residences of Jerusalem's wealthy elite in the pre-70 period have been excavated: the quality of life equalled that in other Near Eastern cities. The ones known best were on the western hill overlooking the temple mount. One particularly impressive two-storey house would have had an impressive view of the bridge, western wall, Robinson's arch, and silhouette of the temple (Avigad, *Herodian Quarter*). The layout revolved around a large central courtyard, from which the various areas of the house radiated. Its large size (600 square m), beautifully plastered walls and ceilings, frescoes and high quality furnishings still give a sense of gracious living. Religion permeated this and other domestic structures; this one had half a dozen mikvaoth and the earliest known representation of the temple's menorah. A nearby house had a finely detailed late-Hellenistic peristyle courtyard, with handsome Corinthian capitals and imported marble opus sectile paving.

Necropolis

Jerusalem's tombs provide some of the most powerful insights into Jerusalem in this period, paralleling both Palmyra and Petra but contrasting in form with their tombs. The tombs were rock-cut with the main functional element being the loculus (niche) or arcosolium (bench with arch), in which an individual body was buried. They too offered the impression of a kind of extended family, of course without the portraits that were common in Palmyra. Burial practices differed in another way: during the late first century BCE and first century CE burials were carried out in two stages, primary burial in the loculi and secondary burial a year later in ossuaries (bone-boxes; Rahmani, *Ossuaries*). This efficient method allowed the tombs to remain somewhat smaller than they might otherwise have been.

The necropolis surrounded the city, with the prime locations being east and south of the temple mount, where many tombs looked straight towards the holiest site in Judaism (Avigad and Geva, 'Tombs', in 'Jerusalem', 747–57). On the east side of the

Kidron Valley, several outstanding tomb monuments showed diverse influences. Zechariah's tomb had a bold pyramidal roof (a 'nefesh'), cavetto moulding (similar to Petra's tombs) and cubic base decorated with Ionic half-columns. The tomb of the Bene Hezir had a simple Doric façade (mid-first century BCE). The tomb of Absalom was topped by a delicately concave conical roof sitting on a drum, which sat on a square base with cavetto cornice over a Doric frieze atop Ionic engaged half-columns (first century CE). At the junction of the Kidron and Hinnom Valleys to the south were the Akeldama tombs (Avni and Greenhut, *Akeldama Tombs*). So important was the temple connection that details in the rock-cut tombs and ossuaries sometimes mimicked the temple details (details of masonry, doors, monolithic ceilings (cf. the Huldah Gates) , perhaps even the façade of the naos). To the west of the old city were Jason's tomb, another Egyptianizing tomb with a pyramidal roof and a single Doric column in the porch (early first century BCE); the Sanhedrin tombs, with various motifs including a porch decorated with acroteria and a pediment that was filled with acanthus leaves and fruit (first century CE). The so-called 'Herod's family tomb' near the King David Hotel looked across the Hinnom Valley to Herod's palace; the complex structure had a burial cave, closed by a rolling stone, with what may have been a pyramidal nefesh. Herod's family tomb, however, was more likely a circular monument north of the Damascus Gate (late first century BCE; Netzer, 'Remains') built in *opus reticulatum* that recalled other circular tombs such as Herodium, Herod's own mausoleum, and the Mausoleum of Augustus in Rome.

Jerusalem's largest tomb was that of Queen Helena and her son Izates of Adiabene, converts to Judaism (50s CE). A 9 m-wide stair led down to a massive door and into a sunken courtyard (26 m by 27 m by 8.5 m deep). It was decorated on ground level with three pyramids (Josephus, *Ant.* 20.95); under the three monuments – no doubt representing her and her two sons – on the west side of the courtyard was a porch with a two-columned façade supporting a Doric frieze above an architrave with carved leaves. The burial chambers, a complex series of interconnected rooms, were entered past a rolling stone.

Synagogue

Sometime in the early first century CE there must have been at least one synagogue, perhaps more. The one essential piece of data comes from the Theodotos inscription, recently discussed from an epigraphic perspective (Kloppenborg Verbin, 'Dating Theodotos'). Three points seem certain: it was a built structure, it predated the destruction of the temple and it was located in the City of David. It may well be that there were a number of other synagogues in Jerusalem, as the literary evidence suggests, but nothing can be said of them.

Aelia Capitolina

The Roman gate at today's Damascus Gate was built in the 40s CE. By that period there was a cardo along the east side of the Tyropoeon Valley, and there probably was one along the west side of it as well, originally running just inside the line of a hypothesized north–south wall. After the two destructions of Jerusalem (70 and 135 CE) the ruins were gradually covered over by Roman rebuilding of the refounded Aelia Capitolina, but there was no wholesale replanning of the city; Aelia's main streets followed the same lines though they were more formal (Kenyon, *Digging up Jerusalem*, ch. 14). After 135, a large new semicircular plaza was created just inside the Damascus Gate, centred around a tall column topped by a statue of Hadrian; both branches of the cardo ran south from the plaza, solving neatly the functional and planning problem created by the meeting of the two streets at such an acute angle, though without the elegance and rationale of the Oval Piazza at Gerasa. Because the northern parts of the city (including Bezatha) had now been included within walls and because much of the southern part of the city either had been destroyed or was occupied by Romans – perhaps by the legionary camp – the city's centre of gravity shifted north-west. A new southern wall was built more or less on the line of the present south wall of the old city, perhaps towards the end of the third century CE.

Aelia was deliberately turned from a monotheistic city that

venerated the God of Israel to a pagan city with several cult sites, with Jews forbidden to enter the city. The Temple of Aphrodite rose above the west branch of the cardo in the same way that the Temples of Artemis and Dionysus did at Gerasa, connected to the street with a monumental stair. A small Temple of Jupiter stood approximately on the site of the earlier Jewish naos, which had been destroyed in 70 CE; in front of it was another statue of Hadrian. Few details are known about either sanctuary. A Temple of Asklepios was located immediately north of the temple mount in part of the area around the Pool of Bethesda (or Sheep Pool); archaeological investigations have found a building with mosaic floor and a group of subterranean caves just east of the double pool; it could date even prior to the destruction of Jerusalem in 70 CE. A market area was north of the rock outcropping on which the Antonia fortress had sat (also destroyed in the siege in 70 CE); it was entered through a monumental gate on the west, parts of which are incorporated today in a monastery and adjacent arch over the modern street. Aelia's forum, also with a monumental arch, was south of the Temple of Aphrodite.

The city was reshaped in this period, but how extensively is uncertain. The city's centre was neither the temple nor the combination of the temple, fortress and palace, for none of these existed. Instead Aelia revolved around the circular plaza with Hadrian's column, the forum with its monumental gate, the Temple of Jupiter and the Temple of Aphrodite, with Asklepios being a minor site to one side. The site of Herod's palace may have contained the Tenth Legion's camp (but that is now disputed), where one of the three large Herodian towers was left as a reminder of the city's strength. Much of the previous city, especially on the south, was eradicated through Roman quarrying and reuse of materials.

Our knowledge of Aelia is limited by the intensity of subsequent building in the Byzantine, Arab, Crusader and following periods. The character of the structures, however, seems more modest than we have seen in the other cities from approximately the same period, especially Gerasa and Palmyra. There is little reason to think anything in Aelia had similarly baroque elements. And this may have been true of earlier Herodian-period Jerusalem as well.

Byzantine Jerusalem

Jerusalem was again reshaped following Constantine's conversion and assumption of power. The forked north–south cardo was retained and colonnaded, remains of the south-west portion can be seen below the modern street level. The plan continued to follow the general lines of Aelia Capitolina, although the city expanded southwards once again, occupying more or less the same areas as in the first century CE. The centre of gravity lay along the west branch of the cardo, and especially on the site of the previous Temple of Aphrodite (both it and the Temple of Jupiter were destroyed at Constantine's request). Since nothing was built to replace the Temple of Jupiter on the temple mount, it lay vacant. For the next three centuries Jerusalem became a city dominated by its churches (Mare, *Archaeology*, ch. 9 for plans and list).

- The destroyed Temple of Aphrodite was replaced with the large Church of the Holy Sepulchre (326–35 CE), a combination of basilica and circular memorial on two sides of a central courtyard; they marked Jesus' places of execution and burial. The church was approached from the cardo, up steps as in the previous Temple of Aphrodite, and through an atrium.
- The Church of the Apostles (fourth century CE), later associated with the upper room and the Basilica of the Holy Zion, lay south of Herod's palace.
- St Stephen's Church occupied a site just north of the Damascus Gate that was traditionally associated with the place of Stephen's stoning (439 CE).
- The Church of St Menas (on the site of the Armenian Cathedral of St James) was named after an Egyptian martyr (444 CE).
- The Empress Eudokia built the Siloam Church (*c.*450 CE) over the Siloam Pool at the south end of the Tyropoeon Valley.
- A Church of the Paralytic (mid-fifth century CE) and then the Church of the Nativity of Mary replaced the Cult of Asklepios north of the Haram al-Sharif. The site was associated with the birthplace of Mary and the home of her parents, Joachim and Anna.

- The Church of St John the Baptist (mid-fifth century CE) was just south of the Holy Sepulchre.
- Justinian built a very large Nea Church with triple nave at the south end of the cardo (543 CE).
- The Basilica of St Peter Gallicantu ('cock crowing') was built on the remains of a monastery (sixth century CE) on the south-east slope of the western hill, over first-century houses claimed as the site of Caiaphas's house.
- The Church of St Sophia was east of the eastern cardo, below the Herodian temenos wall.
- The Church of Our Lady of the Spasm lay just west of the agora.
- On the Mount of Olives were:
  The Eleona Church (before 333 CE);
  Lazarus Church at Bethany (before 390 CE).
  The Church of the Ascension (before 392 CE);
  The Tomb of the Virgin in the Garden of Gethsemane (before late sixth century CE).
- Elsewhere in the city:
  A church under the Monastery of the Cross (fifth century CE).
  Ein Kerem Church, traditionally associated with the parents of John the Baptist (fifth century CE)

This orgy of church-building changed the face of Jerusalem, wiping out or transforming most traces of Roman religion. The spate of church-building had an effect similar to that at Gerasa, though Gerasa's churches were almost as numerous as Jerusalem's and more compactly located. The main circulation routes in Jerusalem were altered as a result of the new dominance of Christian sanctuaries. The street through the market area just north of the Haram became a major link between the city and the holy places on the Mount of Olives. The western cardo now joined the Church of the Holy Sepulchre, the Nea Church and the structures on Mount Zion. The street pattern revolved around an offset or jogged east–west road and a bifurcated north–south road. The general situation, especially the dominance of the two branches of the cardo, was reflected in the famous Madaba map of the sixth century, possibly from the time of Justinian.

Arab Jerusalem

In the early Arab period, following Islam's rapid advance, the city was reshaped again, with another set of shifts in the locations of religious sites. The centre of gravity moved decisively back to its previous location and to the areas south of the Haram al-Sharif. The reason for this was, of course, that what had been the temple mount became the third-holiest Muslim site, with the justly celebrated Dome of the Rock (688–91 CE), one of the noblest structures ever built, marking the site of Muhammad's ascent to heaven. At the south end of the Haram, where Herod's Royal Basilica had been, the al-Aqsa Mosque was constructed a few years later (705–15 CE). The whole area was surrounded once again with a series of structures, including colonnades and schools. Large multi-storeyed palaces occupied the areas south of the temenos.

While some Christian buildings were taken over, others remained in use during the Umayyad period, so that the city came close to having two virtually superimposed religious communities, with Christians mainly on the west and south and on the Mount of Olives, and with Muslims mostly on the east and north, the present general pattern of the city.

Conclusion

Jerusalem has been a monotheistic city for most of three millennia, with only a 250-year period when it was a polytheistic Roman city. One might have thought that it would have been the most stable of cities in terms of its plan and centre of gravity. In fact Jerusalem has undergone more radical changes than other comparable cities in the same region: from a Jewish royal city to a Roman city to a Christian pilgrimage city to the third-holiest site in Islam to a Christian Crusader state and then to Islamic dominance again. The city has been wrenched this way and that during the expansions and contractions and changes in status throughout the periods considered in this book, despite the fact (1) that the core of the city remained relatively constant and (2) that the city's raison d'être, the Rock of Mount Moriah, has continuously been within the walls.

The other cities examined above (Chapters 2 to 5) have all been superseded in the ebb and flow of civilizations; all four have been deserted, with only small and essentially unrelated towns beside – or at Gerasa partly on top of – the ancient city. The continuous occupation of Jerusalem, with what is today an even more important city atop the earlier remains, in part explains the difficulty in describing accurately the structures of the ancient city and their character.

Like Palmyra, especially, Jerusalem had a clear separation between the living and dead, with the necropolis ringing the city and with the most desirable sites for burial being those that were in direct visual contact with the holy place on the eastern ridge. While Jerusalem's necropolis was separated from the habitable areas, the connections between its burials and the central religious site were more than merely proximate visual links; both tombs and ossuaries sometimes had visual symbols of the temple in the Jewish period, so that the dead were as close as possible to the sanctuary itself, both geographically and iconographically.

The fabric of the city itself changed so often that it is impossible to attribute a single continuous character to its structures. Before 70 CE the city's character was opulent but restrained. While there was a strong presence of Hellenistic and Roman elements, still seen in the remains of the tombs that have survived, the city as a whole did not have the character of a pervasively Romanized city. Some buildings such as Herod's palace, of which we have almost no evidence, were probably strongly Roman. The architectural balance between Roman and indigenous elements seen in the surviving tombs was seen just as clearly in the temple, it seems. In the tombs, the mixture is still clear: juxtaposition of classical orders (Ionic, Doric) under Arabian or Egyptian cavetto cornice, topped by pyramids. In the temple, the juxtaposition is more speculative: Roman colonnades surrounded an essentially Near Eastern naos physically arranged within the temenos in an unusual way. The history of such a mixture may have been lengthy, though this cannot be established certainly: it may be that the combination of Hasmonean palace and xystos on the slopes of the western hill may already have had this mixed quality. In this respect, then, Jerusalem shared the character of Palmyra and Petra, cities where the indigenous elements matched or exceeded imported Greek and Roman details. Certainly Jerusalem had some of the cultural expressions of the Roman world: theatre, stadium, colonnades, basilica, for example, but no nymphaeum or bath, it seems. The Roman elements were subsumed within the traditional character of the city: a non-Roman street layout (except perhaps in some northerly parts), a closed yet open sanctuary, its unusual way of relating sanctuary and city.

A comparison of Caesarea and Jerusalem in the early Roman period suggests a significant similarity. The same patron planned one from scratch and extensively changed the other. Both were 'monotheistic' cities. Jerusalem was explicitly so, of course, and it seems certain there were no rival religions at least in the Herodian period. Caesarea was implicitly so, for there is no evidence either literary or archaeological of other sanctuaries or cult centres in Caesarea during Herod's lifetime (see Chapter 5 above). All the evidence of other religions comes later. The aspect of this that is important is that the one expressed Herod's Jewish religion, his 'piety' and his dedication to the God of Israel; the other expressed Herod's *realpolitik*, his participation in the imperial cult and his devotion to his patron Augustus in Rome. If this general assessment of the character of the two cities is correct, it would suggest that Herod saw no contradiction in these two religious convictions – two contrasting and as we would think conflicting forms of monotheism. Herod seems to have held both without tensions between them. To express both seemed natural, for he was both 'King of the Jews and Friend of the Romans' (Richardson, *Herod*, passim).

In the late-Roman period, the city may have seemed more typically Roman, through its refounding by Hadrian, the creation of several important sanctuaries to traditional Roman gods and the inclusion of a forum with monumental gate. This soon changed again in the early-Byzantine period, when the Roman temples were destroyed and new churches built all over the city. And when Islam took over Jerusalem, its relatively tolerant approach to Christianity showed in the parallel developments within some parts of the city, so that there was an almost formal expression of the rivalry of the two religions.

Table 6.1 Jerusalem chronology

Building of second temple	about 515 BCE
Hasmonean period	
Gymnasium/Xystos	early 2nd c. BCE
Hasmonean walls	mid-2nd c. BCE
Hasmonean towers at citadel	late 2nd c. BCE
Hasmonean extensions to temple	late 2nd c. BCE
Hasmonean palace	late 2nd c. BCE
Stone chamber (council?) below bridge	2nd–1st c. BCE
Zechariah's Tomb	late 2nd c. BCE
Tomb of Jason	early 1st c. BCE
Hezir family tomb	early 1st c. BCE
Herodian period	
Antonia Fortress	37–35 BCE
Herodian additions (second wall)	late 1st c. BCE
Hasmonean palace rebuilt	mid-30s BCE
Towers of Mariamme, Hippicus, Phasael	mid-30s BCE
Herod's family tomb	late 30s BCE
Theatre	about 30 BCE
Hippodrome	about 30 BCE
Herod's Palace	23 BCE
Rebuilding of temple	23–15 BCE and up to the 60s CE
Absalom's Tomb	late 1st c. BCE/early 1st c. CE
Theodotos Synagogue	early 1st c. CE
Damascus Gate	40s CE, rebuilt 135 CE
Third wall	40s CE, 60s CE
Queen Helena's Tomb	50s CE

Roman period

Asklepieion	late 1st/early 2nd c. CE
Market and arch	early 2nd c. CE
Triumphal arch and forum	early 2nd c. CE
Semicircular plaza at Damascus Gate	early 2nd c. CE
Temple of Jupiter	early–mid-2nd c. CE
Temple of Aphrodite	early–mid-2nd c. CE

Byzantine period

Church of the Holy Sepulchre	326–35 CE
Eleona Church	before 333 CE
Lazarus Church	before 390 CE
Church of the Ascension	before 392 CE
Church of the Apostles/Church of the Holy Zion	4th c. CE?
St Stephen's Church	439 CE
Church of St Menas	444 CE
Siloam Church (by Empress Eudokia)	about 450 CE
Church of St John the Baptist	mid-5th century CE
Church of the Paralytic (Nativity of Mary)	mid-5th century CE
Church at Monastery of the Cross	5th century CE
Ein Kerem Church	5th century CE
Nea Church (by Justinian)	543 CE
St Peter Gallicantu ('cock crowing')	6th century CE
Tomb of the Virgin	before late 6th c. CE
St Sophia	(?)
Church of Our Lady of the Spasm	(?)
Western cardo	early 6th c. CE
Persian Conquest	614 CE

Muslim period

Muslim Conquest	638 CE
Dome of the Rock	688–91 CE
Al-Aqsa Mosque	709–15 CE

7

Urban design, architecture and religion

Religious expression

Human settlements typically expressed religious aspirations and affiliations more clearly in the pre-modern period than they do in the modern period, often in ways that have given an impression of a religion's domination of village, town or city. For most of recorded history societies and their civic forms have been shaped by religion. The architecture of religious structures has been at the heart of aesthetic expression, highlighting both consciously and unconsciously the nature of the society and exposing its values. The underlying premise of this study is that careful attention to the architecture and urban design of cities, especially religious structures, will tell modern students important things about past cultures.

Not every religious conviction has taken built form, of course, and not all those that have were intended to be deliberately 'aesthetic', but there has been a prevalent aesthetic behind most built religion. Its most basic features are a sense of aspiration, community and otherness, which alone or together result in worship of the divine. This is just as true in small rural villages as it is in major cities. It matters little whether one thinks in small scale of a Berber village with its mosque, a Talmudic village with its synagogue, an Inca town with its 'hitching place of the sun', a Buddhist village with its stupa or an early American town with its white colonial church. At a larger scale one thinks of Babylonian ziggurats, Mesopotamian or Sumerian temples, Egyptian or Greek sanctuaries, Roman or Celtic temples, Christian churches or monasteries. These may display different aesthetics, different aspirations, different communities, different hierarchical arrangements and different power relationships. But on a religious level one must notice the aspirations of the buildings, their communal roles and their concern to express publicly the gods to which the culture owes allegiance.

In the ancient world only a small percentage of the population was urbanized; the majority of people lived in rural towns and villages. I have, however, deliberately not focused on the village or town, though these smaller units of social organization were fundamentally important in understanding civilizations of the ancient world. Despite their inherent importance and interest they are less significant than larger urban centres for the theme of this book. Smaller civic units are usually more homogeneous; they show a less complex sense of the relationship between city and sanctuary, a reduced sense of dynamic competition and rivalry, a more static – but perhaps better woven – pattern of society and religion.

The cities I have focused on have a sufficient degree of religious complexity and diachronic change through successive periods that analysis and hypothesis is warranted. The more complex organization and urban forms of these larger urban conglomerations illustrate better the constant change in the intimate connections between religion and society. The urban layout changed with changing patterns of distribution both of religious and of civic buildings. Through them, the civic leaders gave point and significance to the city's built form, its urban design. There were different patterns for moving through the city, different distributions of structures, different ways to define space, different ways to carry out the functions essential to a city.

Part of what made large urban spaces complex was the variety in the types of religious structures. That variety has not been a major preoccupation in this study, but we should note some of its elements. To begin with, the ways of dealing with death and burial had religious importance, and those arrangements influenced the public image of religions. More important were major sanctuaries, one of which often dominated the city even if it did not always have sole possession of public religious affections. There might have been others, not exactly rivals in the common sense, each vying for some degree of attention. Most major sanctuaries in the ancient period should be thought of primarily as a domus dei, a house for god, where the emphasis was not on the people as much as on the proper facilities and setting for that god. How these temples related to each other in the urban fabric was important. There were also the smaller religious structures intended to foster a strong sense of community for the congregation or group; each was a domus ecclesiae, where the emphasis was not on the god – he was already present with his people – as much as on the people and their needs. In the cities we have surveyed we find such structures, though they have not been very numerous in the periods and cities we have studied: synagogues, Mithraea, churches were some examples. Perhaps surprisingly we have not found voluntary associations that built closely related types of structures, many of which had religious dimensions; the nearest we have come to these strongly communal structures were dining rooms, especially at Palmyra and Petra, in connection with tombs.

Archaeology

The material evidence has deliberately been privileged by building on the extensive archaeological investigations of the last century or more in the five cities. Others who have considered the kinds of issues studied here – classicists, architectural historians, urban historians and art historians – have often used similar evidence. Since it has been less extensively used in the study of religions of antiquity one goal is to draw historians of religion into the discussion (see the three volumes in the Religious Rivalries project, edited by Donaldson, Ascough, and Vaage). Structures for religious uses have shaped and reshaped the urban fabric; the use of archaeological data allows direct insight into the influences religion has had, and also insight into the way those influences have changed with time.

The benefit, indeed the necessity, of using archaeological evidence is readily apparent. The built evidence sometimes provides an alternative approach to that provided by the study of texts in assessing cultures of antiquity; sometimes the two may be in conflict and pose important interpretive problems; sometimes the material world permits scholars to see new relationships or ask fresh questions or revise old assumptions (Wilson and Desjardins, *Text and Artifact*). More often, the two kinds of evidence dovetail neatly. Both texts and material culture, working together, are needed to provide a full and nuanced view of antiquity. In this study, in which we have looked almost solely at the material world, we have found that a vivid picture emerges from archaeology of the Near East: the early and middle Roman periods witnessed a vital and expansive set of architectural developments focused on the urban centres of the region, as vigorous as anywhere else in the Roman world.

Near Eastern context

These Levantine developments were part of the prosperity and peace that began to be seen throughout the Mediterranean world in the last quarter of the first century BCE. The turbulence of the previous couple of decades, the 40s and 30s BCE (and beyond that to the time of Marius and Sulla), which had deeply influenced conditions and events in the Near East, came to an end. The Roman Senate's speedy recognition of Octavian as 'Augustus' in 27 BCE, with all that was entailed in that, set the Roman world on a new trajectory. Augustus's *pax romana*, of which he was so proud, created the new conditions under which the Empire would prosper and expand (Brunt and Monroe, *Res Gestae divi Augusti*).

That prosperity extended as much to cities in the Near East as elsewhere. The prerequisites for the urbanization that followed in the next century or two were the end of internal dissent, centralized power, expansion of trade, increased wealth, reawakened sense of patrons' responsibilities and a heightened emphasis on benefactions. Some aspects of the growth and developments could be seen elsewhere rather obviously: the refounding and redevelopment of Corinth as a Roman colony in 46 BCE, the growth of Ephesus following its selection by Augustus as the capital of the Province of Asia in 29 BCE or the Roman expansion of Pergamum and Athens. Though each case was different, all showed how cities of the classical Greek and Hellenistic world could absorb the new urban elements that Rome wished to foster. They also demonstrated the ways in which this could happen, including facilities for increased international trade, Roman civic life, entertainment, associations, social life and religion, including specifically the imperial cult that followed soon after 27 BCE.

In the Levant many cities had at least a superficial familiarity with late-Hellenistic urban forms, though only a limited number were actually modelled on the cities of Greece or Asia Minor, for the most part cities that had the status of polis. When the effects of the Roman peace with the increased trade and commerce that were closely bound up with it reached the Near East, as they did increasingly in the first and second centuries CE, the expansion under the new impact of Rome was felt most in those cities that were most closely tied to the traditions that went back to the Greek polis.

Romanization

Various roads were taken, from more or less willing and enthusiastic 'Romanization' to resistance. Studies such as this can help to pinpoint some of the inherent tensions that arose in this period both within and between cultures. By emphasizing the role of religion some of the dimensions of those tensions are exposed. It seems clear that we should avoid homogenizing these great cities in a banal way, as if all arose from the same set of conditions, developed as a common response to Rome's influence or expressed a common fusion of elements. Instead we should look for the exciting cross-cultural variations involving Arab, Greek, Roman, Jewish, Christian, Muslim and other influences. A wide range of variations was expressed in multiple ways in the architecture and urban planning, not surprisingly, for buildings are a primary expression of culture, seen in a blunt way in the dominance of huge projects (Bel, the Great Temple, Artemis or the temple in Jerusalem) and in more subtle ways in details, decoration and burial customs.

I have argued with the prevailing consensus that it is wrong to think of the Roman world having fixed borders, beyond which were found primarily barbarians. Boundaries were permeable routes that enhanced contact and movement. Even the well-known static 'barriers' that marked the limits of the Roman areas – and this was true also in the Levant – did not keep others out or Romans in.

I have argued against a common view – perhaps an old consensus in the process of changing – that has held that Romanization virtually obliterated indigenous religions and cultures (see now Cotton, 'Roman administration'). The view that Rome deliberately and progressively imposed its programme on all its territories is not persuasive, despite erudite efforts over the years to support it. Certainly there was a deep Roman influence, and acknowledging this is innocent enough, even if the word has overtones of a kind of de facto policy. It was patently not the case that indigenous cultures had little further influence or effect. Palmyra, Petra and Jerusalem retained their languages. In an ultimate form of resistance to Romanization, Palmyra and Jerusalem rose against Rome, though in different ways at different times. All three demonstrated lively artistic and architectural continuity with their earlier pre-Roman traditions. The continuity was at its clearest not in details but in structures of fundamental importance and significance: the naos of the main temples, buildings for death and overall design elements. Indeed, one could argue that the Roman influences were strongest only in secondary elements such as the peristyle courtyards for temples and street-related features. The evidence is mixed.

There was a more consistent Romanization in the cases of Caesarea Maritima and Gerasa, not perhaps purely Roman cities but closer approximations than the other three cities included here. The reasons for this seem straightforward. First, the cultural inheritance in both cases was not so much that of the surrounding majority population as it was connected with the refounding of the cities, initially in both cases by Seleucid monarchs who were following in the footsteps of Alexander's conquests in earlier generations. Second, in both cases there was a later refounding of the city in the first century BCE or CE (Caesarea by Herod the Great, Gerasa by some unknown process), as a result of which there was a major explosion of building projects. Third, and as a result of the first two, the populations of the two cities seem to have been made up largely of those with Greek or Roman affinities and tastes, and in many cases backgrounds. In the cases of Gerasa and Caesarea Maritima the term Romanization is not exactly the right term, since what was happening was not so much an incremental process as a single major decision, though a decision that fell on fertile ground.

It would be an oversimplification to suggest that in the cases of Palmyra, Petra and Jerusalem there was no openness towards Romanization. Each showed evidence of Rome's influences, whether cultural, architectural, religious or patterns of urbanism. But the two cases (Gerasa and Caesarea Maritima) where Roman inheritance built more directly on earlier Hellenistic patterns of design and building underscored that in the other three cases (Palmyra, Petra and Jerusalem) the process of Romanization, influential as it might have been, was partial and incomplete. Hellenism had, of course, influenced all the cities, but the degree of influence was considerably smaller in some cases. The developments of the early Roman period that might have leaned in the direction of direct Roman influence fell, in some cases, on less amenable ground.

Urbanization

The archaeological remains paint a picture of almost explosive expansion of some of the cities of the Levant between the late first century BCE and the second century CE. The cities considered above did not go through exactly the same steps in the urbanization process (to use the word a little loosely), nor did the expansion occur at precisely the same times, but the developments were comparable and involved comparable features (see Table 7.1, below). This raises the fundamental question considered in Chapter 1, above, about Romanization: Was there a central policy promoting this urban expansion and development?

The distribution of the archaeological evidence throughout the relevant periods, together with the differing administrative arrangements at the time at which urbanization takes off, implies that there was no single model and no particular guiding policy (Eck, *Lokale Autonomie*, passim). The chronology of building developments shows that Romanization had as much – probably more – to do with local goals and aspirations than with an overall empire-wide goal. Jerusalem and Caesarea were earliest in the sequence, driven self-consciously by the ambition of Herod the Great, king of Judea; his goals were to show his leadership and largesse to the Jewish people in the rebuilding and expansion of Jerusalem (30s and later BCE), and to show his adherence to Augustus and behind him the Roman people in the refounding of Caesarea (20s and later BCE). In the two cases, at almost the same time, the same patron took rather different routes, even though there were overarching similarities.

The major pieces in the urban development of Petra, likewise, occurred under local rulers who, even if their relationship to Rome cannot be certainly established, must have had effective control of the Nabatean kingdom at the time (late first century BCE through first century CE). Slightly later, Gerasa began its more deliberate Romanization in the late first century CE with its new plan, new cardo and expanded civic structures, while it was still an independent polis; the developments continued in perhaps an accelerated fashion once it was incorporated into the Province of Arabia after 106 CE. Palmyra, the latest of the five cities to spring into prominence as a major urban centre, did so mainly in the second century CE, during a transitional period of change in status; in its case too it is uncertain when it came under full Roman authority.

In four of the five cases there was fundamental redesign of the city somewhere between the late first century BCE and the early second century CE. Since the local administrative arrangements were different we should be cautious about positing centralized and centralizing causative factors in far away Rome to explain differing patterns of development. The similarities and differences among the five cities are adequately explained in their general outlines either at the local level or in terms of relations between Rome and the local ruler (e.g. Herod, Aretas IV).

At another level the explanation of the rapid urban developments depended on the prosperity and peace introduced by Augustus and continued by his successors throughout most of the next two centuries. Though attention might be directed to Trajan and Hadrian as especially instrumental in these activities, in fact this shortens the period too much and ignores the ambitions and influences of Augustus, with his seminal role in inaugurating the period of prosperity and creating conditions in which a ruler such as Herod would show his gratitude. It was during the Augustan period that Caesarea became the largest harbour on the Mediterranean with very extensive commercial and trade-related facilities, that Jerusalem became famous as a great religious centre and that Petra became one of the great ancient entrepôts.

Monumentalization

The monumentalizing of cities was a major step in the process of urbanization. Nothing emphasized this publicly as much as the construction of colonnaded streets – an innovation of the Roman Near East – that occurred throughout the period. The result is well attested archaeologically; the earliest material evidence was Herod's street along the western wall of the Jerusalem temple, where two handsome but small Doric columns still rest in situ at the north end of the street. They must have been part of Herod's colonnading of that and presumably other streets in Jerusalem. The earliest literary evidence fits well with this archaeological evidence: Josephus comments that Herod was responsible for initiating the innovation of columned paved streets about this time in Antioch (Josephus, *War* 1.425; *Ant.* 16.148, 427). By contrast, there is still neither archaeological nor literary evidence that Caesarea had colonnaded streets in the Herodian period, though it did later. At Gerasa, the south section of the cardo was colonnaded with Ionic columns in mid-century (sometime between 39 and 76 CE), the northern section later in the same century, then the south section made still more monumental in the second half of the second century. This same two-step process occurred at Petra, where the original colonnaded street, which came early in the first century CE, was redone in the second century. The colonnading of streets at Palmyra occurred in the second century in stages, with the earliest attested being the western decumanus and the western section of the cardo (an inscription of 129 CE may imply this), and the rest following over that century.

The streetscape was further monumentalized in other ways. Civic arches (sometimes memorial arches) were built in numerous locations. In Petra at the entrance to the Bab es-Siq (mid-first century CE), a little later the Trajanic arch at the Upper Market and later still the Monumental Arch in front of the Sanctuary of Dushara (possibly late second century CE). In Palmyra there were two single arches at the juncture of the theatre plaza and the cardo (mid-second century CE) and the more important wedge-shaped triple-arched Monumental Arch at the point where the cardo turned towards the Sanctuary of Bel (late second century CE). In Gerasa the dominant arch was constructed beside the hippodrome in honour of Hadrian (130 CE) and late in the same century a triple-arched entry into the Oval Piazza from the rebuilt cardo. In Jerusalem two arches were built at about the same time, one at the entrance to the forum and the other at the entrance to the market. In much the same vein, the junctions of major streets attracted the building of a tetrakionion or a tetrapylon, visible indications of the city's wealth and substance and of a growing civic concern for formal prestige in the urban layout. There was one of each at Palmyra (mid-second and late third centuries CE), one of each at Gerasa (late second and early third centuries CE), and at least one at Jerusalem and one at Caesarea. The surrounding plaza that was usually associated with the tetrakionion/tetrapylon, but not always built at the same time, contributed to the street design and sense of monumentalization.

In most cases the city had one or more nymphaea, often built on a grand scale: there were two at Caesarea Maritima (late first century CE and Byzantine period), two at Petra (both second century CE), one – the grandest of the group – at Gerasa (190–1 CE), and two or three at Palmyra (early to mid-second century CE). Jerusalem is the one city for which evidence of a nymphaeum is lacking. The major streets in most cases were also the setting for propylaeae that modulated the street's rhythm by breaking the regularity of the columns and further adding to its impressiveness. Among the more important examples of this design effect were the Propylaeae of the Great Temple and the Propylaea of the Upper Market at Petra, alongside which the five bridges across the Wadi Musa should be noted; the Propylaea of Artemis with the Propylaea Plaza at Gerasa, as well as the Propylaea of the Temple of Dionysus and, of course, the nymphaeum; the propylaea of the bath at Palmyra; the Propylaea of the Temple of Aphrodite in Jerusalem. It is worth noting that some of these had exaggerated importance because the columns were in imported materials: in the case of the bath and the tetrakionion in Palmyra in pink granite from Aswan.

In some cases we find deliberate large-scale civic efforts to enhance the visual impact of the city: the Oval Piazza at Gerasa (late first century CE) with its central altar was surely the most dramatic, but we should also recall the semicircular theatre plaza and the smaller oval plaza at Palmyra (both early second century CE), the semicircular plaza in Jerusalem at the Damascus Gate (early second century CE) and the semicircular plaza behind the stage at Caesarea Maritima (third century CE). In a category of its own, the paradeisos beside the Great Temple in Petra should be emphasized (late first century BCE) as a rare instance of a public garden. This recitation of monumental street-related structures is impressive partly because many were typically Levantine designs; others were imports from the west.

Other buildings added to the scale of civic improvements. 'Entertainment buildings' were an important element in these developments: in Jerusalem a gymnasium as early as the second century BCE and, in the first century BCE, a theatre and hippodrome; in Petra two theatres, one Roman (first century CE) the other small theatre at Sabra a Greek theatre (late first century CE?); in Caesarea Maritima a theatre and hippodrome (both first century BCE) and later an amphitheatre (first century CE), with subsequent modifications to the hippodrome and at about the same time a new hippodrome (second century CE); in Gerasa a theatre (first century CE) and an odeion (mid-second century CE), along with a third theatre for the Maioumas cult (third century CE) and a hippodrome (mid-second century/early third century CE); in Palmyra a theatre (early second century CE). The evidence for baths is less good, though each city probably had one or more: three baths are known at Gerasa, one at Palmyra, one at Petra, but at both Jerusalem and Caesarea the evidence for baths is found primarily in connection with palaces, until later.

Religion

I have emphasized the importance and the vitality of religion, especially indigenous religion. While this vitality may have faded with the length of time under Roman rule, in the cases of Palmyra, Jerusalem and Petra local religious influences remained relatively strong. The largest and most important manifestations of continuing attachments to traditional religion were the sanctuaries of Bel, Nebo, Allat and Ba'al Shamim at Palmyra; Dushara and al-'Uzza in Petra; and the God of Israel in Jerusalem, together with thin but adequate evidence for synagogues at Jerusalem, Caesarea, Palmyra and Gerasa. The cult of Maioumas in Gerasa was still active in the early Christian period and there was another Maioumas cult outside Caesarea Maritima. The deep strength of Christianity, especially in Gerasa and the surrounding regions and of course in the mother city Jerusalem, should also be viewed as a manifestation of indigenous religion, since for at least its first century or so its history was bound up with that of Judaism. The Christian evidence derived mainly from later periods associated with westernizing and then universalizing tendencies under Constantine and his successors, when what was then viewed as a new religion was given such a vivid built form.

Roman religion in its traditional forms connected with the Olympian gods was also present, though not to the extent one might have expected. Major sanctuaries were dedicated to Zeus, Dionysus and Artemis at Gerasa, as well as to Jupiter, Aphrodite and Asklepios at Jerusalem. No doubt there were a number of other smaller sanctuaries, which have left few remains but can be inferred or noticed in small finds or in the literature. The evidence for purely Roman sanctuaries that took architectural form in Petra and Palmyra and – surprisingly – Caesarea is weak though it was probably a natural tendency at the former two to accommodate traditional gods to Roman cults. It seems slightly odd that these five cities showed little interest in mystery religions: worship of Demeter and Kore was present at Sebaste and Scythopolis but not in ours; cults of Isis and Mithra may have been active, but the evidence is relatively weak except for Mithra at Caesarea Maritima.

Healing, the most popular religious activity of the Roman world, was not strongly present. While an interest in healing was found at other sites, especially the hot springs in the area (Hamath Tiberias, Hamath Gader, for example), the only sanctuary to Asklepios in our five cities was in Jerusalem, almost the last place it would be expected.

Imperial religion became important during the same period, as the process of urbanization was prominent, so it is just a little baffling that it, too, is weakly attested. Pride of place belongs to the Temple of Roma and Augustus at Caesarea Maritima (along with its sister sanctuaries at Sebaste and Panias). Herod's attention to the imperial cult was both obvious and early in its development; in both Caesarea (as well as its harbour Sebastos) and Sebaste the new names announced his intentions clearly. The presence of the imperial cult in Caesarea exposes a sharp contrast with the other sites we have surveyed. Neither archaeology nor – so far as I am aware – literary texts suggests the presence of the imperial cult at an early period in Jerusalem (which is hardly surprising), though we might realistically imagine that the later legionary camp of Legio X Fretensis would have had at least a sanctuary for the standards. There is no evidence at Gerasa throughout the whole period (which is surprising) or at Petra. The fifth of our five cities, Palmyra, had a Caesareum at an early period (first century CE?), so possibly there was an imperial cult centre at some point there; later, the so-called Camp of Diocletian had its sanctuary for the legionary standards.

These civic developments paint a single picture. While the cities varied among themselves in important ways, they shared more in common with the urbanism of the Near East than they did with cities in the western Mediterranean. Both in what they included and what they ignored, they did not easily fit the pattern of thoroughly Romanized and urbanized cities. Only Caesarea seems to have had a library (relatively late in the city's development), a common civic addition in the period. They seemed distinctively Levantine.

Cities and sanctuaries

There were dynamic relationships between sanctuaries and the cities in which they were set. Religious cults dominated cities, in sharp contrast to today's situation. The archaeology of ancient cities allows an appreciation of this dynamic relationship, but it still takes an act of the imagination to understand how important sanctuaries were in defining the cities' culture, religion and character. Some sanctuaries penetrated the fabric of the city, as if the civic machinery were geared up to promote the importance of the cult within the city. Streets and plazas and arches were laid out or redesigned in such a way as to frame or pinpoint sanctuaries. Vistas often focused on the sanctuary. From a distance major sanctuaries dominated the city: Roma and Augustus in Caesarea Maritima overlooking the harbour, the Great Temple in Petra, Artemis and Zeus in Gerasa, Bel in Palmyra and the Jewish temple in Jerusalem.

All five cities included here showed civic pride in a major sanctuary quite clearly, within the city as well as from outside. Palmyra's redesigned cardo and Monumental Arch led the worshipper to the Sanctuary of Bel, even though the cardo did not obviously lead there and the temenos was awkwardly located because of a traditional orientation. In Petra the colonnaded cardo and Monumental Arch formalized the processional way that led to the Sanctuary of Dushara, still in its original location and uncharacteristically oriented north, with the naos's axis across the processional axis. At Gerasa the Temple of Zeus also retained its original orientation though the Oval Piazza integrated it into the redesigned city in a very sophisticated way. The civic design of the great Sanctuary of Artemis emphasized its dominance by a long processional way, designed with great panache, from the east side of the city across the river that bisected it. Jerusalem's ancient sanctuary, without rivals while it stood, dominated the city from its perch on the eastern ridge; Herod extended it into the largest sanctuary in the Roman world, approachable from every direction through related civic improvements such as bridges and overpasses. Finally, Caesarea Maritima's equally dominant central sanctuary, which was approachable from all four quarters, was dedicated to Roma and Augustus and acted as the focus for both harbour and city.

Cities were not static sets of indiscriminately situated monuments but carefully thought-out places to live and work and play and worship. Much of what gave the cities their dynamic form was the magnetism of the sanctuaries. In the same way that they attracted throngs of worshippers on the great festal days – and we have good evidence of this in the case of Jerusalem, at least – they would have attracted other activities to the areas surrounding them. Nymphaea tended to be attracted to the vicinity of the major sanctuary, as at Caesarea where one was built into the platform, or in Gerasa where it was immediately beside the Artemis Propylaea, or at Palmyra where a nymphaeum was near the Temple of Nebo on the cardo. In Petra, the two nymphaea were across the street from each other, just at the point where the cardo bent and there was a clear view along it to the Sanctuary of Dushara.

Sanctuaries influenced the general sense of what were considered to be the best neighbourhoods. The best place to live in Jerusalem was on the western hill because from that vantage point one looked across the Tyropoeon Valley to the temple as well as getting the better western breezes; one wealthy house had a sketch of the menorah, a religiously significant piece of furniture in the temple, etched into the plaster. In Petra, recent excavations on es-Zantur have disclosed early elite houses overlooking the Great Temple and the Temple of Dushara. In Palmyra some of the best houses excavated to date were just below the east wall of the Bel temenos. The same influences were at work in the royal palaces. If area W at Petra, north of the wadi, was a palace, as conjectured, it looked directly at the Great Temple from beside the Temple of the Winged Lions. In Caesarea Maritima, the Promontory Palace looked across a bay at the Temple of Roma and Augustus from beside the theatre and hippodrome. At Jerusalem, the earlier Hasmonean Palace viewed the temple from the east slope of the western hill, while the Herodian Palace, a little farther west but higher up the hill, still retained direct visual contact with the temple.

Civic expressions of power are related to the above. In Jerusalem the location of the royal palace was traditionally significant; in the Iron Age, the palace was beside the temple and within the temenos, and under the Hasmoneans the palace had a kind of symbiotic relationship to the temple, though it was across the Tyropoeon Valley. Under Herod, the city had three foci: religious, military and royal. All three were clearly expressed in the city's built form as dominating structures, visible from almost anywhere in the city. In the case of Caesarea, the city's design also expressed a triple-headed dominance: the three foci were the Temple of Roma and Augustus, the Promontory Palace, and the combination of hippodrome and theatre, or perhaps we might say Roman religion, Roman power and Roman entertainment. Petra and Palmyra also must have had palaces since both were kingdoms in the early-Roman period, but they have not been certainly located so it is difficult to speculate on how royal power was expressed. If, as seems plausible, the palace in Palmyra was underneath the later Diocletian's camp on the west side of the city, two points are worth noting: that it would have balanced almost perfectly the Sanctuary of Bel on the east and that the later explicit Roman expression of power, the Camp of Diocletian, was on the same site. There was no doubt in either case about the powerful presence of religion within the urban forms. About Gerasa (a polis, not a royal city) little can be said, except to note the implicit indications of power in the sanctuaries of the Olympian gods with no monumental bouleutêrion as might be found in cities of the Aegean (though perhaps the odeion served this purpose). It is no accident that some of the cities balanced royalty and religion in the visual and symbolic expressions of power.

Change and stability

I have limited this conclusion to the development of the cities within the Roman period, mainly their high points, though such a synchronic picture might give a false impression, for cities waxed and waned. They were constantly changing, dynamic in a larger diachronic sense. Throughout the periods noted here, religion dominated the cities' functional and architectural forms. Religion and religious sanctuaries shaped the urban fabric, even more in the

Roman period than in the Hellenistic period before it or the Byzantine and Islamic periods after. One of the book's subordinate themes has thus been the interplay between change and stability.

Petra was the most stable in terms of its urban dynamic, with little change in how the city worked over a long period, ultimately traceable, I suppose, to its geographical setting at the end of the long rock fissure that provided its dramatic entrance and the bowl in which the central parts of the city were inevitably set. A fixed physical setting – and its location at one edge of Roman influence where indigenous influences remained stronger for longer? – no doubt contributed to this stability.

Caesarea Maritima, once it had been set on its new course as a planned city, developed in a stable but expanding form. The central sanctuary remained the major religious site for seven centuries, through the Byzantine period; while other features changed (e.g. the hippodrome's relocation, new walls, new administrative centre) its orientation at all periods to the harbour that was its raison d'être gave it a kind of dominant geographical rationale.

Though Gerasa's plan was relatively stable throughout the Roman period, at the transition from a late-Hellenistic city to a Roman city there had been a wholesale shift in the city's urban design, just as at the later transition point when it became Christianized there was another period of substantial change. At both points functions altered and circulation patterns had to be adapted to the new conditions.

One part of Palmyra's growth and development in the middle Roman period was related to its taking over the preeminent trading position that Petra had held earlier. The major reconfiguration of the urban layout, with its new cardo that deferred to the religious sites, was not altogether convincing. Following Zenobia's attempt to hijack the imperial throne and the city's subsequent destruction, the city's contraction created more confusion in the city plan, with a major new attraction in the city's plan in the Camp of Diocletian, at the west end.

Surprisingly, Jerusalem was the least stable in terms of the civic and religious functions. Religious changes were abrupt: from a city dominated by monotheistic Judaism it became a city with multiple

Roman temples, the distribution of which affected civic functions. After Constantine it again became a monotheistic city, a Christian one, with churches scattered throughout and no church on the original holy site, requiring more major changes in urban patterns. Later still it became a centre of Islam with two main structures on the original site, but with some Christian structures continuing to be functional for a long period.

Religion influenced urban circulation. Because the city expanded gradually in the Roman period in broad conformity with the city's character as that was set at earlier moments of refoundation, the best points at which to observe changes in patterns of use were at transition points: Hellenistic to Roman, Roman to Byzantine, Byzantine to Muslim. At those points where we have evidence, the strong pull of the sanctuaries was clear, in Palmyra and Gerasa and especially Jerusalem. Change was less discernible at Petra and Caesarea Maritima. One special aspect of this tendency was the conservatism of religious sites, not invariable but found in all five cities, through which a site was taken over and made to serve new goals, with a new rationale for continued sanctity. Occasionally there was resistance to the use of old religious sites (for example, Byzantine avoidance of the temple site in Jerusalem or major temple sites in Petra) so that the focus of the city altered. Was this, too, evidence of the importance of indigenous religion? Continuity was clear, however, in such varied instances as Muslim adoption of the temple site for the Dome of the Rock, Byzantine reuse of the Temple of Roma and Augustus in Caesarea, Christian use of the sanctuaries of Zeus and Artemis at Gerasa, and to a lesser extent in Palmyra and Petra.

Architecture, urban design and religion

The analysis of civic architecture, urban design and sanctuaries in the Roman world is a useful vehicle for interpreting larger cultural phenomena, relationships and tensions. The built forms and material remains still reflect well, even if not perfectly, ways in which cities and populations absorbed – or did not absorb – important features of the dominant culture. They reflect complementarily whether there was continued adherence to and support for indigenous religious and cultural phenomena; in some cases they provide important evidence for religious rivalry (Donaldson, *Religious Rivalries*; Ascough, *Religious Rivalries*; Vaage, *Religious Rivalries*).

Palmyra absorbed some Roman elements and details; the city fitted comfortably within the Roman world for a considerable period, but it never fully adopted Greek, the lingua franca of the Roman world, only partly accommodated its deities to the Roman pantheon and maintained strong trade connections with powers to the east. Its connections with Rome, we could say, were ambivalent. Jerusalem had had contact with the Hellenistic and Roman worlds from a relatively early period: note the use of Greek, occasional adoption of Greek or Roman institutions, a Herodian building programme that was partly inspired by late-Hellenism and Rome even if not thoroughly. But attachment to the God of Israel was an important counter-pull and that attachment acted as a brake on thoroughgoing Romanization. In fact, the competing tendencies pulled society apart through the first and early second centuries CE, with anti-Roman sentiment surging forward not once but twice. Petra retained a strong interest in its indigenous traditions through the Roman period, even though it already had been relatively accommodating to Hellenistic artistic and architectural ideals in the pre-Roman period.

Gerasa's and Caesarea's contentment under Roman rule evokes no surprise. Both become visible first as Hellenistic cities, both were refounded as Roman cities and both showed a more thorough Romanization in their urban designs. Caesarea was especially interesting because on the one hand it had a single-minded focus on the Sanctuary of Roma and Augustus yet on the other it was the scene of the initial tensions that led to the Jewish Revolt. Though Caesarea did not join the Revolt, its history showed the underlying tensions between commitment to Rome and a continuing commitment to Judaism of a segment of the population.

In recovering the character of the ancient world modern scholars are on the firmest ground when they use the fullest range of evidence, both material and literary. If this study has relied almost totally on material evidence it is not because the literary evidence is unimportant or uninteresting, but because it is already well known and its use has sometimes resulted in a one-sided picture; texts after all are often written by an author who has one or another axe to grind. By gathering strands of comparative archaeological evidence I hope to contribute in the long run to a more nuanced and well-balanced picture of the roles religion and architecture have played in the cultures of the Near East.

After word

I began by commenting on analogies between 11 September 2001 and the Roman world. If, as I have argued, Palmyra and Jerusalem were among the less fully Romanized Levantine cities, their actions against Rome, twice in both cases, should have been significant. I suggest there was consistency between built expressions of one's own culture, commitment to one's own religious traditions and a wish for independence from Rome. Revolts were not always the result of such commitments, but the tendency seems clear.

As this manuscript goes to press in May 2002 international attention has shifted from the 'war against terrorism' that has been centred on Afghanistan to the deeply disturbing continuation of the political, cultural and religious struggles in the regions on which this book has concentrated. It would be a facile mistake to see Israeli/Palestinian or even Arab/western tensions and conflicts as directly continuous with those examined here. It is difficult, however, not to be conscious of the importance, both symbolic and real, of the Haram al-Sharif in Jerusalem, the Church of the Nativity in Bethlehem (from which the Palestinians have just yesterday been removed) or the Cave of the Patriarchs in Hebron. In all three cases – one from the first century BCE, one from the fourth century CE, and one from the seventh century CE – the continuation of 'indigenous religious traditions' is still crucial. They still have the capacity to galvanize resistance to the death.

Table 7.1 Comparative chronological table (dates CE unless indicated)

	Civic/urban	*Entertainment*	*Religion*
Jerusalem	Colonnaded street at temple (22–15 BCE)	Gymnasium (2nd c. BCE)	Rebuilt temple (22–15 BCE)
	Semicircular plaza (130s)	Theatre (30 BCE)	Synagogue (early 1st c.)
	Monumental arch at forum (early 2nd c.)	Hippodrome (30 BCE)	Asklepieion (late 1st c.)
	Monumental arch at market (early 2nd c.)		Jupiter (early 2nd c.)
			Aphrodite (early 2nd c.)
Caesarea Maritima	Harbour and city (22–12 BCE)	Theatre (22–12 BCE)	Roma and Augustus (22–12 BCE)
	Nymphaeum (late 1st c.)	Hippodrome (22–12 BCE)	Tiberieum (26–36)
	Colonnading of some streets (late 2nd c.)	Amphitheatre (early 1st c.)	Mithraeum (late 1st/early 2nd c.)
	Semicircular plaza (3rd c.)	New hippodrome (2nd c.)	Hadrianeum (130s)
		Old hippodrome altered to amphitheatre (2nd c.)	Synagogue (3rd c.?)
		Theatre renovations (2nd c.)	

Urban design, architecture and religion

	Civic/urban	*Entertainment*	*Religion*
Petra	Arch Bab es-Siq (after 50)	Paradeisos (late 1st c. BCE)	Great Temple (late 1st c. BCE)
	Dam and tunnel (49–106)	Theatre (1st c.)	Dushara (late 1st c. BCE)
	Colonnaded cardo (1st c.?)	Bath (1st c.)	Allat/Winged Lion (early 1st c.)
	Arch at Market (early 2nd c.)	Sabra theatre late 1st c.?)	
	Revisions to cardo (2nd c.)		
	Arch at Dushara (late 2nd c.?)		
	Two nymphaea (2nd c.)		
Gerasa	Colonnaded south cardo (39–76)	South theatre (late 1st c.)	Zeus (22–69; 163)
	Colonnaded north cardo (late 1st c.)	North theatre/ Odeion (165/6)	South synagogue (1st c.?)
	Oval Piazza (late 1st c.)	Hippodrome (mid-2nd/ early 3rd c.)	Dionysus (early 2nd c.)
	Memorial arch (130s)	West baths (late 2nd c.)	Artemis (completed 150)
	Nymphaeum (190/1)	East baths (early 3rd c.)	Maioumas (3rd c.)
	Rebuilt south cardo (late 2nd c.)		Synagogue (4th c.)
	at Oval Piazza (late 2nd c.)		
	South tetrakionion (late 2nd c.)		
	North tetrapylon (early 3rd c.)		

	Civic/urban	*Entertainment*	*Religion*
Palmyra	Small oval piazza (129) and decumanus Theatre plaza (early 2nd c.?) Colonnaded west cardo (early 2nd c.) Colonnaded mid-cardo (mid-2nd c.) Colonnaded east cardo (late 2nd/ early 3rd c.) Nymphaea (early 2nd/late 2nd c.) Tetrakionion (mid-2nd c.) Monumental arch (late 2nd c.) Tetrapylon (late 3rd c.)	Theatre (early 2nd c.) Bath, first stage (late 2nd/ early 3rd c.)	Ba'al Shamim (17, 67, 115, 132) Nebo (32 and later) Bel (32, 80–120, 150) Caesareum (1st c.?) Synagogue (3rd c.?)

Notes

Chapter 1: Roman expansion and Romanization

1 The question of Romanization is complex and multi-faceted. At a familial and personal level, it is relevant to note the way princes of client kings, especially, were educated in Rome, sometimes, as in the case of Herod's children, within the imperial household. They usually – though certainly not in all cases – brought back Roman attitudes and convictions, which then informed their future decisions.

Chapter 5: Caesarea Maritima

1 Previously published as 'Archaeological evidence for religion and urbanism in Caesarea Maritima', in Terence L. Donaldson (ed.), *Religious Rivalries and the Struggle for Success in Caesarea Maritima*, ESCJ 8, Waterloo, Ont.: Wilfrid Laurier University Press, 2000, 11-34. The notation has been shortened and altered for consistency, and a few other editorial changes made, especially in the section on 'Relationship to other eastern cities', where the original essay included references to Sebaste; in this version, Petra has been added as one of the comparanda.

Glossary

Acropolis. Citadel or fortified upper part of a city.

Acroterion. Ornamental finials at the peak or lower edges of a pediment.

Adyton. Sanctuary or inner shrine, especially of a Syrian temple.

Aedicula. Shrine, usually used ornamentally, contained within a larger structure, frequently with two columns and pediment.

Agora. Greek public space for civic and commercial purposes (cf. forum).

Ambo. Pulpit in a Christian church.

Amphitheatre. Elliptical or oval theatre-like building for gladiatorial games or combat (e.g. Coliseum).

Anta/is/ae. Projecting ends of side-walls of a naos.

Apodyterium. Changing room in a Roman bath.

Architrave. Structural member, usually stone, spanning between columns or piers.

Ashlar. Regular masonry of rectangular stones laid in regular horizontal courses.

Basilica. Rectangular building, usually with two rows of columns, an apse, higher roof over the central space, lower side aisles and lit by clerestory windows.

Bouleutêrion. Council chamber.

Caldarium. Hot room of a Roman bath.

Cardo maximus. Main street of Roman city, usually but not always north–south.

Cavea. Seating area of a theatre.

Cella. Holy place in a temple in which the statue of the god was placed.

Chôra. The countryside or agricultural land forming part of the polis.

Clerestory. High windows above columns lighting nave of basilica or church.

Colonia. A privileged form of municipal status; originally military colony.

Cryptoportico. Literally, hidden portico; vaulted structure below ground level, usually for storage.

Decumanus. Principal cross street of city, usually but not always east–west.

Domus dei. Literally 'house of god' (Latin); a building not for a congregation but for the god.

Domus ecclesiae. Literally 'house of the community'; a structure primarily to house a group of participants.

Engaged column. Column that projects from but is attached to a wall.

Entablature. Horizontal superstructure carried by a colonnade or wall.

Exedra. Recess, usually semicircular or sometimes rectangular, often seating area in a stoa.

Forum. Roman public space for civic and commercial purposes (cf. agora).

Frieze. Portion of entablature above the architrave, sometimes decorated (e.g. in Doric order, a band of triglyphs and metopes), sometimes plain.

Frigidarium. Cold room of a Roman bath.

Gymnasium. Greek cultural institution, often merged in Roman period with bath.

Hellenistic. Strictly speaking, period between 323 and 31 BCE (death of Alexander to Battle of Actium); culture of that period and its continuation into Roman Imperial period.

Hippodamian plan. Plan of city with streets laid out at right angles, characteristic of Greek cities and sometimes applied to Roman cities.

Hippodrome. A long course, usually round at one end and square at the other, for horse races (Latin, circus).

Hypogeum. Literally, below the earth; a tomb carved out of bedrock below ground level.

Insula/ae. Apartment building, usually occupying a whole block. Sometimes used in town planning to refer to individual city blocks.

Kome. Small town or village.

Lintel. Beam over door or window carrying weight of masonry above.

Loculus. Literally, little place. A niche for burial, usually about 2 m long, ½ m wide, ⅔ m high.

Macellum. Meat market.

Martyrium. Place for depositing relics of martyrs.

Menorah. Seven-branched candlestick, originally part of the furniture of the Court of Priests.

Merlons. Crenellation surmounting wall or entablature, in Syria often of crow-step design.

Mikveh/mikvaoth. A small immersion pool for purposes of ritual purity; some were domestic, some public.

Municipium/a. Town with lower civic status than a colonia.

Naos. Shrine, usually used of the holy place or the inner shrine within which the god dwelled.

Necropolis. Literally, city of the dead; an area in which tombs are found.

Nymphaeum/a. Public fountain; literally place for nymphs (spirits associated with water).

Odeion. Small, usually roofed, theatre (Latin, odium) used primarily for lectures and concerts.

Orchestra. Semicircular area between the stage and cavea in a theatre.

Ossuary. Small carved limestone 'bone box' for secondary burial of bones after decomposition of flesh.

Paradeisos. Park or pleasure ground, often in a royal palace; garden.

Pediment. Gabled end of a roof (i.e., tympanum plus raking cornice).

Peribolos. Wall encircling a temple or precinct.

Peripteral. With a continuous row of columns around perimeter.

Peristyle. A courtyard with columns on four sides; often used of domestic-scale courtyards.

Podium. Platform supporting temple or other structure.

Polis, pl. **poleis**. City (in Greek), usually with appropriate institutions and a surrounding area of land to support it.

Pronaos. Area in front of naos; porch of temple.

Propylaea. An architecturally important entrance to an enclosure, frequently a religious sanctuary.

Scaenae. Stage building of a Roman theatre (Greek = skênê). Scaenae frons was the backdrop of the stage.

Signum (pl. **signa**). Standard or ensign, usually of a legion.

Soreg. Literally barricade (Hebrew) in the Jerusalem temple outside the Court of Women.

Stadium. A long course, often round at one end and square at the other, for foot races.

Stele. Upright stone slab for inscriptions, reliefs, graves.

Stoa. Long, narrow, roofed and colonnaded structure (often two-storeyed); usually found in agora.

Stylos. Column; used in the form distyle (two columns), tetrastyle (four columns), hexastyle (six columns), etc. When used with anta (projecting ends of walls), as in tetrastyle-in-antis, it refers to four columns between the projecting ends of walls in a façade.

Syrian arch (arcuated lintel). Arch over central opening of a horizontal entablature in a columnar façade.

Temenos. Piece of land dedicated to a god; precinct of a temple or sanctuary, enclosing the naos.

Tetrapylon. Square monumental arch at a major intersection with two intersecting passageways.

Tetrakionion. Structure usually of four groups of four columns marking a major intersection.

Theatre. In a Roman theatre the cavea and orchestra were semicircles, the stage was usually as wide as the cavea and as high as the rear row of seats. In a Greek/Hellenistic theatre the cavea was more than a semicircle, the orchestra circular and the stage relatively small.

Theatron. As distinct from a theatre, the term is often used of a more informal seating area.

Tholos. Circular temple-like structure, usually with external columns and conical roof.

Triclinium. Dining room (literally, three benches), traditionally but not always with three benches.

Tympanum. Vertical face of pediment below the raking cornice.

Xystos. Covered colonnade in gymnasium; garden.

Bibliography

Further reading

Chapter 1: Roman expansion

Warwick Ball, *Rome in the East: The Transformation of an Empire*, London and New York: Routledge, 2000; Elizabeth Fentress (ed.), *Romanization and the City: Creation, Transformations, and Failures*, JRA Supp. Series 38 (2000); Robert G. Holyland, *Arabia and the Arabs: From the Bronze Age to the Coming of Islam*, London and New York: Routledge, 2001; Benjamin Isaac, *The Limits of Empire: The Roman Army in the East*, Oxford: Clarendon, 1990; A. H. M. Jones, *Cities of the Eastern Roman Provinces*, rev. edn, Oxford: Clarendon, 1971; Andrew Lintott, *Imperium Romanum: Politics and Administration*, London and New York: Routledge, 1993; Ramsay MacMullen, *Romanization in the Time of Augustus*, New Haven and London: Yale University Press, 2000; Fergus Millar, *The Roman Near East 31 BC–AD 337*, Cambridge, Mass.: Harvard University Press, 1993; C. R. Whittaker, *Frontiers of the Roman Empire: A Social and Economic Study*, Baltimore: Johns Hopkins University Press, 1994.

Chapter 2: Palmyra

Iain Browning, *Palmyra*, London: Chatto & Windus, 1979; Albert Champdor, *Les ruines de Palmyre*, Paris: Guillot, 1953; G. Degeorge, *Palmyre: Métropole du désert*, Paris: Libraire Séguier, 1987; K. Michalowski, *Palmyra*, London: Pall Mall, 1970; M. I. Rostovtzeff, *Caravan Cities*, Oxford: Oxford University Press, 1932; Daniel Schlumberger, *La Palmyrène du Nord-Ouest*, Paris: Paul Geuthner, 1951; Henri Seyrig et al., *Le Temple de Bel à Palmyre*, 2 vols, Paris: Paul Geuthner,

1968–75; Jean Starcky, *Palmyre*, rev. edn, Paris: Libraire d'Amérique et d'Orient, 1985; Richard Stoneman, *Palmyra and its Empire: Zenobia's Revolt against Rome*, Ann Arbor: University of Michigan Press, 1992; Theodor Wiegand, *Palmyra: Ergebnisse der Expeditionen von 1902 und 1917*, Berlin: Keller, 1932; Ernest Will, *Les Palmyréniens: la Venise des sables*, Paris: Colin, 1992.

Chapter 3: Petra

Maria Giulia Amadasi, *Petra*, Milan: Electa, 1997; Christian Augé and Jean-Marie Dentzer, *Petra: Lost City of the Ancient World*, New York: Abrams, 2000; *BASOR* 324 (November 2001) on recent excavations; Iain Browning, *Petra*, London: Chatto & Windus, 1973; Albert Champdor, *Les ruines de Pétra*, Lyon: Guillot, 1972; Nelson Glueck, *Deities and Dolphins: The story of the Nabataeans*, New York: Farrar, Straus & Giroux, 1965; Philip C. Hammond, *The Nabateans: Their History, Culture and Archaeology*, Studies in Mediterranean Archaeology 37, Gothenburg: Paul Åströms, 1973; Manfred Lindner (ed.), *Petra und das Königreich der Nabatäer*, Munich: Delp, 1970; Avraham Negev, *Nabatean Archaeology Today*, New York and London: New York University Press, 1986; Avraham Negev, 'Petra', *NEAEHL* 4.1181–93; Jane Taylor, *Petra and the Lost Kingdom of the Nabataeans*, London and New York: Tauris, 2001.

Chapter 4: Gerasa

Shimon Applebaum and Arthur Segal, 'Gerasa', *NEAEHL* 2.470–9; Melissa Aubin, 'Jerash', *OEANE* 3.215–19; Mohsen M. Aulama, *Jerash: A Unique Example of a Roman City*, Amman: Al-Aulama & Barhoumeh, 1994; Iain Browning, *Jerash and the Decapolis*, London: Chatto & Windus, 1982; Lankester Harding, *Official Guide to Jerash*, Amman: Department of Antiquities, 1944; Carl H. Kraeling, *Gerasa, City of the Decapolis*, New Haven: ASOR, 1938; Margaret Lyttelton, *Baroque Architecture in Classical Antiquity*, London: Thames & Hudson, 1971; Roberto Parapetti, 'The architectural significance of the Sanctuary of Artemis at Gerasa', in Adnan Hadidi (ed.), *Studies in the History and Archaeology of Jordan*, Amman: Department of Antiquities, 1982, vol. 1, pp. 255–60; Fawzi Zayadine (ed.), *Jerash Archaeological Project 1981–1983*, 2 vols, Amman: Department of Antiquities, 1986, 1989.

Chapter 5: Caesarea Maritima

Terence L. Donaldson (ed.), *Religious Rivalries and the Struggle for Success in Caesarea Maritima*, ESCJ 8, Waterloo: Wilfrid Laurier University Press, 2000; Charles T. Fritsch (ed.), *Studies in the History of Caesarea Maritima*, vol. 1: *The Joint Expedition to Caesarea Maritima*, Missoula: Scholars Press, 1975; Kenneth G. Holum, Robert L. Hohlfelder, Robert J. Bull and Avner Raban, *King Herod's Dream, Caesarea on the Sea*, New York and London: Norton, 1988; Kenneth G. Holum et al., 'Caesarea Maritima', *NEAEHL* 1.270–2; Lee I. Levine and Ehud Netzer, 'Excavations at Caesarea Maritima, 1975, 1976, 1979 – Final Report', *Qedem* 21, Jerusalem: Institute of Archaeology, 1986; Avner Raban and Kenneth G. Holum, *Caesarea Maritima: A Retrospective after Two Millennia*, Leiden: Brill, 1996.

Chapter 6: Jerusalem

Nahman Avigad and Hillel Geva, 'Jerusalem', *NEAEHL* 2.717–57; Dan Bahat, *The Illustrated Atlas of Jerusalem*, New York and London: Simon & Schuster, 1990; Dan Bahat, 'Jerusalem', *OEANE* 3.224–38; Meir Ben-Dov, *In the Shadow of the Temple: The Discovery of Ancient Jerusalem*, Jerusalem: Keter, 1985; Kathleen M. Kenyon, *Digging Up Jerusalem*, New York and Washington: Praeger, 1974; Lee I. Levine, *Jerusalem: Portrait of the City in the Second Temple Period (538 BCE–70 CE)*, Philadelphia: Jewish Publication Society, 2002; W. Harold Mare, *The Archaeology of the Jerusalem Area*, Grand Rapids: Baker, 1987; Kay Prag, *Jerusalem*, Blue Guide, London: A & C Black, 1989; Hershel Shanks, *Jerusalem: An Archaeological Biography*, New York: Random House, 1995.

Chapter 7: Urban design and architecture

Werner Eck (with Elisabeth Müller-Luckner) (eds), *Lokale Autonomie und römische Ordnungsmacht in den kariserzeitlichen Provinzen vom 1. bis 3. Jahrhundert*, Schriften des Historischen Kollegs Kolloquien 42, Munich: Oldenbourg, 1999; Seán Freyne, 'Cities of the Hellenistic and Roman periods', *OEANE* 2.29–35; William L. MacDonald, *The Architecture of the Roman Empire*, vol. 2: *An Urban Appraisal*, New Haven and London: Yale University Press, 1986; John Rich and Andrew Wallace-Hadrill (eds), *City and Country in the Ancient World*, London and New York:

Routledge, 1991; Daniel Sperber, *The City in Roman Palestine*, New York and Oxford: Oxford University Press, 1998; John E. Stambaugh, *The Ancient Roman City*, Baltimore: Johns Hopkins University Press, 1988; Leif Vaage (ed.), *Religious Rivalries and Relations between early Christians, Jews and Pagans*, Waterloo: Wilfrid Laurier University Press, forthcoming.

Primary sources

Appian, *Roman History*, trans. Horace White, 4 vols, Cambridge, Mass.: Harvard University Press, 1912–13

Epiphanius of Salamis, *The Panarion*, trans. Frank Williams, 2 vols, Leiden and New York: Brill, 1987–96

Josephus, *Life*, *Against Apion*, *War* and *Antiquities*, trans. H. St J. Thackeray, Ralph Marcus and Louis H. Feldman, 9 vols, London: Heinemann; Cambridge, Mass.: Harvard University Press, 1926–65

Pliny, *Natural History*, trans. H. Rackham, W. H. S. Jones and D. E. Eichholz, 10 vols, London: Heinemann; Cambridge, Mass.: Harvard University Press, 1944–89

Strabo, *Geography*, trans. Horace L. Jones, 8 vols, London: Heinemann; Cambridge, Mass.: Harvard University Press, 1919–32

Tacitus, *The Histories*, trans. Kenneth Wellesley, rev. edn, Harmondsworth: Penguin, 1986

Tacitus, *The Agricola and the Germania*, trans. H. Mattingly, rev. edn, London: Penguin, 1970

Vitruvius, *Ten Books on Architecture*, trans. Ingrid D. Rowland, Cambridge: Cambridge University Press, 1999

Secondary sources

Alcock, Susan E. (ed.), *The Early Roman Empire in the East*, Oxford: Oxbow, 1997

Amadasi, Maria Giulia, *Petra*, Milan: Electa, 1997

Applebaum, Shimon, and Arthur Segal, 'Gerasa', *NEAEHL* 2.470–9

Asali, Kamil J. (ed.), *Jerusalem in History: 3000 BC to the Present Day*, rev. edn, London and New York: Kegan Paul, 1997

Ascough, Richard (ed.), *Religious Rivalries and the Struggle for Success in Smyrna and Sardis*, Waterloo: Wilfrid Laurier University Press, forthcoming

Aubin, Melissa, 'Jerash', *OEANE* 3.215–19

Augé, Christian, and Jean-Marie Dentzer, *Petra: Lost City of the Ancient World*, New York: Abrams, 2000

Aulama, Mohsen M., *Jerash: A Unique Example of a Roman City*, Amman: Al-Aulama & Barhoumeh, 1994

Avigad, Nahman, *The Herodian Quarter in Jerusalem*, Jerusalem: Keter, 1991

Avigad, Nahman, and Hillel Geva, 'Jerusalem: the Second Temple period', *NEAEHL* 2.717–57

Avi-Yonah, Michael, 'Caesarea: the excavation of the synagogue', *NEAEHL* 1.278–80

Avi-Yonah, Michael, and Hillel Geva, 'Jerusalem: the Byzantine period', *NEAEHL* 2.768–85

Avni, Gideon, and Zvi Greenhut, *The Akeldama Tombs*, IAA Reports 1, Jerusalem: Israel Antiquities Authority, 1996

Bahat, Dan, *The Illustrated Atlas of Jerusalem*, New York and London: Simon & Schuster, 1990

Bahat, Dan, 'Jerusalem', *OEANE* 3.224–38

Ball, Warwick, *Rome in the East: The Transformation of an Empire*, London and New York: Routledge, 2000

Barag, Dan, 'The legal and administrative status of Sebastos during the Early Roman period', in Raban and Holum, *Retrospective*, 609–14

Barrett, J. C., 'Romanization: a critical comment', in D. J. Mattingly (ed.), *Dialogues in Roman Imperialism*, Portsmouth, R.I.: JRA, 1997

Bedal, Leigh-Ann, 'A pool complex in Petra's city center', *BASOR* 324 (2001), 23–41

Ben-Dov, Meir, *In the Shadow of the Temple: The Discovery of Ancient Jerusalem*, Jerusalem: Keter, 1985

Berger, Philippe, 'Les inscriptions hébraïques de la Synagogue de Palmyre', *Mémoire de la Société de Linguistique de Paris* 7 (1892), 62–72

Bikai, Patricia Maynor, and Megan A. Perry, 'Petra North Ridge Tombs 1 and 2: Preliminary Report', *BASOR* 324 (2001), 59–78

Blakely, Jeffrey A. *The Joint Expedition to Caesarea Maritima: Excavation Reports*, vol. 4: *The Pottery and Dating of Vault 1: Horreum, Mithraeum, and Later Uses*, Lewiston and Queenston: Edwin Mellen, 1987

Bounni, Adnan, and Khaled al-As'ad, *Palmyra: History, Monuments and Museum*, 2nd edn, Damascus: no pub., 1988

Bowersock, Glen W., *Roman Arabia*, Cambridge, Mass.: Harvard University Press, 1983

Bowersock, Glen W., Appended note P, in Jones, 'Nabatean inscriptions'

Bowman, Alan K., 'Urbanisation in Roman Egypt', in Fentress, *Romanization*, 173–87

Brenk, Beat, Carola Jäggi and Hans-Rudolf Meier, 'Neue Forschungen zur Kathedrale von Gerasa. Probleme der Chronologie und der Vorgängerbauten', *ZDPV* 112/2 (1996), 139–55

Browning, Iain, *Petra*, London: Chatto & Windus, 1973

Browning, Iain, *Palmyra*, London: Chatto & Windus, 1979

Browning, Iain, *Jerash and the Decapolis*, London: Chatto & Windus, 1982

Brunt, P. A., and J. M. Monroe, *Res Gestae divi Augusti: The Achievements of the Divine Augustus. Introduction and Commentary*, Oxford: Oxford University Press, 1967

Burns, Ross, *Monuments of Syria: An Historical Guide*, London and New York: Tauris, 1994

Burns, Thomas S., and John W. Eadie, *Urban Centers and Rural Contexts in Late Antiquity*, East Lansing, Mich.: Michigan State University Press, 2001

Burrell, Barbara, 'Palace to praetorium: the Romanization of Caesarea', in Raban and Holum, *Retrospective*, 228–47

Butler, H. C., *Publications of the Princeton University Expedition to Syria in 1904, 1905, 1909*, 'Division 2, Section A, Southern Syria', Leiden: Brill, 1919

Champdor, Albert, *Les ruines de Palmyre*, Paris: Guillot, 1953

Champdor, Albert, *Les ruines de Pétra*, Lyon: Guillot, 1972

Collart, Paul, and Jacques Vicari, *Le sanctuaire de Baalshamim à Palmyre*, 2 vols, Rome: Institut Suisse de Rome, 1969

Costaki, Leda, 'Palmyra: Plan – Orientation – Religious Spaces', unpublished paper, University of Toronto

Cotton, H., 'Some aspects of the Roman administration of Judaea/Syria-Palaestina', in Eck, *Lokale Autonomie*

Dalman, Gustaf, *Neue Petra-Forschungen und der heilige Felsen von Jerusalem*, Leipzig: Hinrich, 1912

Debevoise, Neilson C., *A Political History of Parthia*, 2nd edn, New York: Greenwood Press, 1968 [1938]

Degeorge, G., *Palmyre: Métropole du désert*, Paris: Libraire Séguier, 1987

Downs, Mary, 'Refiguring colonial categories on the Roman frontier in southern Spain', in Fentress, *Romanization*, 197–210

Donaldson, Terence L. (ed.), *Religious Rivalries and the Struggle for Success in Caesarea Maritima*, ESCJ 8, Waterloo: Wilfrid Laurier University Press, 2000

Eck, Werner (with Elisabeth Müller-Luckner) (eds), *Lokale Autonomie und römische Ordnungsmacht in den kariserzeitlichen Provinzen vom 1. bis 3. Jahrhundert*, Schriften des Historischen Kollegs Kolloquien 42, Munich: Oldenbourg, 1999

Fentress, Elizabeth (ed.), *Romanization and the City: Creation, Transformations, and Failures*, JRA Supp. Series 38 (2000)

Fiema, Zbigniew T., et al., *The Petra Church*, ACOR Publications 3, Amman: American Centre of Oriental Research, 2001

Finegan, Jack, *The Archeology of the New Testament*, rev. edn, Princeton: Princeton University Press, 1992

Fischer, Mosche, 'Marble, urbanism, and ideology in Roman Palestine: the Caesarea example', in Raban and Holum, *Retrospective*, 251–61

Foerster, Gideon, 'The early history of Caesarea', in Fritsch, *History*, 9–22

Freyne, Seán, 'Cities of the Hellenistic and Roman periods', *OEANE* 2.29–35

Frezouls, E. 'Questions d'urbanisme Palmyrenien', in *Palmyre: Bilan et perspectives, colloque de Strasbourg 18–20 Octobre 1973*, Strasbourg: Association pour l'étude de la civilisation romaine, 1976, 191–207

Fritsch, Charles T. (ed.), *Studies in the History of Caesarea Maritima*, vol. 1: *The Joint Expedition to Caesarea Maritima*, Missoula: Scholars Press, 1975

Frova, Antonio, et al., *Scavi di Caesarea Maritima*, Rome: Bretschneider, 1966

Gelb, Susan, 'Architecture and Romanization: Hadrian's visit to the Provincia Arabia', *ASOR Newsletter* 51/4 (2001), 9–10

Gersht, Rivka, 'Seven new sculptural pieces from Caesarea', *The Roman and Byzantine Near East: Recent Archaeological Research*, JRA Supp. Series 14 (1995), 109–20

Gersht, Rivka, 'Representations of deities and the cults of Caesarea', in Raban and Holum, *Retrospective*, 304–24

Geva, Hillel, and Michael Avi-Yonah, 'Jerusalem: the Roman period', *NEAEHL* 2.758–67

Gleason, Kathryn Louise, 'Ruler and spectacle: the Promontory Palace', in Raban and Holum, *Retrospective*, 208–27

Glueck, Nelson, *Deities and Dolphins: The Story of the Nabataeans*, New

York: Farrar, Straus & Giroux, 1965
Graf, David F., 'Hellenisation and the Decapolis', *Aram* 4 (1992), 1–48
Graf, David, 'Nabateans', *ABD* 4.970–3
Graf, David, 'The Via Nova Traiana in Arabia Petraea', in *The Roman and Byzantine Near East: Recent Archaeological Research*, JRA Supp. Series 14 (1995), 241–67
Grainger, John D., *The Cities of Seleukid Syria*, Oxford: Clarendon, 1990
Hammond, Philip C., *The Excavation of the Main Theater at Petra*, London: Quaritch, 1965
Hammond, Philip C., *The Nabateans: Their History, Culture and Archaeology*, Studies in Mediterranean Archaeology 37, Gothenburg: Paul Åströms, 1973
Harding, Lankester, *Official Guide to Jerash*, Amman: Department of Antiquities, 1944
Hayward, C. T. R., *The Jewish Temple: A Non-Biblical Sourcebook*, London and New York: Routledge, 1996
Hirschfeld, Yizhar, 'The early Roman bath and fortress at Ramat Hanadiv near Caesarea', in *The Roman and Byzantine Near East: Recent Archaeological Research*, JRA Supp. Series 14, Ann Arbor: JRA, 1995, 29–55
Holum, Kenneth G., Robert L. Hohlfelder, Robert J. Bull and Avner Raban, *King Herod's Dream, Caesarea on the Sea*, New York and London: Norton, 1988
Holum, Kenneth G. et al., 'Caesarea Maritima', *NEAEHL*, 1.270–2
Holyland, Robert G., *Arabia and the Arabs: From the Bronze Age to the Coming of Islam*, London and New York: Routledge, 2001
Hübner, Ulrich (ed.), *Nach Petra und ins Königreich der Nabatäer: Notizen von Reisegefährten für Manfred Lindner zum 80. Geburtstag*, Bodenheim: Philo, 1998
Humphrey, John H., ' "Amphitheatrical" hippo-stadia', in Raban and Holum, *Retrospective*, 121–9
Isaac, Benjamin, *The Limits of Empire: The Roman Army in the East*, Oxford: Clarendon, 1990
Jones, A. H. M., *Cities of the Eastern Roman Provinces*, rev. edn, Oxford: Clarendon, 1971
Jones, Brian W., *The Emperor Domitian*, London and New York: Routledge, 1992
Jones, Richard N. 'Nabatean inscriptions', in Z. T. Fiema et al., *The Petra Church*, ACOR Publications 3, Amman: ACOR, 2001, 346–9

Joukowsky, Martha Sharp, *Petra Great Temple*, vol. 1, Providence: Petra Exploration Fund, 1998

Joukowsky, Martha Sharp, and Joseph J. Basile, 'More pieces in the Petra Great Temple puzzle', *BASOR* 324 (2001), 43–58

Kahn, Lisa C., 'King Herod's Temple of Roma and Augustus at Caesarea Maritima', in Raban and Holum, *Retrospective*, 130–45

Kanellopoulos, Chrysanthos, 'The architecture of the shops and colonnaded street in Petra', *BASOR* 324 (2001), 9–22

Keay, S., and N. Terrenato (eds), *Italy and the West: Comparative Issues in Romanization*, Oxford: Oxbow, 2001

Kenyon, Kathleen M., *Digging Up Jerusalem*, New York and Washington: Praeger, 1974

Khairy, Nabil I., *The 1981 Petra Excavations*, Wiesbaden: Harrassowitz, 1990

Khouri, Rami G. *Petra: A Guide to the Capital of the Nabataeans*, London and New York: Longman, 1986

Kloppenborg Verbin, John S., 'Dating Theodotos (CIJ ii.1404)', *Journal of Jewish Studies* 51 (2000), 243–80

Kolb, Bernard, et al., 'Swiss-Liechtenstein excavations at az-Zantur in Petra', *ADAJ* 41 (1997), 231–42; *ADAJ* 42 (1998), 259–77; *ADAJ* 43 (1999), 261–77

Kraeling, Carl H., *Gerasa, City of the Decapolis*, New Haven: ASOR, 1938

Kushnir-Stein, Alla, 'The predecessor of Caesarea: on the identification of Demetrias in South Phoenicia', in *The Roman and Byzantine Near East: Some Recent Archaeological Research*, JRA Supp. Series 14, Ann Arbor, 1995, 9–14

Levine, Lee I., *Roman Caesarea: An Archaeological-Topographical Study*, Qedem, Monographs of the Institute of Archaeology 2, Jerusalem: Hebrew University, 1975

Levine, Lee I., 'Synagogue officials: the evidence from Caesarea and its implications for Palestine and the diaspora', in Raban and Holum, *Retrospective*, 392–400

Levine, Lee I., *Jerusalem: Portrait of the City in the Second Temple Period (538 BCE–70 CE)*, Philadelphia: Jewish Publication Society, 2002

Levine, Lee I., and Ehud Netzer, *Excavations at Caesarea Maritima, 1975, 1976, 1979: Final Report*, Qedem: Monographs of the Institute of Archaeology 21, Jerusalem: Hebrew University, 1986

Lichtenberger, Achim, *Die Baupolitik Herodes des Großen*, Wiesbaden: Harrassowitz, 1999

Lindner, Manfred (ed.), *Petra und das Königreich der Nabatäer*, Munich: Delp, 1970

Lintott, Andrew, *Imperium Romanum: Politics and Administration*, London and New York: Routledge, 1993

Lyttelton, Margaret, *Baroque Architecture in Classical Antiquity*, London: Thames & Hudson, 1974

MacDonald, William L., *The Architecture of the Roman Empire*, vol. 1: *An Introductory Study*, rev. edn, New Haven and London: Yale University Press, 1982

MacDonald, William L., *The Architecture of the Roman Empire*, vol. 2: *An Urban Appraisal*, New Haven and London: Yale University Press, 1986

McKenzie, Judith S., *The Architecture of Petra*, Oxford: Oxford University Press, 1990

McKenzie, Judith S., 'Keys from Egypt and the East: observations on Nabatean culture in the light of recent discoveries', *BASOR* 324 (2001), 97–112

MacMullen, Ramsay, *Romanization in the Time of Augustus*, New Haven and London: Yale University Press, 2000

Mare, W. Harold, *The Archaeology of the Jerusalem Area*, Grand Rapids: Baker, 1987

Mendels, Doron, *The Rise and Fall of Jewish Nationalism*, New York: Doubleday, 1992

Michalowski, Kazimierz, *Palmyra*, New York: Praeger, 1970

Millar, Fergus, *The Roman Near East 31 BC–AD 337*, Cambridge, Mass.: Harvard University Press, 1993

Mittwoch, Eugen, 'Hebraische Inschriften aus Palmyra', *Beiträge zur Assyriologie* 4/2 (1900), 203–6

Negev, Avraham, *Nabatean Archaeology Today*, New York and London: New York University Press, 1986

Negev, Avraham, 'Petra', *NEAEHL* 4.1181–93

Netzer, Ehud, 'Remains of an Opus Reticulatum building in Jerusalem', *IEJ* 33 (1983), 163–75

Netzer, Ehud, 'The Promontory Palace', in Raban and Holum, *Retrospective*, 193–207

Netzer, Ehud, *Die Paläste der Hasmonäer und Herodes des Grossen*, Mains am Rhein: Philipp von Zabern, 1999

Netzer, Ehud, 'Tyros, the "Floating Palace" ', in Stephen G. Wilson and Michel Desjardins (eds), *Text and Artifact in the Religions of*

Mediterranean Antiquity: Essays in Honour of Peter Richardson, ESCJ 9, Waterloo: Wilfrid Laurier University Press, 2000, 340–57

Parapetti, Roberto, 'The architectural significance of the Sanctuary of Artemis at Gerasa', in Adnan Hadidi (ed.), *Studies in the History and Archaeology of Jordan*, vol. 1, Amman: Department of Antiquities, 1982, 255–60

Perring, Dominic, 'Spatial organisation and social change in Roman towns', in John Rich and Andrew Wallace-Hadrill (eds), *City and Country in the Ancient World*, London and New York: Routledge, 1991, 273–93

Porath, Y., 'Herod's "amphitheatre" at Caesarea: a multipurpose entertainment building', in *The Roman and Byzantine Near East: Recent Archaeological Research*, JRA Supp. Series 14 (1995), 15–27

Porath, Y., 'The evolution of the urban plan of Caesarea's southwest zone: new evidence from the current excavations', in Raban and Holum, *Retrospective*, 105–20

Raban, Avner, 'The inner harbor basin of Caesarea: archaeological evidence for its gradual demise', in Raban and Holum, *Retrospective*, 628–66

Raban, Avner, and Kenneth G. Holum, *Caesarea Maritima, A Retrospective after Two Millennia*, Leiden: Brill, 1996

Raban, Avner, Kenneth G. Holum and Jeffrey A. Blakely, *The Combined Caesarea Expeditions. Field Report of the 1992 Season, Parts 1–3*, ed. Eve Black, Haifa: University of Haifa, 1993

Rahmani, L. Y., *A Catalogue of Jewish Ossuaries in the Collections of the State of Israel*, Jerusalem: Israel Antiquities Authority, 1994

Rich, John, and Andrew Wallace-Hadrill (eds), *City and Country in the Ancient World*, London and New York: Routledge, 1991

Richardson, Peter, 'Augustan-era Synagogues in Rome', in Karl Donfried and Peter Richardson (eds), *Judaism and Christianity in First-Century Rome*, Grand Rapids: Eerdmans, 1998, 17–29

Richardson, Peter, *Herod, King of the Jews and Friend of the Romans*, Columbia, S.C.: University of South Carolina Press, 1996; Minneapolis: Fortress, 1999

Richardson, Peter, 'First-century houses and Q's setting,' in C. Tuckett (ed.), *Christology, Controversy and Community: New Testament Essays in Honour of David Catchpole*, Leiden: Brill, 2000, 63–83

Richardson, Peter, '3 D visualizations of a first-century Galilean town', with Charles Hixon and Ann Spurling, in Juan Barceló, Maurizio

Forte and Donald H. Sanders (eds), *Virtual Reality in Archaeology*, BAR International Series 843, Oxford: BAR, 2000, 195–204

Richardson, Peter, *Judaism, Religion and Architecture* forthcoming

Richardson, Peter, 'Khirbet Cana (and other villages) as a Context for Jesus', in James Charlesworth (ed.), *Jesus and Archaeology*, forthcoming

Richardson, Peter, 'Khirbet Qana's necropolis and ethnic questions', in Douglas Edwards and Thomas McCollough (eds), *The Archaeology of Difference: Gender, Ethnicity, Class and the 'Other' in Antiquity*, forthcoming

Richardson, Peter, 'What has Cana to do with Capernaum?', *New Testament Studies*, forthcoming

Richardson, Peter, and Mordechai Aviam, 'Josephus's Galilee in *Life* and *War* in archaeological perspective', in Steve N. Mason (ed.), *Josephus, Translation and Commentary*, vol. 8, Leiden: Brill, 2000, app. A, pp. 177–217

Richardson, Peter, and Douglas Edwards, 'Jesus and Palestinian social protest', in Tony Blasi, et al. (eds), *Handbook of Early Christianity and the Social Sciences*, Lanham, Md.: Altamira, 2002, ch. 13

Richardson, Peter, and M. B. Shukster, 'Barnabas, Nerva and the Yavnean rabbis', *Journal of Theological Studies* 34 (1983), 31–55

Roller, Duane W., *The Building Program of Herod the Great*, Berkeley and Los Angeles: University of California Press, 1998

Rostovtzeff, M. I., *Caravan Cities*, Oxford: Oxford University Press, 1932

Schlumberger, Daniel, *La Palmyrène du Nord-Ouest*, Paris: Paul Geuthner, 1951

Schmidt-Colinet, Andreas, 'Aspects of "Romanization": the tomb architecture at Palmyra and its decoration', in Susan E. Alcock (ed.), *The Early Roman Empire in the East*, Oxford: Oxbow, 1997, 157–77

Scully, Vincent, *Architecture: The Natural and the Manmade*, New York: St Martins, 1991

Segal, Arthur, *Theatres in Roman Palestine and Provincia Arabia*, Mnemosyne, Bibliotheca Classica Batava Supp. 140, Leiden: Brill, 1995

Seyrig, Henri, et al., *Le Temple de Bel à Palmyre*, 2 vols, Paris: Paul Geuthner, 1968–75

Shahîd, Irfan, *Rome and the Arabs: A Prolegomenon to the Study of Byzantium and the Arabs*, Washington: Dumbarton Oaks, 1984

Shanks, Hershel, *Jerusalem: An Archaeological Biography*, New York: Random House, 1995

Sperber, Daniel, *The City in Roman Palestine*, New York and Oxford: Oxford University Press, 1998

Stambaugh, John E., *The Ancient Roman City*, Baltimore: Johns Hopkins University Press, 1988

Starcky, Jean, *Palmyre*, rev. edn, Paris: Libraire d'Amérique et d'Orient, 1985

Stieglitz, Robert R., 'Stratonos Pyrgos – Migdal Sar – Sebastos: history and archaeology', in Raban and Holum, *Retrospective*, 593–608

Stoneman, Richard, *Palmyra and its Empire: Zenobia's Revolt against Rome*, Ann Arbor: University of Michigan Press, 1992

Sussman, Varda, 'Caesarea illuminated by its lamps', in Raban and Holum, *Retrospective*, 346–58

Taylor, Jane, *Petra and the Lost Kingdom of the Nabataeans*, London and New York: Tauris, 2001

Tcherikover, V., *Hellenistic Civilization and the Jews*, rev. edn, New York: Athenaeum, 1970

Teixidor, J., *The Pantheon of Palmyra*, Leiden: Brill, 1979

Turnheim, Yehudit, and Asher Ovadiah, 'Miscellaneous ornamented architectural elements in Roman Caesarea', in Raban and Holum, *Retrospective*, 262–304

Tushingham, Douglas, *Excavations in Jerusalem*, vol. 1, Toronto: Royal Ontario Museum, 1985

Uscatescu, Alexander, and M. Martin-Bueno, 'The *Macellum* of Gerasa (Jerash, Jordan): from a market place to an industrial area', *BASOR* 307 (1997), 67–88

Vaage, Leif, (ed.), *Religious Rivalries and Relations between Early Christians, Jews and Pagans*, Waterloo: Wilfrid Laurier University Press, forthcoming

Ward-Perkins, John B., *Roman Architecture*, New York: Abrams, 1977

Ward-Perkins, John B., *Roman Imperial Architecture*, Harmondsworth: Penguin, 1983

Weiss, Ze'ev, 'The Jews and the Games in Roman Caesarea', in Raban and Holum, *Retrospective*, 443–53

Wenning, Robert, 'The betyls of Petra', *BASOR* 324 (2001), pp.79–95

White, L. Michael, 'Urban development and social change in imperial Ephesos', in Helmut Koester (ed.), *Ephesos, Metropolis of Asia*, Harvard Theological Studies 41, Valley Forge: Trinity Press International, 1995, 27–79

White, L. Michael, *Social Origins of Christian Architecture*, 2 vols, Valley

Forge: Trinity Press International, 1996, 1997

Whittaker, C. R., *Frontiers of the Roman Empire: A Social and Economic Study*, Baltimore: Johns Hopkins University Press, 1994

Wiegand, Theodor, *Palmyra: Ergebnisse der Expeditionen von 1902 und 1917*, Berlin: Keller, 1932

Wilkinson, John, *Jerusalem as Jesus Knew it: Archaeology as Evidence*, London: Thames & Hudson, 1978

Will, Ernest, 'Le développement urbain de Palmyre: témoignages épigraphiques anciens et nouveaux', *Syria* 60 (1983), 79

Will, Ernest, *Les Palmyréniens: la Venise des sables*, Paris: Colin, 1992

Wilson, Stephen G., and Michel Desjardins (eds), *Text and Artifact in the Religions of Mediterranean Antiquity: Essays in Honour of Peter Richardson*, Waterloo: Wilfrid Laurier University Press, 2000

Zanker, Paul, 'The city as symbol: Rome and the creation of an urban image', in Fentress, *Romanization*, 25–41

Zayadine, Fawzi (ed.), *Jerash Archaeological Project 1981–1983*, 2 vols, Amman: Department of Antiquities, 1986, 1989

Zayadine, Fawzi, 'Sculpture in Ancient Jordan', in Piotr Bienkowski (ed.), *The Art of Jordan*, Phoenix Mills: Alan Sutton, 1991, 31–61

Index of ancient sources

Index of modern authors

Index of sites and buildings